LITTLE CAESAR

A BIOGRAPHY OF EDWARD G. ROBINSON

Alan L. Gansberg

The Scarecrow Press, Inc.
Lanham, Maryland • Toronto • Oxford
2004

SCARECROW PRESS, INC.

Published in the United States of America
by Scarecrow Press, Inc.
A wholly owned subsidiary of
The Rowman & Littlefield Publishing Group, Inc.
4501 Forbes Boulevard, Suite 200, Lanham, Maryland 20706
www.scarecrowpress.com

PO Box 317
Oxford
OX2 9RU, UK

Copyright © 2004 by Alan L. Gansberg
First Scarecrow Press edition published in 2004.
First published in Great Britain in 1983 by New English Library. Reprinted by
permission.

British Library Cataloguing in Publication Information Available

Library of Congress Cataloging-in-Publication Data

Gansberg, Alan L.
  Little Caesar : a biography of Edward G. Robinson / Alan L. Gansberg.
     p. cm.
  Includes bibliographical references and index.
  ISBN 0-8108-4950-X (alk. paper)
  1. Robinson, Edward G., 1893–1973. 2. Motion picture actors and
actresses—United States—Biography. I. Title.
PN2287.R67 G36 2004
791.4302'8'092—dc22

2003027041

Manufactured in the United States of America.

To M & D,
J, I, B, B
and Maggie

CONTENTS

ACKNOWLEDGMENTS

When an actor is a star as long as Edward G. Robinson was, and so pivotal in the social life of the Hollywood community, everyone with any longevity seems to have an anecdote, a story. I am grateful to the numerous people who shared their memories, or aided me in my search for information.

A special thanks must go to Beulah Robinson, daughter of Robinson's brother Willie, for sharing her time in two long sessions with me. Similarly, Sam and Bettye Jaffe, ever loyal to their friend, opened their home to me, and I am a bigger fan now than I was prior to beginning my research.

This book could not have been written had it not been for the many weeks researching at the Department of Special Collections, Doheny Library, of the University of Southern California. Not only were the Warner Brothers archives available, but also Robinson's personal papers and scrapbooks. My thanks to Dr. Robert Knutson, head of the collections, Edward Comstock, and the rest of the staff for keeping the boxes and mounds of material coming.

John J. Ginelli and Benjamin T. Speiser were personal research assistants, tracking down materials for me.

The list of those who shared their time and recollections or helped me find elusive sources is long, and in no particular order, but with endless appreciation, I thank Mervyn LeRoy, Bob Osborne, George Burns, Irving Fein, Emily Paley, Robert Aldrich, Arthur Gardner, Eban Kandell, Michael Selsman, Juanita Brown, Sue Davis, Barbara Lowenstein, Tommy Furlong, Pat Furlong, Christine Foster, Paul Hunter, Neil Steinberg, Bill Haber, Phil Weltman, John Babcock, Gena Rowlands, Esme Chandlee, Josh Logan, Ron Lyon, Bob Abrams, Stephen Pinkus, Don Segall, Don DeMesquita, Milton Sperling, Lionel Stander, Albert Maltz, Joseph Roos, Sam Yorty, Dorothy Sinclair, Suzanne and Stephen Macht, John Forsythe, Wally Grauman, Jack Haley Jr., Sally and Al Burton, Connie Gerber, Karen Lustgarten, Ivan Ladizinsky, Nilsa Rios, Terry Gobright, Agatha M. Gansberg, Martin Gansberg.

In addition, my thanks, love, and admiration go to Donald Freed and Patty C. K. E. Freed, who were there from the beginning; and to Arthur Ross, who helped to fill in the unpublished gaps about the time of the black- and graylisting. I'd be lax if I didn't thank Sherry Huber for seeing the property as viable. And, of course, a special love and gratitude to Gina Friedlander, who was understanding when my attention was at 910 Rexford Drive.

PROLOGUE

The house at 910 Rexford Drive in Beverly Hills sits today like so many other palatial homes in the golden ghetto, built to be large, to reflect the affluence the motion-picture industry brought to Los Angeles. As automobiles zip past on their way to Coldwater Canyon, the Tudor-style structure is probably hardly noticed. Because of the wall and high foliage, the house can barely be seen from the road. Perhaps only tourists, armed with a guide to the movie stars' residences, will know that this was once the home of Edward G. Robinson.

Edward G. Robinson. The cocky, ebullient tough guy. He was Little Caesar, the quintessential gangster success and failure story. Robinson had defined for the huge Great Depression moviegoing audience the idea of the snarling, immigrant antihero—a vicious and unrepentant underdog going down in a hail of bullets.

This was his image. An image as important to his continued success as his brilliance on the screen. The image had paid for the priceless pieces of art that surrounded Robinson at home. The image that brought him fame.

Yet, 910 Rexford Drive is more than just another affluent structure. Because Robinson collected the best art available, the home was a mecca for the intelligentsia who flocked to Hollywood during the 1930s and 1940s. Robinson's Steinway piano was autographed inside by the greats in the music world. His personal mementoes contain the affections of the greatest artists of canvas. Writers, directors, producers, and actors all flocked to his parties or dropped by welcome and unannounced to see his collection.

The gathering of the creative individuals does not tell the entire story. Robinson wanted his home to be the mecca. If not a salon, it was certainly the meeting place for many major Hollywood events that were mere by-products of the screen work.

Flashback to December 9, 1938, and Robinson is playing host to the notables of the screen world—Joan Crawford, Melvyn Douglas, Jack Warner, Myrna Loy, Spencer Tracy, James Cagney, Groucho Marx. The event is the meeting of the Committee of 56 of the Anti-Nazi League, so named because the number equaled the signatures on the Declaration of Independence. It was organized to begin a month of radio broadcasts and rallies nationwide, all aimed at convincing President Franklin Delano Roosevelt to arrest the menace of Hitler and Nazi Germany.

Robinson could be seen that night, looking taller than his 5'6" frame allowed, his cigar bouncing from hand to mouth, or used to accentuate a point with a flip through the air. The house was, indeed, more than the spot where his wife, Gladys Lloyd, had become one of the most successful hostesses of Hollywood, or where their son, Manny, was growing up. It was a place where Robinson could live the life his father, Morris Goldenberg, had wanted for him: a life surrounded by the finer things in life, even lived slightly above his means to keep the ambition strong. And, even more importantly, Robinson was actively involved in humanistic causes, both for his own people and for the good of all mankind. He was, on the night of December 9, 1938, in his glory. His political activities as a liberal Democrat, as a militant activist, had brought the town together for a cause he held dear. This was the essence of America, the land to which he had emigrated. In a few weeks he would begin work on *Confessions of a Nazi Spy*, which would startle the public with its political message.

Fast-forward to October 1947. The mood in Hollywood has changed since the war. The cast of characters in the movies has changed. Joan Crawford has found herself without a studio. Norma Shearer and Greta Garbo have retired. In a year, Henry Fonda would depart for Broadway, and the studio system itself would be challenged in court.

As always, as the American Dream changed, so did its double—the American film. Dream and film had always walked hand in hand. Now, for many in the film community the dream would begin to slide toward nightmare, as if a film of terror were unreeling. The invasion of the reputation snatchers and the character assassins was about to begin.

But Edward G. Robinson was, at first, virtually oblivious to the change. In 1947 he was enjoying his greatest year since he left the safety of Warner Brothers in 1943 and in October 1947 was filming *All My Sons* while studying his script for *Key Largo*, which would follow. Both vehicles had the substance he had craved in all his scripts but had not always received from the studio. And even if he would be sharing star billing with two more-attractive men—Burt Lancaster and Humphrey Bogart— with just weeks before his fifty-fourth birthday, it was better than other stars could do after they had reached their peak, and solid work for any actor.

But the week of October 20, 1947, would not be a normal period of filming and script meetings. Robinson was aware that the House Committee on Un-American Activities (HUAC) had convened in Washington, D.C. He had reason to be concerned with the proceedings even before they began—hadn't his name been whispered as one with Communist connections? For several months there had been press reports that the FBI listed Robinson's name among those who had been Red sympathizers.

Eddie didn't fear the FBI. J. Edgar Hoover was an old friend, or at least so Robinson thought. They had exchanged many letters and autographed photos. He was unaware that the FBI had compiled a growing file of his alleged left-wing wrongdoings, even suspecting him of espionage. Eddie didn't fear skeletons in his cupboard, because he saw none there. Yes, he had been politically active, a leading Hollywood liberal, but he was a loyal member of the Democratic Party, a fan of FDR. Hadn't Eddie and Melvyn Douglas once bought FDR's lucky felt hat at an auction, only to give it back to the president so he could use it during the next campaign?

Unfortunately, some fellow actors saw Eddie in a different light. In his testimony before HUAC, Adolphe Menjou implicated Robinson as being sympathetic with the "Communist" side in recent labor squabbles in Hollywood. Eddie could have lived through that, but what came the next day was another matter: testimony that would shatter Robinson's destiny. On page one of the *New York Times* on October 23, 1947, Howard Rushmore, the former film critic for the *Daily Worker*, and a man who admitted to having been a member of the Communist Party from 1936 to 1939, was telling HUAC that "the *Daily Worker* regarded Charles Chaplin and Edward G. Robinson as what we call in the newspaper business 'sacred cows,' people you trust favorably. I don't know whether or not [Robinson] is a Communist, but for ten years he has been joining front organizations and is still doing it."

The same day the president of the Screen Actors Guild testified. The hero was "clad in a tan gabardine suit," according to the *Times*, "wearing glasses, a blue knitted tie and white shirt." When he entered the room, "there was a long drawn-out 'ooh' from the jam-packed predominantly female audience." The president told HUAC that, indeed, actors as well as writers were Communists and that they had attempted to take over SAG, but had been thwarted. He never mentioned Robinson by name but said that the American Committee for the Protection of the Foreign Born was "a Commie front"—and Robinson was one of its key sponsors.

The president of SAG was, of course, Ronald Reagan, who would play a leading role in Robinson's personal horror film during the next five years. Reagan, Menjou, Rushmore—they would all participate in shattering an image that had survived for sixteen years as one of the most striking on the silver screen.

910 Rexford Drive can still be seen as a symbol of the American Dream, even a decade after Robinson has died, and thirty years after the

shattered image began to rebuild. Edward G. Robinson had come to America to escape one form of persecution. His adopted land had given him a rags-to-riches biography, and he had returned the gifts by being generous with those riches, and generous with his time. He had worked toward making America a land of peace, and thus the world. The country thanked him by putting him through another form of persecution, one that challenged the patriotism he held dear. He survived, but both Robinson and America had changed.

1

THE IMMIGRANT

My mother may have given birth in Rumania, but I was born the day I set foot on American soil.

—Emanuel Goldenberg aka Edward G. Robinson

Jews had been living in Rumania since pre-Christian times, and the Goldenbergs could trace themselves back for two hundred years, long before the Treaty of Berlin, which in 1878 had granted Rumania complete independence on the condition that all inhabitants be given equal political and civil rights. They were provisions that were never followed. Jews had to pay a special poll tax, were excluded from professions, and barred from universities.

Morris and Sarah Goldenberg already had four sons when Emanuel—who would find fame as Edward G. Robinson—was born on December 12, 1893, at 671 Strada Cantemier in the Jewish section of Bucharest. Synagogue records—long ago destroyed—would have listed their fifth son as Menashe ben Yeshayahu Moshe, his full Hebrew name. Before him were four brothers—Zach, Jack, Oscar, and Willie. A short time later Max, son number six, would come into the world, and nine people, including Sarah's mother, would fill the small quarters. For the first few years of his life, after he outgrew his crib, Menashe would sleep with his grandmother, a short, feisty, and independent woman.

Their family home—a small two-story structure connected to several other houses surrounding an all-purpose courtyard—was in an area where Jews were assigned to live but was not a ghetto in the classical sense. There was no gate keeping them enclosed at night, although few dared to leave safe territory. There were some trees, a little greenery, a park, however small, but mostly cobblestone and brick, inhabited by devout, black-frocked Jews and the handful who had adapted secular dress and, if it meant relief from poverty, secular culture.

Bucharest was a crossroads culture, with western European influences, oriental influences, Russian influences, and of course the native touch. The Jewish community was well rounded as well. Yiddish theater had its origins in Rumania, thanks to the establishment of a troupe in Jassy by Abraham Goldfaden in 1876. The Jews had their own subculture, with foods featuring olive oil and black olives. The emancipation of the community, and the subsequent assimilation and even conversion to Christianity, was slower in Rumania than it was in Germany, Hungary, and even Russia. Because the country had not been under the czars, there was no pale of settlement that had kept other generations of eastern European Jews on the move. Most families like the Goldenbergs had roots, if not in Bucharest itself, at least in the territory. Morris had been born in Jassy.

Relatively speaking, the Goldenbergs were comfortable albeit far from rich. Anti-Jewish laws had rendered 40 percent of the workforce unemployed, but Morris Goldenberg worked from dawn to dusk as a house builder and tinsmith, and there was always food on the table. Morris was devout. The Goldenbergs were urbanized, but far from emancipated. It was a traditional Jewish home. On Friday nights the white tablecloth would be taken out, and the family *benched licht*—lit the traditional candles—and would eat the Sabbath meal and enjoy a little bit of festivity, with Morris delighting the children with Yiddish anecdotes and stories. If they were good, Emanuel and his brothers would even be given a taste of Sarah's homemade cherry brandy. Religious training for the sons was adhered to, and they learned their Hebrew along with Yiddish, Rumanian, and German, which was the dominant language of business among Christians.

Papa Goldenberg had a love for the world, a sense of discovery that he transmitted to young Emanuel, who was nicknamed Manny. Morris liked to stroll outside the Jewish quarter with his young son beside him, stopping for tea and cakes in a café. There was even time for occasional frivolity: Years later Robinson would recall attending a short silent moving picture with his father, a Western that neither of them felt was particularly good. He also recalled attending a stage version of Jules Verne's *Around the World in Eighty Days* and being enchanted. For years he thought the actors had made up their lines as they went along.

Some of the sights were not as lovely as Papa would have wanted. Leaving the Jewish sector was more than an adventure; it meant leaving the safety zone. The Goldenbergs were Jews, and subject to insults, and all too often, violence. During one mob attack, Jack Goldenberg, son number two, was hit on the head by a brick. His skull was cracked, and he lay convulsed by fever for many days. Although it was never treated by a doctor, the wound healed, but periods of blackouts and forgetfulness followed. Eventually, in America, his mysterious ailment would become the family tragedy and a living reminder of the anti-Semitism they had left. Jack would die aged twenty-eight in an institution, having lost all sense of reality. The wound never truly healed for him, nor for the family. To his last days the memory of Jack could make Robinson's eyes fill with tears.

Morris Goldenberg was no fool. He knew there was no future for his family in Rumania, a country that had banned all public education for Jewish children—*his* children. By 1899 there had begun a series of organized marches of thousands of Jews across Rumania to Austria and then to the United States, the promised land. More than 70,000 of the 200,000 Rumanian Jews emigrated between 1900 and 1906, and the Goldenbergs were among them.

As in most immigrant histories, the family didn't travel as a group. First brother Zach went, then Jack and Oscar. In New York, Zach found work in the upholstery business, Jack became a metalworker, and Oscar a cabinetmaker. New York was wonderful, they wrote back home: There were no restrictive laws; the younger boys could be educated in public schools. Money was sent, and finally Papa Goldenberg realized he would have to leave Manny, his other two sons, his wife, and his mother-in-law, and see for himself just what this New York was all about. It meant leaving the five practically defenseless in Bucharest, but the decision was made. Papa left.

It was two years before Morris sent for the rest of the family, but the call to come to America was the easy part. Sarah, her mother, and her three remaining sons had to find their way to Vienna via a network of wagons, trains, and just plain walking—an "underground railroad," as Robinson would later call it. From Vienna, with the help of various Jewish organizations, the five made their way to the port of Le Havre, in northern France. Exhausted, weary and tattered, they were then subjected to the most arduous part of the journey—traveling steerage across the Atlantic Ocean. Young Manny was sick all the way, so sick he prayed for a quick, painless death. But, like all immigrants who had made the same journey, the Goldenbergs were kept alive by the thoughts of the riches that awaited them in America.

This paradise was not to be found when they landed at Castle Garden on Lincoln's Birthday in 1903. The tearful reunion with the older Goldenberg men had to wait, as the five new immigrants were detained overnight and forced to sleep on the floor because of the holiday.

Morris and his older sons were there to meet them, but Manny could hardly recognize his father after the separation. Morris would later tell the story of the reunion and laugh about his Manny. As the family walked toward him, he saw each one holding more than his or her share. Even Max, the youngest, dragged two suitcases along behind him. At the rear was Manny, fixing the creases in his clothes and carrying but one small bundle. Looking at Max and Manny, Morris laughed and called his fifth son "the white-collar man." They knew from the beginning that Manny would work with his brain, not his hands.

The "heaven" that Morris took them to on Manhattan Island was not lush: It was a tenement on Broome Street surrounded by a Lower East

Side that has since been romanticized but was, nonetheless, an overcrowded slum. What Manny saw was decrepit building standing next to decrepit building. There were trees only in small enclaves. Everywhere else there were people, pushcarts, commotion. Yiddish was being spoken, true, but with different accents, with words added from the speaker's old country. Morris had found a job with the Ever-Ready Battery Company. It was not to his liking, but it would have to do.

It is a tribute to their strength that the Goldenbergs did not lose their spirit in America, as many had done. Their home in Bucharest had been clean and well kept, even if old; their neighborhood there had stood for two hundred years. The Lower East Side had been a haven for the incoming poor for a much shorter time, but if the history of the Broome Street building had been written, it might have told of Irish, German, German Jewish, and even some Russian or Rumanian Jewish tenants before the Goldenbergs. Sarah turned it into a home immediately. The traditional mezuzah went on the doorpost, the silver candlesticks on a prominent shelf, and the floors were cleaned and scrubbed again until the filth, and memories, had gone. Bucharest had been crowded, but America was even more cramped, and several brothers were forced into each bed. It fueled the fervor of the older ones to make it, to succeed, if only to escape the conditions.

Yet the essence of America was apparent to all of them. In Rumania Jews (and Greeks for that matter) had been oppressed and segregated: In America a multitude of peoples, creeds, and even colors lived side by side. And away from the old political oppression and the strict, rabbinically directed communities, Jewish life was also different on the Lower East Side: Skullcaps need no longer be worn outside the synagogue. Being American was important. Anarchists and Communists would hold festive balls on Kol Nidre, the eve of Yom Kippur—the Day of Atonement, the holiest festival in the Jewish calendar; families would quarrel as one member joined the Communists, another the Labor Bundists, and still another the Republicans. Yiddish papers were split politically; Jews, Italians, and Irish would join together to fight for labor unions and better conditions. Diversity in opinion was not just allowed, it was expected.

Robinson, as an adult, would say that this view of the melting-pot culture that was America had made him feel the country was, indeed, special. It was a feeling that would remain with him for the rest of his life, even while his adopted country was battering away at his soul for being politically too liberal fifty years later.

Although Manny spoke Yiddish, Rumanian, and German and read Hebrew, he knew no English when he entered PS 137. Yet he had an ear for languages, a talent that would, in a few years, prove the making of his acting career. Manny learned English relatively quickly. He listened hard to his teachers, Anglo-Saxon Americans whom he would call "Mrs. Washington" and "Mr. Lincoln" because that is the image they held for him. He became aware of his accent, and he worked to rid himself of it, to sound like his classmates who were born in America. No, to sound even better. Within a year he was proficient, so adept that he did not remember ever having an accent, except perhaps a bit of New York sharpness.

Morris and Sarah went to great lengths to retain the family spirit and ties they had brought with them. Friday-night meals were still the highlight of the week, with the candles, the cherry brandy, the pressed white tablecloth. They were also scenes of rapid-fire talking and joking, with Morris displaying his talent for storytelling. As Manny grew older he learned to appreciate his father's gift and emulate it when he, too, found an audience.

Morris also taught his sons to improve themselves, as he did by running a candy store and leaving the battery business behind. His motto was, "Always live beyond your means. It will make you work harder." Manny listened, he believed. He knew that English, and subsequently success, would not just be learned at school. Manny spent hours poring over newspapers, both American and Yiddish—and there were many of both to choose from in those days. Clad in the short pants boys wore in 1905, he spent his afternoons in the affluent splendor of the Astor Place Library reading books, among them classics such as Jack London's *The Sea Wolf* (in which he would star when it was made into a motion picture thirty-five years later). From reading he also learned about politics. Since the *New York Evening Journal* was his favorite newspaper, its publisher, William Randolph Hearst, and its chief columnist, Arthur Brisbane, became Manny's first American heroes. He didn't know the term "yellow journalism," for which Hearst was famous, but he did know that Brisbane attacked the "trusts" and the "monopolies," the very forces of evil as seen by the immigrants on the Lower East Side.

Occasionally, he would turn to the drama section and read the reviews, memorizing the names of the greats—Ethel Barrymore, Henry Dixey, and especially the Jewish ones: Alla Nazimova, Oscar Hammerstein. It would be years before he'd attend a Broadway show, and at this stage, his theatrical experiences were sparse—a Yiddish theater presentation, an amateur drama in school or at one of the settlement houses.

Manny had no inkling that someday he would be on stage with the greats and later be a name to be reckoned with himself. As his grades moved from the Ds of his first report card to the B+ and A marks that knowledge of the language brought, Manny dreamed of being a lawyer, perhaps even a savior of the lower classes around him. He explained to his attentive family one night at dinner that he didn't want to be a corporate lawyer, or a pawn of the moneyed class, but a criminal lawyer, "with the object of defending those who lacked the power or the money or the sense to defend themselves."

This desire was part of his goal to be the perfect American, fit and sound in every way. His mind was growing, thanks to the hours in the library. His spirit was soaring with each morning's unfurling of the flag, the Stars and Stripes. But nature interceded in one way, in that he was far from an athlete. In one grade school incident, he lost consciousness and almost drowned in a neighborhood swimming pool. His heart stopped and only quick resuscitation saved him, but he hated pools forever after. His home in Beverly Hills would have an art gallery, but no pool.

A year or so later he began going to the gym instead of the library several afternoons each week in the hope of building his physique—one last try to be the perfect American. The constant exercise, overzealously practiced, brought him to the brink of nervous collapse. He was, thereafter, an enthusiastic spectator.

After his term at PS 137 was up, he moved on to PS 20, a school from which such luminaries as George and Ira Gershwin, Jacob Javits, and Paul Muni—later Robinson's greatest rival—also were graduated. By this time Manny knew he'd always be last in athletic competition, so he had turned to pursuits he felt he could master. He discovered he had the ability to articulate thoughts and stories, just as his father did at the dinner table. Still only twelve, he decided to take the big step and try his elocution on an audience. Armed with an essay entitled "Keeping Our Streets Clean," he stood up and spoke before an auditorium gathering at PS 20. It earned him applause and the guts to walk over to the University Settlement House. There, with speeches borrowed from worn, paperback novels, he tried his hand at dramatic recitation. His endeavors were greeted with shouts of "Hey Manny, yawr a regulah achtuh," in the thick street En-glish of his peers. Up on stage he was accepted.

Public speaking brought him a bit of personal success, a niche from which he could find self-esteem, and a soapbox from which he could articulate his ideas and persuade the other young minds to his current way of thinking. His parents continued to dream that Manny would be the lawyer he talked of becoming. But then, for at least a short time, religion entered Manny's life. Aged twelve and a half, as he began to study for his bar mitzvah—the ritual of manhood in which all Jewish boys participate—Manny announced that the prospect of becoming a rabbi was appealing.

So he studied. He walked across the Williamsburg Bridge to Brooklyn in order to find a teacher whose training was more spiritual. Morris and Sarah were shocked: A Jewish boy—*their* Jewish boy—should be a lawyer, a doctor, not a rabbi. Manny was firm, he would not be dissuaded. He saw preaching as a chance to move the minds and spirits of men as only the best religious teachers had done.

When the day came in December 1906 for him to rise to the bimah—the synagogue pulpit—and read from the ancient scriptures, he was ready. The Rivington Street Rumanian Jewish Congregation—which still stands today—was filled with the masses that Manny wanted to steer toward righteousness. He read from the Torah, the scriptures. Then he stood facing the mass of faces, of men with prayer shawls on top of their heads or around their shoulders. He spoke. They listened while he read his speech in Yiddish. They remained still while he read it again in English. It was, he would laugh later, the longest bar mitzvah speech in the history of the congregation, but the men sat still and listened. Yet, when he finished, there were no cheers, none of the lift that speaking before a more secular congregation at the settlement house had brought. But there was praise: The men told his father he was a savior of his people. A rabbi he would be.

Morris was a wise father. He couldn't forbid his son to become a rabbi, but he could coax him in another direction using the sort of psychology that came naturally to parents of his generation. The week after the bar mitzvah, Morris took Manny to a yeshiva to propose him for the rabbinate. Manny looked around. The boys were not sitting in a classroom with a "Mrs. Washington" or a "Mr. Lincoln" and discussing a myriad of subjects and ideas: They were hunched over on benches, listening to a black-frocked, bearded old man read from the Bible. To a boy whose mind and dreams took him to wide-open spaces, this looked like a prison. He reconsidered.

"I found there were other ways of doing good," Manny would say later. He announced his intention of being a lawyer or an engineer again. "I couldn't be sanctimonious twenty-four hours a day anyway."

Inside himself he knew he was addicted to applause, even if he could not yet admit it; Manny loved the feeling that the faces of the crowd were listening to *him*, to words from his mouth. Six months after his bar mitzvah he was appointed to produce and direct the commencement exercises at PS 20. He rehearsed his classmates on top of the roof on Broome Street, saving the commencement speech for himself. Borrowing heavily from Teddy Roosevelt's second inaugural address, he delivered the words, manipulating the crowd in a way that would make any politician proud. When he finished there was applause, a commodity lacking at the synagogue.

Manny received good grades at PS 20 and was accepted at Townsend Harris High School uptown. The entire Goldenberg clan followed, moving to the Bronx, where Morris opened what Warner Bros. publicity would later call an antique store, but what was really a secondhand store, a place to find rare and unique little items, or *tchotchkes*, a Yiddish word that can mean anything from a trinket to an unrecognized gem. Robinson would later recall that few items in the shop were precious, but Morris had a feel for quality, a sense he passed on to his most inquisitive son. The son would later utilize this knowledge in his obsession with collecting works of art. Even as a youngster wearing short pants, he would find his way to museums and art galleries, look around, then head back to the Astor Library to discover, in books, what he had seen and why it was renowned.

But politics, not art history, was Manny's major interest in high school. Townsend Harris was a high school filled with achievers, with young men who were eager to become involved with the issues of the day. For Emanuel Goldenberg, who was already a member of the Young Folks Political League, politics was a natural extension of his desire to communicate his idealism.

Once again Hearst was Manny's man. It is a matter of political record that William Randolph Hearst ran as an independent candidate for mayor of New York in 1909—his second try for the office. What Hearst probably never knew was that Manny Goldenberg became one of his most vocal supporters, despite the fact that, at fifteen, he was unable to vote. If Hearst never knew Manny by name, his campaign committee did. They found him at Townsend Harris campaigning for their man and decided to put him on soapboxes throughout the boroughs. Manny was all too eager to cry out against Hearst's opponents—Democrat William Jay Gaynor, a puppet of Tammany Hall, and Republican Otto T. Bannard. At one point, Manny was driven by automobile to preach the gospel according to Hearst in Manhattan's theater district. It was the first time Manny had been in an automobile; it was the first time he had seen Broadway; it was the first time he had attracted the attention of total strangers with his words, with his ability to use the textures of his voice. He was strong; he was emotional; he was full of energy.

Hearst lost. And Manny had passed through Broadway almost oblivious to the theaters around him. But he had tasted politics firsthand and he had enjoyed it. When he returned to Townsend Harris, no political argument was too soft. Manny debated with his schoolmates both inside and outside the classrooms. His sympathies were always with the underdog, always with the weak.

No doubt that is how he now saw himself, realizing that he'd never be tall. At most he was 5'6," maybe closer to 5'5," and he was forever trying to make himself look taller. His face was already far too broad to be considered handsome, his hair was black, and his eyes a deep brown. Even his complexion was swarthy. He compensated by dressing better than his peers (a trait he would carry into his adult life), with good, clean if old suits, worn with an intelligent manner.

With the confidence he had acquired during the Hearst campaign, he fought for the causes he believed in. He argued. He debated. When one classmate was honored with a gold watch Manny thought was undeserved, he marched to the principal's office and demanded that the honor be revoked. Often he won his fights. Whatever he lacked in physical stature he was already developing in charisma. He was nominated for class president against one James Donahue, a tall, articulate, and better-looking young man of Irish descent.

The campaign almost tarnished his image of America. It became Jew against Irish, or kike against mick. Manny and Jim were aghast, and they squelched the name-calling by walking arm in arm in front of the student body. Manny could not tolerate prejudice in America. The election came, and like Hearst, Manny lost. But his friendship with his opponent lasted a lifetime. Donahue went on to become a respected judge in New York.

Morris and Sarah thought that their son, with thoughts of the pulpit behind him, would become the lawyer or engineer they hoped for. Manny paid lip service to their dream, but increasingly, his real joy was in the arts and, without even realizing it, he was being drawn into the dramatic world. He acted in school plays whenever he had the opportunity, usually relegated to playing the parts of adults.

He was graduated from Harris in 1910, knowing full well that he could not be satisfied with law as a career, although Manny dared not tell his parents. He entered the City College of New York, Class of 1914, thinking he would dabble in a number of different courses of study for a while and find himself.

Actor Sam Jaffe was also at CCNY then, Class of 1912, and he and Manny Goldenberg met, thus beginning a friendship that would last until Robinson's death in 1973. Jaffe was, like Manny, not yet sure that acting was a legitimate career goal and was studying math and physics. "I used to see him on campus," Jaffe recalled. "I didn't have much contact with him in college, but he made his presence known in school. He was always a figure you'd notice. He was active in causes, always wanting to help people. Wanting to help people ran like a red thread through his life."

But Manny primarily wanted to help himself. He enrolled in math and science courses and almost flunked out of school. Instead of attending class sessions he began to find oppressive, he'd sneak into music classes or the school auditorium and listen to rehearsals. He was absorbed in trying to find a direction, a worthy goal.

One day during his sophomore year in English literature class, he was called upon by Professor William Otis Bradley to recite Antony's soliloquy from *Julius Caesar*. In a 1956 interview with the *New York Post*, Otis recalled the scene: "I happened to look up and there was Robinson, lost to the world. His hands were clenched at the side of the desk. I never before or after saw a student so deeply affected. He was beside himself. He was trembling. Tears welled in his eyes and ran down his cheeks. I saw then that he had dramatic imagination."

Buoyed by Bradley's reaction, Manny used the soliloquy to audition for the Elizabethan Society, the CCNY dramatic club, and was accepted. He threw himself into a self-education in the arts. He went back to the Astor Library to read all he could on the great actors, dramatic critics, and playwrights. He read the great playwrights' work. After these sessions, he would stroll through the bookshops that then stood on Fourth Avenue, buying books and inexpensive reproductions of the work of great artists such as Rubens, Goya, Rembrandt. On weekends he'd buy a seat in the balcony of a Broadway show, or even a lesser production in the Bronx. After much introspection, Manny knew. He wanted a career on the stage.

But he dared not tell his parents, not because he feared their disapproval or rejection, but because his immigrant soul told him that his parents had not sacrificed so he could go into such a profession—precarious and without a guaranteed future.

"He asked Adolph Werner, who was head of the German department, for help in going into the theater," Sam Jaffe still remembers. Werner tried to discourage Manny but finally "gave him a letter for Mr. Benjamin Roeder, who was David Belasco's casting director. I remember that he had to wait until Roeder returned from a vacation, but eventually he got to see him."

Roeder was sufficiently impressed to get Manny an audition for the Sargent School, soon to be known as the Academy of Dramatic Arts, on whose board of directors Roeder served. But Franklin Sargent was also on vacation, and by the time the audition could be arranged, it was late summer of 1912, only days before Manny was to begin his junior year in college. Standing before Sargent on that hot August day, Manny did not know what to expect from the deacon of drama, a master of unnerving silences and penetrating stares. He did not really know what an audition meant. When Sargent asked him to perform a monologue, he blanched, then fell back on the one piece of dramatic work he knew well—the Antony soliloquy. Sargent thanked him, and Manny went back to the Bronx expecting to return to CCNY.

As the autumn session began, Sargent contacted him. He was accepted and awarded a full scholarship. But that seemed the easy part. He now had to tell Morris and Sarah. They were not pleased: They argued with him; they warned him of the likelihood of failure, of painted ladies, and an unnatural life. But his brothers backed him up, Morris and Sarah gave way, and Manny was on his way to becoming an actor.

Although Warner Bros. publicity would later boast that Edward G. Robinson had received a degree from CCNY, had studied law, and eventually earned a master's degree from Columbia University, he did not. Instead, he dropped out of college and studied at the best acting school America had to offer at the time.

2

FROM THE BRONX
TO BROADWAY

I'm not so much on face value, but when it comes to stage value,
I'll deliver for you.

—Edward G. Robinson

As Manny Goldenberg threw himself full force into the rigorous syl-
labus of the Academy—movement classes, scene work, fencing,
dance, elocution—Sargent knew he had a prospect who, with the right
dedication, could make a living on the stage. After only a few weeks at the
Academy, Robinson was taken aside by Sargent and given what was a
"suggestion," but was nonetheless to be followed: Change your name to
something, shall we say, more Anglo-Saxon.

Manny gave it some thought. Although he was still living at home in
the Bronx with his parents, they would just have to understand this new
step. He agreed to change his name. He sat for long hours with a friend,
Joseph Schildkraut, nicknamed Pepe, but they were unable to come up
with anything suitable. Then one night he went to see a British drawing-
room comedy called *The Passerby*, a play long since forgotten. From his
vantage point in the rear of the Criterion Theater balcony, he could hear
the actors but was having trouble seeing them. He heard a butler on stage

say, "Mrs. Fiske, there's a Mr. Robinson to see you," and the name stuck in Manny's mind.

Robinson. It was a name other Jews had found suitable when they changed their names. Robinson it would be. For a first name he wanted to retain the initial E, so he chose Edward, after the then king of England. One couldn't get more Anglo-Saxon than that. He retained the initial G as a reminder of who he really was.

Sargent gave his approval to the new name and Edward G. Robinson it would be. From that point on only family members would call him "Manny." He would be, to all new acquaintances, "Eddie." Although Manny would experiment with his name in theater programs during the next few years, Edward G. Robinson was the name he would stick with.

With a name chosen, Robinson was ready for his real stage debut under the auspices of the Academy. Late in 1912 Sargent cast him as Consul Bernick in the Academy's production of *The Pillars of Society* by Henrik Ibsen at the Carnegie Lyceum. Although Robinson had to act with the indignity of lifts in his shoes, it was worth it, as casting people and theatrical producers would be in the audience. The production ran its allotted span, but it turned out not to be the showcase that would get him work. There were no offers.

He heard that the Loew's Theater chain had open tryouts, so he put together an adaptation of *The Bells* by Henry James, the story of a man who is haunted by the faint memory of a murder he committed years earlier, and who, under hypnosis, dredges the incident up from the depths of his soul.

Calling his one-act play *The Bells of Conscience*, Robinson performed for the Loew's casting men. They liked it and booked him for four split weeks at their Plaza Theater on Lexington Avenue. Asked what name he wanted for the marquee, he gave them "Edward G. Robinson," the first time he had needed to do so professionally. When he arrived at the theater, he saw the sign "Edward G. Robinson in *Bells of Conscience*" awaiting an audience. It was to be another fifteen years before his name was again above the title on Broadway.

It gave Robinson confidence that *Bells of Conscience* had been favorably received, although the forum was technically vaudeville. He was now, in his own estimation, a professional. He had his first suit, purchased for the production, and a felt hat bought secondhand on Seventh Avenue.

Still, no work came, and he returned to classes. His pal Pepe Schildkraut was the son of Rudolph Schildkraut, one of the premier actors of the Yiddish theater, and Pepe mentioned that his father was looking for a short-term replacement for a small role in his current play, *Number 37*, at the West End Theater. Robinson jumped at the chance, and Schildkraut senior agreed. Since the play was in Yiddish—Robinson would have preferred English, although Yiddish was his first language—he chose the name Edward Golden for the program. He rehearsed with the great Schildkraut, more than a little awed.

Robinson—or Golden—had one scene in the second act, played entirely with Schildkraut. He was a district attorney in his fifties, but it was not unusual for younger actors to play older men in the Yiddish theater. The first time he walked out on stage and faced Schildkraut, he promptly forgot the lines. Panic-stricken, he dashed off stage to find the prompter and a copy of the script. When he returned on stage he discovered Schildkraut ad-libbing snatches of dialogue from previous plays to an audience oblivious to any crisis. When the performance ended, Schildkraut insisted Robinson take a bow, which the young actor did.

"So what was wrong, young man?" Schildkraut whispered when the curtain finally came down.

"I forgot my lines," Robinson responded, full of grief and apology.

"So what was such a problem?" shrugged Schildkraut. "All you had to do was ask me and I would have told you."

Robinson had learned a professional lesson that night. *Number 37* would be the only time he performed on the Yiddish stage, although even today Hollywood friends and colleagues insist he was a Yiddish theater veteran.

What Robinson needed now was work, having fulfilled the requirements of the Academy. It was 1913, he was still just nineteen, and he was without prospects: He haunted the theater district making the contacts that he hoped would bring him the beginnings of a career. The great George Arliss (who had not yet gone to Hollywood) was kind enough to respond to young Robinson's inquiries and suggested that he be dedicated, the old "if you want it badly enough you'll have it" adage. Robinson listened. He became the personification of dedication. While others enjoyed a more hedonistic life and sexual dalliances, he knocked on doors of agencies and wrote letters to producers. Occasionally, there was interest in at least seeing him, but there was little work for a young character actor. Even his sturdy Anglo-Saxon name could not hide his ethnic looks, and though relatively slim, he had not grown since high school.

An actor with an obvious disadvantage often comes up with a gimmick to get work, and Robinson thought of a line that he thought was convincing. When he went for interviews and was, as usual, surrounded by tall blond Adonises, he'd say to the agent or casting person, "I'm not much on face value, but when it comes to stage value, I'll deliver for you." The Wales Winter Agency listened, partly to get him off their backs, partly because they were loosely associated with the Academy and wanted to keep Sargent's good will—and a steady flow of blond Adonises.

The S. M. Stainbach Stock Company was in need of an apprentice, to fetch and carry for the stars, pull curtains, run errands, and when needed play bit parts. Was Robinson interested? He was, of course. He went home, told Morris and Sarah of his good fortune, and set off for Binghamton, New York, to earn the princely sum of $25 per week, which even then was a pittance.

It would be nice to say that Robinson was discovered and vaulted to stardom in Binghamton. Alas, this was not the case. He toured with the company to Albany, New York, and did get to act, in plays such as *The Traveling Salesman, The Man on the Box*, and *The Gamblers*. As an extra he often played a few parts in each play, and the stage manager allowed him to use Edward G. Robinson as billing for a small part and Emanuel Golden for bits. The one role that salvaged the weeks he spent with Stainbach was a chance to play Sato in a production of Eugene Walter's *Paid in Full*.

Not accepted by the cast since he was lowest in rank, Robinson spent most of his free time—the little he had—by himself. One night in late April 1913, he struck up a conversation with a lady in a restaurant; they ended up in his room, and he experienced his first sexual encounter. Robinson would later report that it was less than satisfying, and when he returned to New York, dedication to work again became his driving force.

Summer was spent back in The Bronx, again pounding the pavements in hope of work. Morris and Sarah gently suggested he try to get reaccepted at CCNY, perhaps to earn a diploma in something else at which he could make a living. As September approached, Robinson almost agreed.

But Wales Winter rescued him from such a fate. The Orpheum Theater in Cincinnati wanted him for their autumn season. He rushed to Wales Winter to sign the contract. Unlike the extensive contracts Robinson would sign in later years, his first real acting assignment was finalized on one sheet of paper. On it, J. Herman Thuman, manager of the Orpheum, engages Edward G. Robinson of 835 East 152nd Street for "a thirty-week season, more or less" at $40 per week. The manager agreed to pay Robinson's expenses to Cincinnati, and back to New York, only if the manager gave two weeks' notice prior to discharge. The management would furnish costumes for period plays, but Robinson would have to supply modern dress. Gross commission of 5 percent each week for the first ten weeks' salary was to be sent to the Academy. If the season were to run the full thirty weeks, Robinson would earn a two-week vacation without pay. Finally, in lieu of a morals clause, there was the simple "insubordination and intoxication instant dismissal."

When he got to the theater, Robinson realized that the shiny contract had no real meaning—the other actors still ignored him. He wasn't good-looking, and he was playing very small parts. One such part, as petty thief Dick the Rat in *Alias Jimmy Valentine*, would be a hint of what was to come for Robinson, but no one in Cincinnati noticed him. It was a theater with a proscenium arch and no desire for experimentation. Robinson earned his money, but he was less than pleased and gladly returned to New York when the Cincinnati season ended in twenty-two weeks.

Back in New York there was again no work, although Robinson continued to attempt to sell himself as "not good on face value, but good on stage value." He read of auditions for a tour of *Kismet*, and realizing they still needed someone for the part of Nasir, he presented himself on stage as someone who could play a fifty-year-old man in the Caliph's Court, borrowing from lessons learned with Rudolph Schildkraut. Harris Grey Fiske, the producer, liked what he saw, and Robinson was sent to Canada.

The show toured in Ottawa, Montreal, and a few other cities, and Robinson's salary was $25, back at the level he had received from Stainbach in Binghampton. There was one difference, though; now he was accepted by the other cast members as a real actor. One dancer in particular, Leah Salisbury, became a good friend, and more than a decade later, then a literary agent, she would remember him and send him a copy of a book by W. R. Burnett with the suggestion that he read it. The book was *Little Caesar*.

Kismet lasted only a few weeks on tour, for when World War I broke out in Europe, Canada, a member of the British Commonwealth, was thrown into the conflict. All theaters were closed, and Robinson found himself without a job, pounding the pavements of Broadway once more.

Prospects were bleak, so Robinson did what most other actors tried when unemployed—vaudeville. He put together a script aptly called *Electrocution* and won a chance to play it at Hammerstein's in New York. It was canceled after a few performances because the management thought it was too depressing for an audience of ticket buyers concerned with a war overseas that might touch home. Hammerstein's tried him again in another skit, this time playing a Chinese, but it lasted only a few weeks, typical for vaudeville.

It was not until early 1915 that Robinson, who was again contemplating a return to CCNY for a degree in education, got what was to be his big break. Adolph Klauber was general manager and casting agent for Arch and Edgar Selwyn, well-known theatrical producers who also dabbled in moving pictures. Klauber had a property entitled *Under Fire* by Roi Cooper Megrue that was perfect for the times—a story exploring the warlike nature of Germany, filled with scenes involving the allies, the British, Belgian, and French, fighting against the kaiser. It meant a large cast, and to minimize costs, Klauber had been instructed to find actors who could double up on parts, no easy task considering the variations in dialects that would be needed.

There was a certain young actor in New York who had become adept at doubling parts, who was fluent in French and German and their dialects, and who always promised "stage value." Klauber decided to give Robinson a chance. For $60 weekly, Robinson found himself playing a Belgian spy (complete with goatee), a Belgian peasant (hysterically screeching "The Germans are coming"), a German officer (the one who comes), and a Cockney soldier in the trenches. So impressed were Klauber and the Selwyns, they fired a few actors, gave Robinson $20 more per week, and gave him a few more international roles. He billed himself at the opening as E. G. Robinson.

Their instincts were right. When *Under Fire* played Boston, the *Boston Globe* singled out their discovery and noted: "The most versatile actor in *Under Fire* is E. G. Robinson. He plays three widely different roles, but so clever is the actor's makeup that it is difficult for the audience to realize that the same man who acts the French spy in the scene at the Belgian inn is a moment later the outraged Belgian peasant, close after he has been shot by the Germans. Later, in the third act, he is one of the wounded soldiers in the Cathedral, 'somewhere in France.'"

That was out of town, but when *Under Fire* opened at the Hudson Theater in New York, on April 12, 1915, the critics again noticed the energetic young actor who was spending as much time changing costumes as he was on stage. *Vanity Fair* singled out the character work, including Robinson. *The Theatre Magazine* indicated, "E. G. Robinson is admirable as André" (the spy).

Broadway, reviews, a decent salary, even a few interviews, which he loved. Forget CCNY. Edward G. Robinson was a working actor, and one who had a wonderful showcase. Interviews called him "a veritable league of nations" for his multicharacter work.

With his newfound success, Robinson cast off The Bronx boy forever. He bought an entirely new wardrobe, all first class, remembering what Morris Goldenberg had always told him about living beyond his means so he'd work harder. He strutted down Broadway carrying a cane, wearing spats: a dandy, a man of class and distinction, a man girls wanted to date. And date he did, always taking a taxi and doing it right. But he remained celibate, on the whole, still a child in his approach to women. Sex "left me stuttering and sweating," he would say later.

The Selwyns came through again when *Under Fire* had run its course and cast Robinson as Fagan, a criminal, in *Under Sentence*, a play by Mergrue and Irvin S. Cobb. Robinson was attracted to the play because it dealt with prison reform and therefore had a "message." It had a healthy run.

With two successes under his belt, his bubble burst with *The Pawn*, in which he played a Japanese. It looked good at first—one of the Chicago newspapers printed a caricature of Robinson—but *The Pawn* lasted only two weeks at the Fulton Theater in New York. Robinson went straight into *Drafted*, playing a German officer, but it flopped before it even reached New York. In November 1917, producer Arthur Hopkins cast him in *The Deluge*, a play by the Swede Henning Berger. Pauline Lord starred, and Robinson had a crush on her. The play didn't get off the ground.

He licked his wounds and went to Buffalo to play a French Canadian named Batiste in a play entitled *The Teacher of Goshen Hollow* produced by George M. Cohan. Its name was shortened to *The Little Teacher* by the time it got to Broadway, and Robinson was in another success.

By spring 1918, though, Robinson knew he would soon be drafted into the army and probably sent overseas to fight in France. Oddly enough, although he now wanted to contribute, Robinson had registered as a conscientious objector, noting on his application "unless my country needs me." In 1914 he had been pro-German, a sentiment he blamed on the fact that the Germans were fighting Rumania and Russia, countries he felt to be his mortal enemies, and also on the isolationism of his hero

Hearst. It was the sinking of the *Lusitania* in 1915 that had changed Robinson's views.

In July 1918 Robinson asked George M. Cohan to write a letter to the intelligence bureau for him. Robinson hoped it would get him into the secret service. He enlisted in the navy, but the hoped-for appointment from Washington was not to come through. Instead, he was sent as a sailor to Pelham Bay in the Bronx to do clerical duties and peel potatoes. When the armistice came in November, Robinson was still sitting in Pelham Bay, and he was bitterly upset. Ironically, a few days later his appointment to the secret service came through, but it was too late: He had seen the effects of the war, the mutilated bodies on their way back from the trenches. "I turned them down," he would say later in interviews. "I realized all along that I was right. That war is not right." This pacifism would also lead him to vote for Eugene V. Debs, the Socialist Party candidate for president in 1920, in large measure because the Socialists had not supported the U.S. involvement in World War I and were vehement in their opposition to bombing cities.

The war had also matured him—he was almost twenty-five when it ended—and he knew he could no longer be content to live with his parents in the Bronx, no matter how easy it made his life. He took a job with the Garrick Players in Washington, D.C., as the first step toward severing the apron strings.

After a few months he returned to New York and went into rehearsals for *Dark Horses* in the spring of 1919, playing an Anglo-Saxon role for what was quite probably the only time on stage. Rehearsals were interrupted by a strike when the actors joined together to form Actors Equity and had to fight for its recognition by the producers. Once again he was on a soapbox on Broadway, but unlike before, for Hearst, he was now preaching his own cause. Robinson learned many lessons during those strike weeks, particularly when George M. Cohan, the man who had been his sponsor in his attempt to join the secret service, snubbed him when they passed on the street. It was then he realized the true nature of the relationship between actor and producer. In the 1930s he would have many fights with the likes of Jack Warner and Hal Wallis, always aware that he was an employee.

Dark Horses opened as *First Is Last* in September 1919 and lasted a few weeks, enough time to make a star of Richard Dix, but left Robinson out of work again. He was hired to play Satan in *Night Lodging*, by Maksim Gorky, produced by his friend Arthur Hopkins, which opened a few days before Christmas and had a healthy run, until the summer of 1920.

Broadway was now dominated by the new flapper age, but Robinson was still married only to his career. He was still the dandy, now a known figure in the theater district. He'd occasionally try a speakeasy at night but rarely had much to drink. The flapper age was not to his taste. To pass the time after the closure of *Night Lodging*, he again haunted the art galleries and began to invest in a few prints. He was now living at home again in The Bronx, however reluctantly, and when he dated, Robinson would see his companions to their apartments or hotels in a taxi around midnight, then head for The Bronx.

In September, he was cast as Pinsky—a Jew—in *Podelkin*, an anti-Bolshevik play produced by Booth Tarkington and starring George Arliss, who had been Robinson's hero. Another lesson was learned. Arliss the actor was aloof and not particularly helpful or interested in his admiring supporting players. *Podelkin*, despite Arliss's presence, flopped within a month. A star does not necessarily carry a production. (Ironically, years later Robinson would star in another anti-Communist play, *Darkness at Noon*, a play with similar characters—but his reasons for taking the part would not be purely artistic.)

Out on the streets again, Robinson was awaiting word from Arthur Hopkins about work when he bumped into his old acquaintance Sam Jaffe, whom he had not seen since their casual encounters at CCNY. Jaffe too, like Robinson, had decided to give the theater a try. It had been rough going, Jaffe remembers:

> I had been on tour with a show, I was back with no work and I met Eddie on the street. He looked different than he did at CCNY. Not just older, but

there was a manner about him. I remember he was wearing a hat and carrying a walking stick. We talked and I told him the difficulty I was having in getting a job. He said, "Why don't you go see Arthur Hopkins. He sees everyone." I did, and Hopkins cast me in a small part in *Samson and Delilah*, in which Eddie played a very prominent role. Later, when we went on tour with the show, our friendship was cemented. What attracted me to him as a friend? He was a wonderful actor. You just had to look at him on stage. And he was very moral.

Samson and Delilah starred Jacob Ben-Ami, the great Yiddish star, in his first English-language production, a backstage comedy in which Robinson played a part that reminded Broadway insiders of Oscar Hammerstein. Jaffe was The Prompter, with his back to the audience most of the time. Robinson and Jaffe were drawn together partly because of their horrified reaction to Ben-Ami in rehearsals and on stage. He went to great lengths to upstage his fellow actors, was a ham, and—to Robinson and Jaffe—overacted to an astonishing degree. Nevertheless, when the show opened in November it was an instant hit, Ben-Ami especially, and they were guaranteed numerous weeks of work and then a road tour. It was a good, steady income. Robinson had worked his way up to $200 per week as his going rate.

Artistically, though, he felt barren. He was searching for more, tired of being a supporting player, bouncing from part to part. He talked Hopkins into letting him skip matinees of *Samson and Delilah* to play a larger role in *Elvind of the Hills*. He was able to do a few of these matinees but was still unhappy.

Hopkins had become a good friend and sensed Robinson's restlessness. He suggested Robinson try something different—a moving picture. The Selwyns had got together with a fiercely independent immigrant named Sam Goldfish (later Goldwyn) and were producing motion pictures in Fort Lee, New Jersey. Although some stage actors still felt films were beneath them, Robinson suppressed any such feelings, coaxed by a challenge and a hefty salary—more than he had made in any one week as an actor.

Fields of Glory was the name of the film—a melodrama starring Dorothy Gish and written by Irvin Cobb—and was, of course, silent. The experience, from the outset, was jarring to Robinson the stage actor. Scenes were shot out of sequence, so Robinson's final dialogue was the first thing he was asked to do. He couldn't figure out what to do with the dialogue, since this was silent. He was supposed to invent his words and worry about gestures, broad gestures. The latter wasn't a problem. Fitting into this new technology was. Robinson saw the rushes and was aghast at the way he looked on screen, at his mannerisms, his dark and brooding appearance.

He talked it over with Gish. He would quit. She tried to reassure him that rushes meant nothing, that films were edited and cut with subtitles. It would all work out. Robinson was not convinced. He was determined to quit, to leave this abomination called movies behind him forever. He marched into Goldfish's office to demand to be released from his contract when the producer pulled a surprise of his own—Robinson would soon discover that film producers were to have the upper hand. Goldfish *wanted* Robinson to leave. He wasn't satisfied with the work either but promised Eddie that some day they would work together again (not until *Barbary Coast* in 1935).

Robinson was dumbfounded, as many were by Goldfish, and hurt. It was the first time anyone had told him his work was not up to par. He licked his wounds by accepting an engagement in Denver, Colorado, at Elitch Gardens. It gave him a summer with some time for rest and relaxation, as he worked in a number of inconsequential audience favorites, and every so often got lucky with a girl. With a salary of $150 per week and fewer expenses, Robinson spent the summer freed of money worries. He was also happy to be away from the humidity of New York and away from his parents' apartment. Only he and Oscar, who would never marry, lived at home now, and Robinson was sure it would break his parents' hearts if he left finally before finding himself a wife.

While in Denver, Arthur Hopkins sent Robinson the script for a play entitled *The Idle Inn*, which Robinson recognized as the English-language adaptation of a favorite Yiddish folktale. When he returned to

New York, Robinson told Hopkins he would be delighted to play the role of the father of the bride for the marriage sequence. He reminded Hopkins of Sam Jaffe's work in *Samson and Delilah*, and his friend was cast as the bridegroom. His enthusiasm ran high, until he discovered that Hopkins had engaged Ben-Ami, by now a Broadway as well as Yiddish theater legend, to play the lead. History repeated itself. Ben-Ami gave little to the actors on stage but was beloved by the audience, who in turn neglected the other actors as well. Were it not for his long-standing relationship with Hopkins, Robinson would have quit. Luckily, there was not time for a confrontation between Ben-Ami and Robinson: The play opened before Christmas in 1921 and lasted only a few weeks.

Hopkins revived *The Deluge*, still in love with the play, and cast Robinson in it again. It gave Robinson work for the winter, but that was all. By spring he was out of work and gladly returned to Denver for another season of stock. At the Elitch Gardens his picture was on the cover of the program. He was a star in Denver, but he yearned for the same status in New York, and for a vehicle that would give him a chance to stretch himself.

The Theater Guild, established in 1919, was the perfect forum for Robinson. Its purpose was to encourage new playwrights and serious productions, just what he wanted. In September 1922 he had his chance. He was cast as Louis in the French farce *Banco*, produced by the Guild at the Ritz Theater. Alfred Lunt, who starred, would later heap praise on Robinson as an actor, but the production was doomed and lasted only a few weeks.

Unemployed and frustrated, he was approached by John Robertson and offered a role in a movie Robertson was directing to be called *The Bright Shawl*. It meant six weeks or more in Havana, Cuba. Again it was a silent film, and there would be the same pitfalls as with *Fields of Glory*. But it also meant more money than he was used to, and besides, Robinson was already an aficionado of cigars, and the best came from Cuba. He backed down from his vow never to do another movie, and not long after Columbus Day, Morris, Sarah, and Sam Jaffe were on the pier to wish him bon voyage.

Cuba was a stark contrast to America in 1922. There was no Prohibition, so Robinson and stars Dorothy Gish and Richard Barthelmess drank and caroused. The Robinson who had always been an avid reader and had in recent years been devouring only the best in magazines and nonfiction didn't open a book. When the shooting of the plantation melodrama was over, he returned to New York embarrassed with himself for having made a movie he thought "silly" and having lost his sense of art.

The Theater Guild saved the day. He was cast in two roles—the Button Molder and Von Eberkopf—in *Peer Gynt*, the Ibsen classic. Starring was Pepe Schildkraut. When *Gynt* opened in February, Robinson felt like an artist. But *The Bright Shawl* was playing in New York at the same time and it was for this work that he was most recognized on the street. He was aware also of the contrasts between the live theaters—old, cramped, with wooden chairs—and the new movie palaces, built in splendor. He was beginning to have doubts, but no more film offers came his way. If they had, he might have taken one.

Peer Gynt lasted its six-week run, and Robinson was offered what was, up till then, his most exciting project. He would originate the role of Shrdlu in Elmer Rice's *The Adding Machine* for the Guild. The play, which deals with the effects of the mechanized modern world on the worker, suited his talents and political temperament. It was—and remains—an extraordinary play but was a risk. The cautious Robinson, in need of a change but fearing the results of his appearance in the play on his career, used the name Edgar G. Robinson when the production opened in March. It was controversial, but *The Adding Machine* helped set a standard, for both Rice and Robinson. It gave Robinson prestige but did not help him pay his mounting bills. The play closed after seventy-two performances, hardly a hit.

A string of flops followed: *The Voice* closed in Chicago, and another Hopkins production, *Launzi*, died quickly. *The Royal Fandango*, which starred Ethel Barrymore, one of the theater's grandes dames, again thrust Robinson into someone else's star vehicle. But her name didn't carry it; it opened and closed in November, and he was out of work again. (Also in the cast of *Fandango* was Spencer Tracy, and this was the only time they would work together.)

This was the heart of the 1920s, a period in which Broadway flourished. Musicals had never been so lively. Mae West had been thrown in irons for being too daring. Women were voting. Aware of the changes, Robinson decided to shy away from the Guild and try something highly commercial. He was offered the role of Ed Munn—the heroine's lover and later husband—in *Stella Dallas*, a tale of frustrated mother love that would become a great film. He took it and promptly fell in love with the star, Leslie Carter, in rehearsals. The crush lasted only a few days and was based on his admiration for her ten years earlier. But Carter took Eddie seriously, and for the first time in his career Edward G. Robinson, character actor, was fighting off the advances of his leading lady.

The morality that had attracted the friendship of Sam Jaffe ruled him, as it would time and time again. Robinson bowed away from Carter, as he would from virtually every leading lady in years to come. The man who, at age thirty-one, was still living at home in The Bronx was also sexually ethical, or indeed shy. His affairs, even in the easy, often promiscuous, atmosphere of the theater, were rare.

After *Stella Dallas* closed, Robinson took a trip to Europe by himself. It was far from a sobering experience but instead reinforced who he was and who he wanted to be. The Robinson of Broadway—dapper, suave, cigar and walking stick always in hand, but always surrounded by people who wanted directions to the latest speakeasy—found a reaffirmation of his ambitions and of his earlier interests in Europe. In Paris he bought dozens of prints of paintings by the masters and returned to New York accepting that he was a serious performer (albeit fond of a good story and an old Yiddish gag).

He returned to work with *The Firebrand*, again starring Pepe Schildkraut, and was rewarded with a long run and his caricature in the theater pages of the *New York World*. It was a comedy, a tale of the lives of the Medicis, and had the aura of Europe, the ambiance to which Robinson felt he belonged. He could no longer see himself in The Bronx, and he approached his parents with the decision that he would leave, expecting tears and threats. He got neither. Their immediate reaction was to enlist his brothers to help make furniture for their actor son.

Within a few weeks he had a small apartment at the Guilford, a building on East 46th Street that attracted many from the arts world. Finally, he was leaving the family hearth and was out on his own.

3

IN SERVICE TO THE BROTHERS WARNER

Though Gladys and I were married for twenty-five years there was always a thin wall between us. The wall never came down.

—Edward G. Robinson

Pepe Schildkraut was only too glad to help his old friend make himself at home in the Manhattan scene—a scene that now need not be ended by midnight taxicab rides to The Bronx. Robinson found himself going to a sort of salon that regularly met at the home of Emily Paley, who, in the 1980s, would remember him as a "darling man. A truly nice person. And very bright." She was Ira Gershwin's sister-in-law, and her parties were filled with a long list of New York's leading creative talents: Ira and George Gershwin, Leopold Stokowski, Sol Hurok, Walter Damrosch, Joseph Schildkraut. These musical influences persuaded Robinson to purchase a piano, but it was a player piano, a Steinway Ampico, since he never learned to play more than a few basic tunes.

Being part of a crowd also meant he had to reciprocate invitations, and Robinson began eagerly to take his turn hosting parties at his apartment. The crowd was a mixture of what New York had to offer, never wholly actors (the pattern for Robinson's future parties).

At one such gathering a stockbroker acquaintance brought his date, a member of the cast of *Lady Be Good*, the latest Fred and Adele Astaire vehicle. She was Gladys Lloyd, the daughter of sculptor Clement Cassell. Although she was from Philadelphia, her roots were Welsh and partly New England. She was also a Quaker, divorced, and the mother of a daughter, lively, bright, bouncy, and even lovingly flighty. Robinson by contrast was a total professional, a somewhat solemn Jew who needed and could handle a gentle ribbing from time to time. Opposites, perhaps, but Robinson would later insist he fell in love at first sight. Gladys, who was just seeing her career revived, had reservations. But she aroused his manhood, an element of his persona that he inhibited.

After that night he asked her out, took her for champagne dinners at the Lafayette Hotel, an "in" spot. He was fascinated by her background; she was less than thrilled with his Jewishness. He wanted to be with her, she didn't refuse. Robinson canceled his plans to tour with *Firebrand* and, instead, opened in two Theater Guild productions in November 1925—*Androcles and the Lion* and *The Man of Destiny*, classic plays by George Bernard Shaw.

Gladys's indecision wore down, and they soon started dating steadily, though he dared not tell his family that he was thinking of marriage with a non-Jewish woman. No one in the immediate memory of the family had married a "shiksa," and he agonized about being the first.

By February 1926 he was sure Gladys was the right woman for him, but instead of marrying her, Robinson took the role of Rob Feiwell in the Guild's production of *The Goat Song*, a work that is often considered the best production of the celebrated actors' group. *The Goat Song* starred Robinson's old friend Alfred Lunt and his wife, Lynne Fontanne, and, perhaps prophetically, dealt with life in the Danube in the seventeenth century when a demonic child born to an aristocratic family turns into a killer, a monster who brings revolution and tragedy to the country. Robinson's character was a Jewish meddler, in the play for some comic relief, as a symbol of the commoner. New Yorkers were horrified, completely unaware of the grotesque parallels with the advent of Adolf Hitler in Germany. It was a much discussed effort that brought Robinson criticism for the way he played his character—some said it was too Jewish, too stereotyped. But most importantly, he was noticed.

Stature brought him into the best New York circles, and Gladys was on his arm. This also made the columnists take notice of him, and Robinson and Gladys Lloyd became "an item." Silently, his brothers and their wives would read about the pair but dared not ask if Lloyd were a stage name. They sensed the woman their brother was seeing was not a Lowenstein or Lilienthal in disguise. They said nothing to Manny—as they still called him—and certainly nothing to Morris and Sarah. The columns said Eddie and Gladys were out dancing, dining, drinking, but when he went home to the Bronx, no questions were asked. His parents knew he had long since abandoned the dietary laws learned in their kosher home; they knew he had become modern; they tried not to think about it.

The success of *The Goat Song* prompted the Guild to offer Robinson a slot in their new repertory company, which he accepted when they offered him the role of General Profirio Diaz in *Juarez and Maximilian*, a dramatization of the Mexican fight for independence. It appealed to his political sense and was also written by Franz Werfel, the author of *The Goat Song*.

Since the Guild season would not begin until the autumn, Robinson decided to spend the summer of 1926 doing what he thought would be an innocuous little play in Atlantic City. The play was *We Americans*, a celebration of the spirit of the country that Robinson—once Emanuel Goldenberg—held so dear. He was cast as Morris Levine, the father of a Jewish clan. He loved the part, the play, the message. *We Americans* was such a hit out of town that it seemed destined for Broadway and to bring Robinson not only a noticeable role, but also more money than the $200 per week the Guild had offered. He asked to be let out of his *Juarez* contract, but the Guild refused.

Sadly, he left *We Americans* in Atlantic City. His part went to a Yiddish theater star named Muni Weisenfreund, later Paul Muni, who became Robinson's chief rival at Warner Bros. Muni never admitted that he received his first break in English-language theater because Robinson had left the show of his own accord. Robinson would always envy Muni's success with the Morris Levine character he had originated. For the rest of their lives they were, at best, civil to each other. They carried on what Hollywood loves to call a feud, and Robinson would have to endure losing many a film role to the better looking and less typecast Muni. Ironically, Muni would even do the film version of *Juarez*.

But at the time he was satisfied with *Juarez*. The title character never appeared and Diaz—Robinson—was the voice of revolution, liberalism, and justice, a role that Manny Goldenberg had rehearsed on the soapbox for Hearst fifteen years before. The play did well, and in keeping with the repertory concept Robinson and Lunt were cast in *Ned McCobb's Daughter* at the end of November. From there he went into *The Brothers Karamazov*.

He also took the big step and married Gladys. On January 21, 1927, they were wed in a $25 civil ceremony in Medina, Pennsylvania, by a justice of the peace. His new wife had filled the lonely void in his life, but Robinson was filled with anguish. Like other Jewish men who married out of the faith in those days, he could not bring himself to tell his family. He was unaware that Rhea, brother Willie's wife, had read the item in a column and had told the other brothers and their wives. But Morris and Sarah still did not know, and Morris never did know. He died of a stroke a few weeks later, with his Manny missing a performance of *The Brothers Karamazov* to be at his side. For a week Manny sat shivah—the mourning period—with his family and never mentioned Gladys. No one mentioned Gladys. His anxiety over the secret marriage caused Robinson to contract bursitis, but he continued to work on stage and keep the true nature of his private life a secret from his family.

One by one the family members let it leak that they knew Manny had married Gladys. They came and they met her. They liked her. Robinson eventually went to the Bronx and told Sarah and brother Oscar, still at home, that he had been married for several months. He felt like Al Jolson in *The Jazz Singer*, the first "talkie," which had just taken New York by storm. Sarah was stoic. She agreed to meet Gladys at their new apartment on 11th Street in Greenwich Village. It was an anxious time, but Sarah looked around and saw a beautifully decorated apartment; she saw an attractive wife and a good home. The barriers were broken down, and Sarah accepted the marriage and Gladys.

"By the time I was born and could remember, my grandmother was crazy about Gladys," recalled Beulah Robinson, Eddie's niece and Willie's daughter. "I guess you couldn't help but love her. In my recollection, Gladys always saw to it that there were flowers in my grandmother's apartment in her later years. They would send little orange trees from California. Gardenias too. My aunt would see that my grandmother had great-looking hats made by Mr. John. They adored each other. My aunt was a special person, really unique. Anyone could see that."

That trauma over, Robinson's physical ailments disappeared. He decided that the money he was receiving from the Guild was not enough to support a wife with expensive tastes that matched his own, so he departed, a move that sparked the drama critic R. Dana Skinner in *The Commonweal* to write (May 11, 1927): "As to Mr. Robinson, it is one of those baffling mysteries why the Guild should allow him to leave. Quite on a par with Alfred Lunt and Dudley Digges in general ability, he is the most versatile actor I have seen on the New York stage."

The most versatile actor spent the summer of 1927 in Atlantic City trying out a play by Jo Swerling entitled *The Kibitzer*, a cigar store merchant who was always butting into the affairs of his neighbors. The play needed work done on it and didn't make it to New York then. But waiting for him back home was a play called *The Racket* by Bart Cormack. Robinson was asked to play Nick Scarsi, a gangster very much like Al Capone, who was terrorizing Chicago. It was not a character about whom he was very enthusiastic, but it was a starring, not featured, role, at the amazing salary of $650 per week. He could not turn it down.

The opening night did not go as planned. The Scarsi character was supposed to be shot from offstage, but the gun didn't go off, and Robinson pulled a knife from his pocket and stabbed himself. He was humiliated.

Here he was, playing a treacherous, evil gangster, not the classy, highbrow roles that had brought him notice at the Guild. The Scarsi character was alien to him, a world apart from the cautious, artistic person he knew himself to be.

But on the morning of November 23, 1927, he woke up to the best reviews of his life. He was no longer a utility player, he was a Broadway star. His name was above the title for the first time since *Bells of Conscience* in 1913. Robinson was the toast of Broadway. Alexander Woollcott, part of the Algonquin crowd, rushed to do an interview and told New York readers: "I suppose there never was a more wildly inappropriate mask worn in the history of nomenclature [than Edward G. Robinson]. His *nom de guerre* suggests office furniture and routine and a suburban house with a hose to water the geraniums. But he, himself, is a short, swarthy, electrical creature of formidable dramatic power and hands that can weave a hypnotic ballet in the motivating of a scene."

He agreed to tour with the show. In Philadelphia a critic said, "We cannot wax too enthusiastically about *The Racket*." The next stop was Chicago, author Cormack's hometown, and the city banned the show, fearing Capone and his gang would react with violence to the dramatization of their actions. The story played the national press, and by the time the show reached Los Angeles, it was the hottest ticket in town.

Robinson was unaware that all of Hollywood was waiting to see him on April 14, 1928, when *The Racket* opened. He had been bathing in the Southern California sun, marveling at the palm trees, comparing the climate to Cuba (the only other warm-climate locale he had visited), but not paying attention to the film colony. Among producers and studio moguls who saw his performance were Mervyn LeRoy and Irving Thalberg. Film and contract offers were made. But thinking back to *Fields of Glory* and *The Bright Shawl*, Robinson rejected them all. He wanted no part of California or Hollywood. Instead, when *The Racket* closed in Los Angeles, he headed up to San Francisco to do the play there and in a few weeks was back in New York, where he went into rehearsals for a play by Hugh Walpole entitled *A Man with Red Hair*. It opened in November, again with sterling reviews. Robinson, wearing a red wig, monocle, and psychotic smile, again kept the audience spellbound. One critic noted, "Robinson proves in his present characterization of a sadistic lunatic that he is without peer in this particular field on the legitimate stage."

A Man with Red Hair earned Robinson $500 weekly plus 10 percent of the gross, but remembering his father's dictum to "live above your means," he was spending money as fast as he could make it. When he was in *The Goat Song*, he had bought his first oil painting—that of a cow—and now prints were not enough, he wanted the real thing. Gladys coveted furs and wanted their apartment to be a showplace. They entertained often or went out on the town. They saved very little money.

So, when Walter Wanger approached Robinson in late 1928 and asked him to appear in *The Hole in the Wall*, a film he was producing for Paramount in Astoria, Queens, Robinson didn't refuse right away. He listened when Wanger persuaded him that, unlike his earlier efforts, this was a talkie; he could continue to appear in the play and leave the soundstage at noon on matinee days; Claudette Colbert was to star, and she too had stage experience. Besides, the money was good, and he agreed to do the film.

Robinson was reminded right away that film salaries were bigger than stage. The budget sheets for the picture list his salary as $1,350 per week for five weeks, plus an additional $225 per day for recording and a share of the profits. Films were lucrative, indeed. He started shooting in Astoria on December 3, playing a gangster called "the Fox," who is in love with Colbert, a woman seeking revenge against a matron who had her jailed for kidnapping the matron's daughter. The Fox eventually turns himself in so that the Colbert character can marry the newspaper reporter she really loves. In his first major screen role, Robinson did not get the girl.

It didn't matter to him because he never bothered to see the entire cut film. He did see the rushes, though, and he realized that to survive in motion pictures he would have to subdue his stage mannerisms. The hands and gestures were reduced; the voice became less sharp and mannered. With Colbert's help he had turned *The Hole in the Wall* into his personal acting school.

Doing a film did not endear him to the entire theatrical community, many of whom were determined not to go before the cameras just for the money. Although he had long since left the Theater Guild, one of its directors, Herbert Biberman, called for sanctions against Robinson because he had chosen to make the film. Biberman contended that Robinson had "a moral agreement" to be true to the stage. Biberman, who would later become one of the Hollywood Ten, insisted that Robinson was an intellect and "the Movement" needed him.

Biberman aside, Robinson was now the toast of Broadway. He got together with Jo Swerling and revived *The Kibitzer*, the play they had closed in Atlantic City two years earlier. Robinson shared writing credit when he opened in the play in February 1929, and it was a huge success. His name was above the title; again his caricature—he loved them—was in several newspapers, including the *Jewish Daily Forward*, and all over New York, people of every ethnic persuasion were telling each other "not to kibitz." Robinson had brought a new word into the English language.

It looked like a long run until Robinson discovered that without his knowledge Swerling and producer Patterson McNutt had sold the film rights to Paramount. By summer a film version starring Harold Green was playing at a tenth of the cost to patrons just blocks from the Royale Theatre. Within weeks the audience had dried up and the marquees came down. Robinson's stage version had been forced to close.

No stage work followed. The Depression was on its way, and money was tight. His actor friends were debating whether to go to Hollywood. Some were moving to the Coast; others, like Pepe Schildkraut, were keeping their base in New York but gladly taking the long trip west for the money. And big money it was too; stars were getting $1,000 per week on Broadway, but the sky was the limit in Hollywood. Trusting Pepe, Robinson left Gladys in New York and traveled to Hollywood with his old friend to appear in *Night Ride*, a Universal picture directed by the same John Robertson who had cast Robinson in *The Bright Shawl*. In *Night Ride* he had third billing and played a gangster who kidnaps a reporter (Schildkraut) in order to escape the police. He dies in the end, and Pepe gets the girl. But Robinson got the notices—critics called him "a polished actor" on the screen. He had learned his lessons well.

Hollywood took notice. Irving Thalberg offered Robinson the male lead in *Sunkissed*, a film MGM was planning based on Sidney Howard's play *They Knew What They Wanted*, which had been a Broadway success. It was inviting and the salary would be $2,500 per week. He agreed to stay in Hollywood. Production began on October 10, but within days Robinson was ready to quit. His costar, Vilma Banky, was not a stage actress. He was playing a fifty-year-old man with all the pathos he could muster, but she was stumbling through her part as the waitress who marries the older man, although she really loves the farmhand.

When the production ended on December 6, he was at his wits' end. The film had been shot out of sequence. Vilma Banky had been less than adequate as a leading lady, although she had top billing, and ironically the title had been changed to *A Lady to Love*. The only enjoyable aspect of the film was that he got to smoke cigars in front of the camera as part of his character. To get through the work, "I needed to depend on a smoke," he told director Victor Seastrom.

Of course, although he outwardly detested Hollywood, saying he yearned to get back to New York, there were other considerations. The Depression had hit, it was December, and winter was waiting back east. In sunny California, though, Thalberg invited Robinson to his elaborate beach house, where Robinson sat around the pool chatting with Joan Crawford, Louis B. Mayer, and Norma Shearer. The conversation seemed vacuous to Robinson—meaningless gossip and chitchat about the industry. These people were not the Gershwins, or Sol Hurok, or the others who made up his New York crowd. He felt superior.

Still, he liked the money. After the MGM picture was finished, he accepted Universal's offer to make *Outside the Law*, directed by Tod Browning. One more picture and one more weekly check for $2,500 wouldn't hurt. But artistically, he was again unhappy. In *Outside the Law* Robinson was a hood named Cobra Collins, who, setting a pattern for future films, dies at the end of the picture. When production ended, Robinson didn't wait to be lured with other offers. He got on the train and headed for New York.

Universal was not through with him though. As he traveled toward New York, he was greeted at each stop with telegrams from Carl Laemmle Jr. asking him to return to Hollywood to replace Jean Hersholt in *East Is West,* playing a Chinese "chop suey king" who purchases Lupe Velez as his slave. Robinson resisted the film company's pleas all the way to New York where, he later claimed, they offered him $100,000 if he'd return to California and finish the picture.

He discussed the offer with some Broadway friends. They told him to take the money. He discussed it with Gladys. She was tired of sitting in their apartment alone and wanted to be with him. Gladys also thought that she could have a career in motion pictures, riding on his coattails. She agreed he should do it, and Robinson left for Hollywood, expecting Gladys to join him later.

East Is West was less than a masterpiece, and Robinson spent much of his off-camera time dodging the advances of Lupe Velez, who was known to see all her leading men as notches on her bedpost. He resisted, as he always would with leading ladies.

In March *A Lady to Love* opened and was a huge success, much to Robinson's surprise. The audiences flocked to the MGM film to see Vilma Banky, perhaps, but MGM's scouts told them the short, swarthy Robinson was causing just as much interest. Mayer and Thalberg decided they wanted Robinson for their stable of "more stars than there are in the heavens."

He was summoned to Thalberg's office on the MGM lot in Culver City. The actor who had never earned more than $750 per week on the stage was offered a three-year contract that would have guaranteed him $1 million, but there was a catch. Robinson still saw himself as a New York actor. He wanted to be tied to MGM for only half a year and given at least four months per year to appear in a play. Thalberg was adamant in his refusal. MGM molded careers, he told Robinson, and Thalberg and L. B. Mayer would be the only ones to decide where and when Robinson worked. The terms were not acceptable to Robinson. He turned MGM down and walked out of Thalberg's office, never to work for the film company during the "Wunderkind's" lifetime.

When he stepped out into the warm noon sun, it suddenly struck Robinson that, during the Depression, he had turned down a million dollars. He began to shake, fell to his knees, and retched uncontrollably for several minutes. His agent had to help the stage star to his feet and practically carry him to the car, as onlookers stared in amazement.

Robinson returned immediately to New York, to the emotional security of the stage, of Gladys and their crowd. He agreed to play the lead in *Le Marchand de Paris*, renamed *Mr. Samuel* and adapted from a French success. He was to have billing above the title and be paid a top Broadway salary. But *Mr. Samuel* was a flop. Just as Robinson had seen years earlier when he played support to Ethel Barrymore in *Royal Fandango*, stars alone do not attract an audience. *Mr. Samuel* was more than just a bitter disappointment: It showed Robinson that audiences are fickle, that nothing in show business is guaranteed. Each night he went on stage to a half-filled theater. After five or six performances the anger was building inside him. He had turned down $1 million, taken a job worth $1,000 per week, and was about to be unemployed.

At the fifth performance Hal Wallis, a top executive at Warner Bros.–First National, came backstage to see Robinson and offer him a contract. It was worth less than MGM had offered, but with some haggling, Wallis and Jack Warner were willing to give Robinson time off each year to do theater. Robinson and Gladys discussed the contract only briefly. Their minds were already made up. He signed and headed for the Coast.

There has been much written about Hollywood contracts during the studio-dominated period of the 1930s and 1940s. All too often they are described as enslavements. While that may have been the case with actors the studio discovered, Robinson was a stage star and as such had more status. He never had to sign a seven-year contract and was always able to retain some level of story approval, a level that increased as his star rose in the Warner Bros. firmament. His contract in 1930 was for four pictures in his first year at $35,000 per movie. Later, in February 1931—after *Little Caesar* made him a box office smash—he would sign a revised contract for four pictures his first year and three his second.

Through the years he would be alternately friendly and hateful toward the Warners, particularly Jack. Harry Warner would be the godfather of Robinson's son and the one he would turn to for favors. Jack, shrewd boss that he was, was someone Robinson would always respect but would come to mistrust. Robinson soon came to know Jack's foibles: He was fond of putting on a thick Yiddish accent for visitors; he would absorb subordinates' ideas and make them his own; he constantly put his brothers in their place; and he very firmly held the strings that controlled his actors.

Gladys and Eddie did not think to give up their Greenwich Village apartment when they went west. They kept it and rented a similar two-bedroom suite at the Chateau Elysée Apartments on Franklin Avenue, not far from the middle of Hollywood. Unable to drive, Robinson was forced to take taxis to the studio until he was provided with a driver.

What they saw in Hollywood was a community growing as fast as the developers could make deals—real estate and films always competed for preeminence as the biggest moneymakers in the movie colony. East of their apartment was Los Feliz, an area filled with splendid mansions that had housed the silent stars, where Cecil B. DeMille and W. C. Fields still lived. Just to the north was Beachwood Canyon and a five-hundred-acre housing development called Hollywoodland, with its huge thirteen-letter sign in an almost religiously symbolic position on the hills overlooking the town.

On Hollywood Boulevard, the Roosevelt Hotel was just three years old and the scene of spectacular banquets. Across the street Grauman's Chinese Theater was a symbol of Hollywood Babylon with several star footprints already in the courtyard. Sid Grauman also owned the Egyptian Theater three blocks away. The entire boulevard from La Brea to Vine was fashionable for Los Angeles, even if it didn't compare to the Fifth Avenue of Robinson's beloved New York.

Gladys and Eddie would eat at one of the hotels or at the Musso-Frank Grill on the boulevard, or try the Brown Derby, Perinos, or the Ambassador Hotel on Wilshire Boulevard, a business district that still attracted the movie colony. On Sunset Boulevard were many of the studios, centers of constant activity.

Warner Bros. was located on Sunset Boulevard between Van Ness and Bronson—the site of Golden West Broadcasters today—but due to a shortage of sound equipment, a good number of the films were shot at newer studios in Burbank, where government regulations insisted they were technically produced by a subsidiary called First National. So pressed for sound equipment was the company that the Sunset studios would be hooked by telephone wire to the audio equipment—located in Burbank—and would film during the morning and afternoon. By 7:00 P.M., First National would take over and shoot through the night.

In the early weeks Robinson got along well with the Warners and with Wallis. They were all the sons of immigrant Jews, although his bosses were native born. Still, they could share jokes in the Yiddish dialect while being very modern and American at the same time. If the Warners weren't interested in art for art's sake as Robinson professed to be, at least they outwardly gave every impression they hoped films would move away from melodramas and train robberies and into the realm of adaptations of serious fiction and biographies. This appealed to Robinson, as did the star system that provided him with almost royal treatment.

He was quick to learn that star treatment wasn't a guarantee of quality—a lesson taught when he was assigned to *The Widow from Chicago*. Robinson played Dominic, a gangster chieftain who is captured when he's tricked by the heroine and hero (Alice White and Neil Hamilton). Robinson was not pleased with *The Widow* which was only sixty-four minutes long. He considered it lightweight, although when it opened in December, he received good notices. Once again he felt he was playing Nick Scarsi from *The Racket*. He had only third billing, and very little actual dimension in the script.

Neither Eddie nor Gladys mixed easily with the Hollywood stars, seeking out friends from New York instead. They thought about calling it quits, but the $2,500 checks that arrived at their apartment each week helped. Robinson completed his work with resentment, convinced he'd never be happy in the movies. He counted the days until he could leave for the four months he was contractually allowed to do theater.

It was a four-month option he was never to take up. A few days after *The Widow from Chicago* was completed, Wallis summoned Robinson to his office and showed him a script based upon a successful novel by W. R. Burnett. Robinson knew the novel. Leah Salisbury, his dancer friend from the *Kismet* tour, had sent him a copy months earlier. The book was *Little Caesar*.

4

LITTLE CAESAR

Some people have youth, others beauty. I have menace.

—Edward G. Robinson

As in all great casting stories, the role of Enrico Cesare Bandello did not fall into Robinson's lap. When Wallis gave him the script, he said they were considering Robinson for the part of Otero, Little Caesar's most loyal soldier, although in truth that was probably a ploy because Jack Warner was not sure what he wanted.

While Robinson was reading the script, Warner was having story conferences with Mervyn LeRoy, the young director to whom he had assigned the project. In later years Warner, LeRoy, and Robinson himself would all claim credit for the casting. LeRoy had seen Robinson in *The Racket* when it played in Los Angeles and also knew Robinson's work in New York—he had even seen a smattering of the vaudeville Robinson had done. He was aware that Robinson could play a gangster. Warner was also convinced that Robinson was a possibility, a strong one, but his instincts told him that a young hopeful named Clark Gable—who was being touted by Wallis's agent-sister, Minna—might be good for the part as well. He tested Gable and was appalled by the good-looking actor's big ears and wide-eyed features (it did not dawn on him to pin the ears back). He rejected Gable and suggested Robinson to LeRoy, assuming full responsibility for the choice.

Wallis, who had always favored Robinson for the part, was more than amused when Robinson stormed into his office and demanded not the supposedly assigned part of Otero, but Rico himself. Robinson ranted and raved in front of Wallis, cigar in hand, street accent wearing through his normally impeccable stage diction. The man who stood before Wallis *was* Little Caesar (Robinson had come dressed in black overcoat, homburg, and white evening scarf). Robinson told Wallis that the script needed rewrites. They would be done. Wallis conferred with Warner and LeRoy. A test was ordered. When they saw it, they knew there was no other choice, and Robinson was cast, still less than interested in playing yet another gangster but willing to go along for the good of his contract and his mounting bills.

With Robinson pushing, Francis Faragoh wrote a second draft for the picture, one which Robinson told Wallis he thought "read like a Greek tragedy." In it, a small-time hood named Cesare "Rico" Bandello joins a big-city mob run by Sam Vettori (Stanley Fields), but under the control of Pete Montana, the real chieftain (Ralph Ince). Rico overthrows Vettori and ruthlessly takes over the gang, kills the city crime commissioner, and wreaks terror, only to be defeated by his former best friend, Joe Massaro (Douglas Fairbanks Jr.), who is able to turn state's evidence when Rico weakens and cannot kill his pal. It was a script with good three-dimensional characters, even if the years have taken a toll on its bite.

Mervyn LeRoy was still active in 1983, with an office in one of Sunset Boulevard's most exclusive buildings. On the wall behind his desk is a still-life painting by Robinson, which the star gave him many years after their first triumph together. He still treasures it and the memory of his friend: "Eddie was a wonderful man and a great actor. Later in his career he did things in one or two takes, but not with me on *Little Caesar*. He would do anything for you if it turned out right, if he trusted you. I never had any trouble with him. I gave them trouble. I told Eddie that I was trying to make out that Rico was a great man, a powerful man, who knew what he was doing but was not always a villain. Eddie agreed with that."

Little Caesar took thirty-one days to shoot in July and August, and Robinson had to furnish his own wardrobe. Although the work went well, the cast and crew were spooked by reports—they turned out to be true—that Al Capone had a spy on set to see how they were doing. After all, the Rico character was loosely based on him.

LeRoy realized early on that Robinson was a serious actor who tended to be anxious about his performance and about how he looked on the screen. But it was that very harsh voice and squat but powerful appearance that LeRoy and Warner wanted, and LeRoy tried to keep the set lively, to allay Robinson's fears, by pulling pranks (such as nailing Robinson's cigar to props). Their relationship, despite LeRoy's admiration for Robinson, was a trifle uneasy throughout; LeRoy was about seven years younger than Robinson, and each felt he had to prove himself to the other.

The levity on the set worried Wallis, and he put a stop to the pranks, insisting that they were hurting Robinson's performance. Today, LeRoy insists, "Eddie was always fooling around. He was a great comic and a great actor. He knew what he was doing. He knew comedy and he knew drama. He was a genius in everything he did."

The scenes in *Little Caesar* that the mild-mannered and pacifist Robinson found the most difficult were the ones involving guns. Robinson was unable to shoot his prop gun without blinking, so the problem was eventually solved by taping his eyelids open for the key scene in which he had to shoot and kill the crime commissioner. He also had trouble staying still under fire. The art of screen violence had not yet been refined; there was no explosive charges that could be taped to the actor's body. When they were to shoot Rico's death scene, steel plates were pinned inside Robinson's clothing, covering his stomach. Special-effects wizard George Daly had it all worked out: machine-gun bullets—blanks, of course, but still dangerous—were to be shot into the plates. Robinson, very gun shy, kept moving off target and would have met his own end along with Rico's, had Daly not taken note of the nervous movements.

Today *Little Caesar* is remembered largely for the image of Rico/Robinson snarling "Yeah, yeah, awright you guys" type of dialogue. Robinson claimed he never used those words or that tone and in later years could never mimic his own work. In truth, the famous snarling was not in the script. LeRoy was not satisfied with the ending as written, in which Rico, hiding on the streets, overhears a reporter and a cop talking about reports in the newspaper planted by Sergeant Flaherty (Thomas Jackson) calling Rico a coward. In the script, Rico confronts the men and, to prove who he is, tosses a diamond ring at them. They at first think he's a bum with cheap costume jewelry, until the reporter looks at the ring and realizes it's real.

LeRoy decided instead to have Rico overhear two bums reading the newspaper. He grabs the paper from them, reads the put-down, then goes to the phone to call Flaherty and challenge him. In this key phone conversation Robinson, moving with the scene and character as he went along, punctuated his one-way conversation with the famous "Yeah, yeah" and "Yeah, see . . .," which inadvertently became his trademark.

Warner Bros. also came into conflict with the censors, who objected to Rico's dying words as written—"Mother of God, is this the end of Rico?"—and the scene had to be reshot with the ending that is on virtually all available prints: "Mother of Mercy, is this the end of Rico?"

Since there was no score and little excess footage, the eighty-minute movie was ready for the theaters very quickly, but Warner held it over until January 1931, hoping to get the most mileage from his $250,000 investment (this was no Christmas picture). They chose as a prologue for the film the proverb "For all that take the sword shall perish with the sword." They were ready for the January 22, 1931, premiere in New York.

The house was packed at the Strand Theater that night. The title *Little Caesar* rolled up, followed by Robinson's name, then those of Douglas Fairbanks Jr., Glenda Farrell, and the rest of the cast. The first view of Robinson is of his stubby fingers turning back the hand of a clock. From that point on the audience was mesmerized. By midnight Robinson was the hottest property at Warner Bros.—topping Ruth Chatterton, William Powell, and Kay Francis.

When the critics' notices appeared, there was no question that Robinson was a hit, although he cringed when one wrote, "He speaks with a New York public-school accent." They also noted his broad features and his high sloping forehead, but suddenly what he had always considered ugliness was transformed into charisma. Within twenty-four hours long lines developed outside the ticket booth, stretching to 47th and 48th Streets. Fistfights and even a near riot ensued as patrons clamored for tickets. Police had to be called in to keep order on several occasions. Robinson had become a household name.

Warner, Wallis, and LeRoy had not realized what the Little Caesar character would mean to the Depression audience, how it would strike a nerve. Robinson's diminutive size and lack of conventional good looks, plus his dynamo energy, had made him an underdog archetype for the masses, people who thought of themselves as underdogs and victims of the economy and ruling class. Rico had killed, but he had killed an affluently dressed member of the establishment. "I probably expressed a feeling that millions of people had about their own lives," Robinson would say in an interview in the 1960s. "I think the popularity of my role can be attributed to the public preoccupation with the American dream of success. Rico was a guy who came from poverty and made it big. Rico made it straight up the ladder and everyone could identify with his climb."

One of the few detractors was W. R. Burnett, the man whose book had started it all. He was furious that there was not a single member of the cast who was of Italian descent. Burnett also shot off an angry letter to Wallis accusing him of having made Rico a homosexual involved with Joe (Fairbanks). He cited as proof two scenes—when Rico cannot pull the trigger and kill his former best friend and mutters, "That's what I get for liking a guy too much," and in the sequence in which Rico is propped up at the head of his bed talking to Otero (George Stone), who is resting at his feet, his eyes filled with loving admiration for his gangster boss. Wallis always denied that there was any homosexual undercurrent. Yet, Burnett never had anything but praise for Robinson himself.

Warner Bros., too, knew immediately that they had to capitalize on their new star. Anyone who saw Robinson in public could sense the awe in which the public held him: Clerks in stores would wait on him first, always shaking nervously; children would cross the street rather than walk within feet of Little Caesar. The actor who was afraid to fire a prop gun was now Public Enemy Number One. The Warner Bros. publicity machine moved into action. There were Little Caesar bookmarks, posters, and souvenir books. Robinson was thrust into interviews, although when he told his life story, Warners cautiously made sure it was reported he had wanted to be a "minister" rather than a "rabbi." (They wanted to play down his Jewishness, and Robinson would put up with the charade for about a year, before releasing his real name.)

Gladys was put to work to bolster the image. She wrote an article for a fan magazine called "Confessions of a Gangster's Moll" about what it was like to be married to the notorious Little Caesar. Meanwhile, *The Hollywood Reporter* slipped in an item to help the studio create the image it wanted for its new leading star. "Robinson wreaks his fury on ham and cheese sandwiches at lunch," a gossip column presented!

Off screen and out of the public eye, Robinson and Gladys were having problems with their marriage. She was envious of the attention paid to him; he longed for New York; and they were both bored. Holed up in the Franklin Avenue penthouse, they had little to do. Robinson found the movie crowd dull and gravitated toward those who had been on the New York stage, like himself. Gladys was pushed by the studio into attending teas, which she found less than stimulating, and she finally rebelled against spending one more day shopping. There were constant quarrels, with Gladys pushing over and over again for her chance to be in films. Robinson gave in and agreed to talk to Warner about it. He was told there would be no contract for her.

And there seemed to be no work for him. After *Little Caesar* he sat for five months watching his fan mail pile up, but there were no scripts. Warner did not know what to do with him, until he noticed that James Cagney, whose screen image was equally tough, had also just made it big in *The Public Enemy*. It was decided to put both new stars in a movie, which would naturally have to have a crime and gangland background.

That movie was *Smart Money*, the story of Nick Venizelos (Robinson), a small-town barber who has small-town luck with gambling and is persuaded by his friends and employees, including Jack (Cagney), to try his luck in the big city. Nick agrees and winds up first making a killing and then dead, penalized by the mob for being too successful. Another death scene. Cagney and Robinson got along famously on the set, under the watchful eye of Alfred Green, who directed. There was much in common between the two stars. They were both Hollywood illusions, in a way: short, dynamic men manipulated by the camera to seem tough and domineering. Oddly enough, Cagney had a long list of credits in the Yiddish theater, despite his Irish-Norwegian ancestry. It was a bizarre twist in a way: Robinson, the Jew, had but one Yiddish theater credit, while the Irishman from Hell's Kitchen always delighted in throwing a line or two of Yiddish into his films. The two traded Yiddish gags and became friends.

Robinson also managed to talk Wallis into casting Gladys in the small but featured role of a cigar store girl who is also the source of poker game locations. It made it possible for them to drive to the studio together and for a few weeks masked the problems that plagued their marriage.

After *Smart Money*, Warners teamed Robinson with Mervyn LeRoy again for *Five Star Final*, based on the play by Louis Weitzenkorn. It was a part more to Robinson's liking and became a film that endures dramatically. In it, Robinson portrays a city editor on the fictional *New York Gazette* who, pushed on by his boss, dredges up a twenty-year-old scandal and gives it front-page prominence. The lives of innocent people are subsequently mangled—including that of a fragile young woman (Marion Marsh)—and Randall (Robinson) wields his paper to crusade for truth in the fourth estate.

With a budget more than twice that of *Little Caesar*, although he got the same $35,000 salary, *Five Star Final* was Robinson's biggest film to date. Robinson would always regard his role as one of the most important of his career—"It fits into my reform-the-world complex," he would tell interviewers.

Robinson and Gladys, who had also had a small part in *Five Star Final*, were sent by Warner Bros. to New York for the June premiere of *Smart Money* at the Winter Garden Theater. Welcomed back by family and friends, Robinson still felt like an actor, not a star, until the night of June 18, when *Smart Money* had its premiere. Several thousand fans crowded the streets outside the theater as the stars arrived. When Robinson's limousine pulled up in front of the theater and he stepped out onto the red-carpeted sidewalk, the crowd became a mob and mounted police had to keep them in line. Robinson and Gladys were so overcome that he almost failed to notice his name on the marquee in twelve-foot-high letters.

His popularity was soaring, and Robinson, with Warner's blessing, decided to make out of it what he could, *while* he could. Like most actors he was very concerned about making money, and as they always lived beyond their means, Robinson agreed to go out on a personal tour that summer with a schedule designed by the Radio-Keith-Orpheum Theaters. It was vaudeville, technically, but at salaries that would top $5,000 per appearance in the larger cities. Robinson dressed as Little Caesar would walk out on stage, do a Rico routine about "the mugs" in the audience, then talk about life in Hollywood. It took all of twenty minutes. He tried it first in New York, Brooklyn, Boston, and Newark.

The manager of the Brooklyn RKO Albee Theater was not impressed and sent a memo to the main office calling Robinson's performance "fair." His reception in Brooklyn was "disappointing," thought Albee manager Fritz Jean Hubert. The first ten minutes were rated as "nothing," the next five as "a few snickers," and the ending as "slow." Drawing power? Hubert thought, "Fair. Will not hurt business. Should be OK for the family houses through the middle West. No speech necessary at any performance so far, and the week is half over."

It did not matter what Hubert thought; Robinson turned out to have drawing power throughout the country. While performing for a week in St. Louis, Robinson found many of the supposedly "family" women in the Midwest found him attractive sexually. "Dear Mr. Robinson," one fan wrote, in a note delivered to the stage door. "I saw you Sunday night. You were marvelous. I am just crazy about you, and Mr. Robinson, I am under thirty. I don't wear glasses and I don't wear flat heels. Hay Hay! From your friend in South St. Louis." The man who had been a virgin until the age of twenty, and who had never been predisposed to womanizing, was now a sex symbol!

The year 1931 had been a success, and the September premiere of *Five Star Final* would be the ultimate triumph. *The Hollywood Reporter*, which was celebrating its first anniversary as the bible of the movie industry, headlined, "*Five Star Final Wows!*" and added, "Picture is one of the greatest since the inception of talkies. Tremendous box office appeal."

At this point, Robinson could have activated the clause in his contract that guaranteed him four months in which to do theater work. He did not. Although he felt his New York friends treated him as a real person, not a celluloid image, he returned with Gladys to Franklin Avenue in Hollywood and learned how to drive a car—a sure sign that he was adapting to California life (he purchased a Chevrolet, although Warners thought he should drive something more flashy). If he didn't like Hollywood, he was now accepted: William Powell and Robinson competed in the press about their hat collections; Joan Crawford sought him out for her pool parties; and the Robinsons seemed entrenched in Hollywood society.

Before leaving for vacation in November, he made *The Hatchet Man*, one of the four films he was contractually obligated to do for release in 1932. Directed by William Wellman, he played a Chinese gang lord with a sense of honor and morality. Loretta Young was his wife, a woman who didn't love him but had been promised to him by her deceased father. In the end Robinson saves her from the man she has run off with. He doesn't die, but he doesn't exactly get the girl either. Dudley Digges had a supporting role in *The Hatchet Man*, a sweet irony for Robinson since he had once been featured in a play when Digges had his name above the title on the marquee. But it was the only part of the film Robinson savored.

After three pictures he was proud of, he sensed *The Hatchet Man* was routine. Yet, his accounting ledger told him that he and Gladys would have an income surpassing $300,000 for 1931. *Little Caesar* was one of the highest-grossing films of the year, with *Cimarron, Daddy Longlegs, Min and Bill,* and *Trader Horn.*

In November, then, rather than look for a stage property, Robinson and Gladys left for London. He was greeted on his December 17 arrival by a newspaper headline proclaiming, "Al Capone of the Screen Arrives in London." An entire continent had never seen him on Broadway but had discovered him through the cinema. Page boys at his London hotel shivered when he passed by, and Robinson and Gladys basked in the spotlight. In interviews, he didn't talk about saving the world; he said he liked British beer.

The New Year of 1932 was celebrated in Paris, a double celebration since Robinson had been declared one of the top six male box office draws of 1931. With his Hollywood money he bought a Renoir. A week later, in Rome, Edward G. Robinson, born a common Jew in Bucharest, had an audience with the pope. They chatted briefly about how movies can influence an audience.

Back in Hollywood at the end of January, *The Hatchet Man* was getting special treatment from the Warner Bros. publicity department. The handout for the film, which had just opened, had Chinese characters and read, "Perhaps you can't read Chinese, but in any language it means you must see Edward G. Robinson in the greatest picture of his career—*The Hatchet Man.*" Another proclaimed the film "Will clear your consciousness as no motion picture ever did before." Robinson and Gladys could walk down Hollywood Boulevard and see the fliers in the gutter, his image left for the sweeper. They could also see queues at the box office for a movie that Robinson knew could never have been a success were it a stage play.

He went to work with LeRoy again on what he hoped would be a better vehicle, *Two Seconds,* the story of a sour murderer who is unrepentant about murdering his wife and dies in the electric chair. It was not a good film. Years later, LeRoy had no memory of it, and Robinson could never recall details for interviews. When it opened in May, the *New York Daily News* gave it bad reviews, but movie patrons lined up in Brooklyn, and *Two Seconds* made a decent profit.

He was next assigned, for his summer work, to a Howard Hawks project, *Tuna*, a name that was quickly changed to *Tiger Shark*. It was another action melodrama, about a crusty fisherman whose jealousy eventually causes his death (in other words, Robinson again didn't get the girl). Nor did he have a particularly good time during shooting. He was wary of the project the minute he heard from Warner that it would be shot in the water off Catalina Island. Robinson disliked swimming (he had, after all, once almost lost his life in a grade school swimming pool), and although Warner and Wallis assured him a stunt man would do most of the work in the water, this turned out to be far from the case. In the climactic sequence, his character—Mike Mascarena—has to drown in close shot, a task no stunt man could undertake. Robinson himself was thrust into the water to feign death for four hours in a shark-infested area. On another day a cameraman had actually been rescued only seconds before a real tiger shark swooshed by, ready for lunch.

Robinson was shaken after the experience and given time to rest before he was to begin his next assignment, *Silver Dollar*. It was a well-deserved relaxation, and Robinson, matured in Hollywood ways, used the time to rediscover his political consciousness. The Manny Goldenberg who had been a political activist in Townsend Harris High School had become submerged in Edward G. Robinson, movie star, insulated from the two realities of those Depression days.

Robinson, who had by this time grown away from the politics of Eugene V. Debs and become a Democrat, immersed himself in the campaign for Franklin Delano Roosevelt, the party's nominee for president in 1932. It was not a popular choice to make in Hollywood. The moguls and producers were often staunch Republicans—particularly Louis B. Mayer—and they didn't want their stable players involved in anything controversial, let alone the campaign of a Democrat. But Robinson would not be silenced. He spoke up at parties, he appeared at rallies, he sent donations.

As Robinson embraced Roosevelt's plans for solving the Depression, the publicity department at Warner Bros. sent out releases noting that the star liked pipes, Chinese jade, caricatures of himself, paintings, Tudor furniture, and cutting and pasting player piano rolls into special arrangements. While Robinson campaigned for the Democrats, Warner Bros. had a graphologist do his handwriting analysis and published the results—he was an aesthete, impressionable, unostentatious, candid, and cultured. *Silver Dollar*—based on H. A. W. Tabor's life—tells the story of a Kansas farmer who becomes a reckless Colorado silver baron only to be ruined when the country adopts the gold standard. Production on the film, in which he was again directed by Alfred E. Green, ended on September 8, and Edward G. Robinson, movie star, and his wife left for New York, where on September 29 they were at Yankee stadium to see his favorite team beat the Chicago Cubs 5-2 in the World Series. The movie star got his picture in the papers with the caption reading, "Edward G. Robinson of movie fame with Mrs. Robinson." Less coverage was given to the fact that Edward G. Robinson, born Emanuel Goldenberg, was campaigning for Roosevelt.

Robinson began carrying a silver dollar in his pants for luck about this time, partly because of the movie and partly because it was during filming that Gladys had discovered she was pregnant. Although she had a daughter, Jeanne, who lived with them from time to time—mostly extended visits—Gladys had assumed she would never have another child, and Robinson had thought he would not be a father. Now all was going well. The career was moving smoothly; intellectually, he felt he was growing again. And wherever they were—Hollywood or New York—they were part of the industry's social register.

When Roosevelt was elected in November, Robinson and Gladys decided to take the plunge and throw their first Hollywood party at Chateau Elysée for a stream of movie people who came and went well into the night. Gladys was a superb hostess and the event was successful, but the economic conditions in Hollywood and political rumblings in Europe were dampening the gaiety. Robinson's salary was cut 15 percent as Warners faced bankruptcy; Kay Francis, who had been the reigning queen of the lot, had her salary cut by an amazing 35 percent, a sure sign that her career was coming to an end.

Salary cut or not, Robinson and Gladys traveled to Denver for the December 1 premiere of *Silver Dollar*, a lavish affair at which the cream of the city dressed in period costumes. By the end of the night Warner Bros. was certain it had another hit, but the Robinsons were on their way to New York where Gladys was to rest in the Essex House pending the March birth of their child. She was not expected to have an easy pregnancy. In her late thirties, she was fragile and would require almost constant doctor's care. A full-time nurse was hired.

Robinson wanted to be with her, and a few days before Christmas, he called Darryl Zanuck, still a production chief for Warners—he had not yet started 20th Century—and asked permission to remain in New York until Gladys gave birth, forgoing any film assignments. Zanuck agreed, but a few days later Jack Warner reneged on that agreement. Robinson was told that back in California a new project, *The Little Giant*, was awaiting and, when he objected, was told he could stay in New York but would be taken off salary. Robinson had learned another lesson about movie moguls: Although their top box office draw, he was still an employee, and it was a lesson that was to change his attitude to movie making forever.

But for the time being, with Gladys's agreement and her doctor's approval, he returned to Burbank to shoot *Little Giant*, directed by Roy Del Ruth. The film's title was obviously concocted to cash in on Robinson's previous great success. *Little Giant* was set after Prohibition, with Robinson as "Bugs" Ahearn, a bootlegger turned beer baron, trying to make it in California society. He lusts after Helen Vinson but ends up with the brighter and more efficient Mary Astor. At last he got the girl!

Once again, filming was a horror, partly because he was anxious about Gladys, but also because everything that could go wrong seemed to do so. In one sequence he is playing polo with Helen Vinson, a chic society woman. As written, her horse bolts and Bugs Ahearn takes off after her, pulling her onto his horse, thus saving her life. The scene was to be shot on mechanical horses fixed high up in front of a moving backcloth, with steel platforms below. Although Robinson was anything but athletic and

Vinson was not used to such activity, rehearsals went well at first. When the actual filming began, it was an entirely different matter. Vinson's mechanical horse started moving faster than she had expected, and when the time came for Robinson to grab her, she took hold of him too firmly, and the two of them started to slip off their horses. Robinson screamed for the director to stop, but the noise from the horses and fans on the set drowned his voice. In a desperate attempt to save them, Vinson tried to push Robinson back on his horse, but instead they both toppled over and landed hard on the steel platforms below. Robinson was badly bruised in his shoulder and hip, while Vinson received hairline fractures that meant shooting was held up for a week while she recuperated in a hospital. Both suffered pain and discomfort for the rest of the time *Little Giant* was in production, and Robinson would be one week later in returning to Gladys. The sequence itself, ironically, ended up on the cutting-room floor. But as meager compensation, *Little Giant* netted Robinson an extra $3,000.

He immediately headed back to New York when filming was completed to discover that his mother, Sarah, had been looking after Gladys in his absence. The pregnancy hadn't been easy, as Gladys had had to spend the last few months in bed, but on March 19, 1933, she gave birth to a healthy son at Doctors' Hospital. Photographers and reporters haunted the hospitals, and the child's birth made national headlines.

In proper American tradition, Gladys insisted that the child be named for his father: Edward G. Robinson Jr. Big Eddie was appalled—that just wasn't done in Jewish families. Gladys was firm, though; she had already agreed that the son could be raised as a Jew and wanted Eddie to bend on this one point. He did. Eight days after his birth, Edward G. Robinson Jr. was the star attraction at his bris—the ritual circumcision performed on all Jewish males. Sarah and the rest of the family were in attendance, along with good friends such as Sam Jaffe. Since the family called Robinson "Manny," as they had always done, the son was dubbed "Little Manny." Robinson approved of that. In Hollywood, the child was just Manny Robinson.

The new father celebrated the birth of his son by investing $20,000 in paintings—two Pissarros, a Degas, and a Monet. It was the Depression, and dealers wanted to make sales, so he was able to pay in installments. He now had a collection, however small.

The Robinsons had a big decision to make. If they were going to raise a child, they needed a house, a permanent base, to be together. As Robinson was now a famous face, there was no place to hide in New York City, where walking down the street meant being recognized. Hollywood was more insulated, with homes only miles from the studios, and a town used to celebrities. Much to their surprise, they elected to plant their roots in California.

Robinson returned to the Coast, leaving Gladys and Manny in the care of Sarah. Warners put him in front of the cameras for *I Loved a Woman*, in which he played an art student forced to take control of his father's meat-packing plant. He becomes corrupt but manages to have Kay Francis in his arms at the end. *I Loved a Woman* would, as shooting progressed, represent a turning point in Robinson's approach to moviemaking, but in the early days there was only one thing on his mind—the house he had rented on Arden Drive in Beverly Hills, owned by the Hearst family. Gladys, Sarah, Manny, and a nurse joined him during the shooting, and while they were settling in, Robinson became less and less enamored with the script. He appealed to director Alfred Green for changes, but he was ignored. Determined not to do inferior work, Robinson stormed into Wallis's office, and after much argument, writers Charles Kenyon and Sidney Sutherland were told to comply. The result was a film that Robinson always felt was good.

Yet, more and more, he was becoming aware of his status as mere employee. For instance, Robinson injured his knee during filming of *I Loved a Woman*, but Warner Bros. agreed to pay the $30 medical bill only so he would sign a four-week extension of his contract. That, and the *Little Giant* disagreement, which had forced him to leave a pregnant Gladys, was still fresh in his mind. So, when his contract came up for renewal, he demanded changes. He wanted story approval and the chance to be lent out to another studio. He was forty years old and wanted to stretch himself professionally.

Story approval was not unprecedented. Arliss had it, as did Chatterton. But Robinson went after it with a vengeance. His new contract, dated July 11, 1933, guaranteed his services to Warner Bros. for three films each year, to be made from stories and scripts sent to him on specified dates, and approved by him. Even before Robinson signed the papers, Wallis was receiving memos from Roy Obringer, production head, stating that the screen tough guy was rejecting scripts with the same ease as the gangsters he played ordered executions.

The list of rejections mounted, most of them projects that never got off the ground—*Grand Slam, Lawyer Man, The Machine, Kingfish* (about Huey Long)—all stories of gambling, attorneys, political corruption. Instead, Robinson approved a script based on the life of Napoleon, with what he considered a dream part. He recommended Ernst Lubitsch and Frank Borzage as directors. He was put off. The same fight would occur each year for several years.

Many of his choices were poor. *Dark Hazard* appealed to him because it was based on a novel by W. R. Burnett, but the story of a gambler who loses all failed at the box office. His next film, *The Man with Two Faces*, was based on a play entitled *The Dark Tower* by George S. Kaufman and Alexander Woollcott. Robinson portrayed a brilliant stage actor and director who, in disguise, kills his sister's (Mary Astor) evil husband. It didn't do any better on the screen than it did on the stage. After fighting for story approval, Robinson had made bad decisions, and Warner whispered around town that he was box office poison.

But he would not back down from his insistence on better scripts, and once again, in 1934, he battled with the studio. He telegraphed Jack Warner: "Dear Jake, Have been waiting around for months for a good story STOP Why won't you dig one up for me STOP Am happy about the Napoleon adaptation STOP It is extraordinarily good STOP Regards and *mazel tov*. Eddie Robinson."

Warner didn't answer until he read in *The Hollywood Reporter* that Frank Borzage was to direct *Napoleon, His Life and Loves* at another studio and was considering Peter Lorre and Charles Chaplin for the lead. He agreed to do the Ernest Pascal script that Robinson seemed to want, lined up Robert Florey to direct, and listed Bette Davis as his choice for Josephine (a plum part for the latter since she was still doing second features for the studio).

Robinson, perhaps overzealously, reacted by demanding script changes, and Warner went for the gut by canceling the project in retaliation. Robinson was then forced to practically beg for the role, even offering to do the film for a mere $60,000 (only three-quarters of his contractual fee). Warner just laughed. Instead, he offered Robinson *Babbit*. He rejected it. Warner offered *The Story of a Country Boy* by Dawn Powell. Robinson rejected it.

Warner had had enough. He suspended Robinson on April 28, claiming there were no suitable stories for him, and Robinson went home to Rexford Drive to sit and wait. The family had moved there after less than a year on Arden Drive, and it was not an unpleasant place to be. A large Tudor-style mansion, 910 Rexford had French-style windows, high ceilings, and three floors, with guest quarters on the third floor and a studio where Robinson would paint and sketch. There was no swimming pool.

But there were also bills. The paintings purchased after Manny was born were hardly paid for. Sarah had developed a heart condition, and a badminton court was taken down and replaced by a guesthouse so she wouldn't have to climb stairs. The salaries of Manny's nurse, a maid, and a butler-valet added to the expenses. Gladys did not find it easy to contain her extravagance for clothes, and even their food bills were higher than normal, since they had agreed to keep a fully kosher home, including kosher meat and two sets of dishes, whenever Sarah was with them.

Robinson needed a salary. In June producer and friend Lester Cowan wrote to Jack Warner regarding story possibilities for him. They included an unnamed project described as a pirate movie—a "Little Caesar" of the high seas—and he also suggested the possibilities of Captain Blood or Captain Kidd. Cowan urged Warner to make a quick decision, bluffing that Robinson might have other commitments. Warner wouldn't move quickly. Robinson remained on suspension.

Robinson's pleading eventually paid off. Pressed for cash, Warner could taste the money a loan-out would bring in, and he finally agreed to a deal with Harry Cohn that sent Robinson to Columbia for *The Whole Town's Talking*. The project seemed right. It was based on another book by W. R. Burnett, who seemed to have a knack for inventing characters suitable for Robinson. In this yarn, Robinson played the dual role of a milksop hardware clerk who, through no fault of his own, is the double of a ruthless hood. Meek Arthur Ferguson Jones is mistaken for the hood—Killer Mannion—when the latter breaks out of jail. Jones is released by the police, but not before there is front-page publicity. Mannion, now aware that he has a double, holds Jones hostage, allowing him to work by day but using the identity papers the police have given Jones by night in order to continue his life of crime. But when Jones hears Mannion's gang making fun of him, he poses as Public Enemy Number One and orders the gang to kill Mannion, who they think is Jones. Jones then captures the gang for the police and is a hero, winning the heart of Jean Arthur.

It looked like a winner. It was a solid comedy and a good script—written by Robert Riskin and Robinson's collaborator from *The Kibitzer*, Jo Swerling. Cohn was ready to go ahead with filming no later than August 8. Cohn was in the process of negotiating with Al Santell to direct when Robinson, determined to look out for his own career, stepped in once again. Santell, whose credits included Mack Sennett one- and two-reelers as well as *Daddy Longlegs* and the 1930 version of *The Sea Wolf*, was not acceptable to the star. He wanted John Ford. Cohn and his general manager, Sam Briskin, were furious, but Cohn, who didn't waste a penny if he could help it, had already spent money developing the picture. Reluctantly, but shrewdly, he lured Ford away from RKO, where he was all but signed for a film, and booked him to direct *The Whole Town's Talking*.

It was a good move and a good movie. When *The Whole Town's Talking* opened for general release at the beginning of 1935, it was a sensation (and the first of Robinson's films to be shown at Radio City Music Hall). Robinson had established himself in comedy as well as gangland drama. Warners, too, couldn't have been more pleased: The loan-out, to which he'd agreed in order to get Robinson off his back, now looked like a shrewd Warner plan. Everyone was happy. There was talk in Hollywood about Robinson being nominated for an Academy Award, and Warner's happiness faded abruptly. No studio wanted to lose face by having one of its stars win an award for a film shot at a rival studio. There would be no award nomination. Warner saw to that.

The Whole Town's Talking became more to Robinson than just a hit movie. It pushed him back into the top box office lists and made Eddie and Gladys one of Hollywood's favorite couples, rivaling Frederic March and Florence Eldridge, and Melvyn Douglas and Helen Gahagan. The house on Rexford Drive was increasingly full of friends, there was money, and there were good times.

Yet, Robinson could never be satisfied with mere movie stardom, and he was slowly becoming a leading political activist in the film community. While others were trying to ignore Adolf Hitler and Benito Mussolini, he was trying to organize support against their regimes. It would be another year before these efforts would culminate in the Hollywood Anti-Nazi League, but for now, Robinson would turn parties into political forums, both he and Gladys finding it difficult to warm to anyone who could not see the coming doom, and who did not support FDR's New Deal.

Warner turned a deaf ear to his star's political machinations—as a Jew he couldn't fault Robinson for attacks on Hitler—but he wanted to use the renewed appeal the Columbia film had given Robinson to put the star back to work. And Robinson was eager to get back to work for his home studio. Memos of the time show that he approved the script for *Filthy Lucre*, a Dashiell Hammett thriller. Warner changed his mind about doing it, however, and instead wanted Robinson to do *Stiletto*, the story of a Sicilian forced to leave Italy because he has fallen afoul of the Mafia. He moves to America, joins the police force, and fights gangsters in his new country. Robinson was hesitant to do another gangster-oriented film, but the script came at a time when he was being audited by the Internal Revenue Service for the year 1933. Since he was to play the good guy, he agreed.

Warner was delighted, or so Robinson assumed. He allowed the casting news to be leaked to the industry trade papers. But Warner's other leading actor-star, Paul Muni, was giving him the same sort of script arguments as Robinson, and to teach them both a lesson Warner shelved *Stiletto* and went into discussions with Robinson about *Dr. Socrates*, originally to be a Muni vehicle, the story of a doctor involved in the underworld. Robinson saw a chance to snatch a role from Muni and agreed. When Muni got wind that Robinson was to play the part, he demanded that Warner return *Dr. Socrates* to him. It was just what Warner wanted. Muni was cast, and Robinson was offered the role of the leading gangster in the film. He was furious, unwilling to play number two to Muni, and immediately refused. (Robinson got the last laugh on this one, though. When the movie opened it earned Muni some of his weakest reviews.)

There was no going back to *Stiletto* after the *Dr. Socrates* incident. Robinson and Warner were hardly speaking, but Robinson's agent and lawyer were pressuring Warner to lend out their client again until things cooled off. Although Warner was, at first, hesitant, he agreed to listen to offers. They came quickly. Universal wanted Robinson and Charles Laughton to star in *Sutter's Gold*, about the California gold rush. Warner procrastinated, and then about a week later Sam Goldwyn, king of the independents, and Robinson's first film employer, asked for the loan of Robinson for *Barbary Coast*, a tale of gambling, corruption, and love in San Francisco during the gold rush. Warner hesitated again, but Goldwyn was not a man to be defeated when he wanted something or someone. After weeks of negotiations, on July 10 Robinson was lent to Goldwyn, with Warner receiving twice his star's $80,000 salary.

Robinson's excitement abated very quickly when he reported to Goldwyn's studio. Although one of the costars was an old New York pal, Frank Craven, the leading lady—who was to have top billing—was Miriam Hopkins. Although loved by audiences, she never got the same adoration on set, for Hopkins, a beautiful but cunningly selfish actress, was obsessed with upstaging other actors. On *Barbary Coast*, she had costume approval and insisted on a headdress that would make her several inches taller than Robinson. He fumed when director Howard Hawks asked him to stand on a box for his scenes with Miriam. But Robinson won round one, and Hopkins worked in her stocking feet.

Hopkins liked to improvise her lines, rearranging the words in the script to suit her perception of style. Robinson was the consummate professional who, by this juncture, was already known as an actor who loved rehearsals but liked to shoot his scenes in one or two takes. Hopkins would say a line one way in rehearsals then change her mind when the cameras were rolling, thus irritating Robinson beyond endurance. He became edgy, tempers flared, and as a result he felt his performance suffered, while she seemed quite satisfied with her own. Hawks was either powerless to stop her or didn't want to bother.

Hawks and Robinson, after two weeks of shooting, were not getting along well. (Hawks, however, respected talent, and years later he said Robinson, Muni, and Walter Huston were the best actors he had worked with in Hollywood.) Robinson had brought politics into the off-camera discussions, and as a result the politically divided set became tense with heated emotions and flare-ups. Hawks, a conservative, had found an ally in Hopkins, whose views could often be antebellum Southern. Robinson argued that FDR's New Deal policies would help bring the Depression to an end, and also that more should be done in Hollywood to help get actors, directors, and other film artists out of Germany (some were already trickling in).

It got worse. In one scene in the gambling palace that Robinson (Chamalis) owns, Hopkins (Swan) was to sip champagne. Hopkins decided she was allergic to the drink and proceeded to sneeze during each take. After more than twenty takes the bottle was empty and Hopkins was on the floor! Filming was halted for the day, and the assistant director and other crew members were blamed for not keeping a closer eye on her. Robinson thought this unjust—as he had at Townsend Harris High School when he thought the wrong student had been given an award—and it all became more than he could take. A few days later Robinson reached breaking point. He lit into Hopkins with all the verbal force he could muster. She was selfish, she was temperamental, he had seen prima donnas like her on Broadway. He had had it. She feigned an apology, and Hawks moved in to break it up, calling an early lunch.

All during the break Robinson steamed. He was furious with Hopkins, furious with Hawks. Sides were being taken. Cast members Joel McCrea and Walter Brennan, who were against the New Deal in political discussions, sided with Hopkins. Authors Ben Hecht and Charles MacArthur stopped by to pat Robinson on the back and agree that Hopkins was a pain.

By 1:00 P.M. the cast and crew were assembled again, and Robinson and Hopkins kissed and made up for appearance's sake. The scene called for Robinson to slap Hopkins, never an easy thing for an actor to make look realistic. Hopkins promised to say the lines as written and admonished Robinson to do it right—hit her hard the first time. The actor who had to have his eyes taped open to prevent his blinking at gunfire, the pacifist who declared all wars to be unjust, did just that. When the time came to slap Hopkins, he slugged her, whacking her with such force that she fell to the ground. Hawks yelled cut. Robinson and Hopkins glared at each other, there was a pregnant pause, then the crew began to cheer. Little Caesar, the snarling underdog, had won the common man to his side again. Hopkins was humiliated and returned to her dressing room, where she sulked for several hours.

As Robinson sat in his dressing room, ashamed and embarrassed, waiting for Hawks to call him back to the set or release them for the day, he could hear the crew talking about how marvelous he had been by punching the bitch. Hadn't she wanted it done in one take? they laughed. It was on that day, perhaps somewhat erroneously, he was dubbed "One-Take Eddie" by the crew. As he sat there he tried desperately, but unsuccessfully, to brush the growing smirk off his face.

Hopkins behaved for the last week of shooting *Barbary Coast*. The conservative element on the set was quiet, the liberals chatted happily. Hopkins barely spoke to Robinson. Even her phony gaiety and exaggerated manners had disappeared. There was no smile on her face. That is, until October. When *Barbary Coast* opened Sam Goldwyn had an instant hit. So did Hopkins. It was she who had stolen all the headlines.

With *Barbary Coast* finished, Warner was glad to get Robinson back on his lot. They had purchased the Robert Sherwood play *The Petrified Forest* as a vehicle for him. Robinson readily agreed in an August memo to play the part of Duke Mantee, the gang leader whose appearance at an isolated café heralds the death of a loner intellectual and the salvation of a waitress. Bette Davis, now a star thanks to *Of Human Bondage*, was Warner's choice for the waitress, and he already had Leslie Howard set to repeat his stage performance.

Robinson would later claim that he backed out of the film because he didn't want to play another gangster. Although Warner allowed him to say that publicly to save face, the memos of the studio reveal another story to be true. Humphrey Bogart had played the Duke Mantee part on Broadway and yearned to tackle it on film, a medium he had temporarily abandoned because, like Robinson, he was tired of playing hoods (his were all still supporting roles only). Although Mantee too was a gangster, it was a leading role, and Bogart correctly saw it as his ticket to movie stardom.

Bogart's loyal friend Howard sent a telegram to Warner demanding that Bogart be cast. Robinson was told that Howard, not he, had the necessary clout, and Bogart won. There were no hard feelings. Robinson and Bogart would work together numerous times and become friends and even political allies.

However gracious Robinson was in defeat, there were still no parts for him, and he sat out the rest of 1935 and the beginning of 1936 until he finally agreed to accept the role of Johnny Blake in *Bullets or Ballots* (which ironically would have Bogart as the fourth-billed hoodlum and Blake's archenemy).

Robinson played a maverick cop who loses his shield, decides on his own to infiltrate the numbers rackets, and eventually leads the police to the gangster's den, as he dies from a bullet wound earned in a shootout with Bogart.

Bullets or Ballots was plagued with problems and was not a particularly happy experience for Robinson. A few weeks after the filming began on March 16, Joan Blondell, Robinson's love interest, developed a throat infection and was off for a week. In April, Sarah Goldenberg took seriously ill, and Robinson flew back to New York expecting her to die. She was made of stronger stuff and survived, but seven days were lost. To make up for lost time, cast and crew were working from 2:30 P.M. to 4:00 A.M. on many days, an exhausting schedule. The film finished seven days behind schedule, earning Robinson an extra $75,000, but it was little consolation. Topping it all was an argument with Warners' accounting department, which insisted on charging Robinson $75 for a coat purchased for his character in the film. Robinson had taken it to New York with him and when he returned decided to keep it. Jack Warner eventually stepped in and admitted it was ridiculous to charge for the coat.

Bullets or Ballots opened in May, only days after Robinson, Blondell, and Bogart had gone on the popular radio show *Hollywood Hotel* to perform a sound-only version. This extra publicity heightened audience interest, and the film set box office records in New York, earning $11,500 in its first two days. As a further publicity stunt, Warner Bros. had arranged for Robinson to be stopped in full view of photographers while carrying a suspicious violin case. Photos of him were taken while he alternately expressed both fear and defiance at this intrusion of privacy by the police.

Meanwhile, Warners once again had no vehicle for him. Smarting because Muni had been given the part of Louis Pasteur and was now their prestige player, Robinson pressured Warner for a similar biographical film. Warner leaked to the press that he was planning to do a picture about Beethoven with Robinson, and the actor readily agreed. But scripts and commitments to directors and research were unforthcoming, and Robinson knew he was being fooled by Warners' press agents.

Gladys had gone to Great Britain in February to investigate film possibilities in London. Her charm with British producers had gained offers, and Robinson agreed to do a film for Alexander Esway that would be distributed by Columbia. Entitled *Thunder in the City*, the original script was written by Aben Kandell, coincidentally another Rumanian Jew who had grown up on the Lower East Side and gone to the same public schools as Robinson, albeit a few years later.

Warner, realizing the Beethoven film would not be made, gave Robinson his permission, and Robinson left for New York, where he was to board the *Normandie* for Southampton on June 17. The scene on the pier at West 4th Street the day he left buoyed his spirits, showing him he was still popular. Press reports record a "mob" of fans there to see him off and maybe get an autograph. Also on board, although not yet a big star, was Henry Fonda.

Robinson sailed to Britain with Kandell, who had a vivid memory of the trip and of the real-life Little Caesar. He recalled:

> Eddie was a modest man, he was warm. He was funny and generous. You couldn't have found a better guy.
>
> We were on the boat. He was alone, I was with my wife. But I met this English girl. A knockout. You couldn't have dreamed of a better situation, but not for me, because I was with my wife. Now, you have to understand that at that time there was no one more important than a motion picture actor. Wherever we'd go with Eddie in England, we'd see reporters. You'd think he was a senator or something.
>
> So my hands were tied with this girl. But I knew from Hollywood that Eddie and his wife were always fighting. I tried to fix Eddie and this girl up, but he was scared shitless even though Gladys was 8,000 miles away. I'd become good friends with him, so I figured I'd prod him on with this chippie, because she was willing. He was a movie star, after all.

Robinson kept his fidelity throughout the voyage, but even after he checked into the Strand Hotel in London, Kandell did not stop trying:

> We continued the friendship with the girl in London. She owned a beautiful house in Mayfair, and she invited us for dinner. Eddie was the guest of honor, but still he wouldn't give in. I just marveled at his restraint. I couldn't conceive of a guy not taking advantage of a situation like this. But maybe that's my corrupt point of view.
>
> I'm not a trained psychologist, but I don't think Eddie was very sexually oriented. He had his art collection. He was always fighting for the democratic

way of life. He was not a gambler. He was not a boozer. He was an inveterate smoker, and Freud might have had something to say about that. He always had something in his mouth. But I'm not Freud, so I won't hazard a guess. I will say that Eddie's passion was his work.

The work was not going well. *Thunder in the City* was a weak tale of an American who goes to Britain on business and stumbles on distant relatives who are impoverished aristocrats. He helps them back to wealth and when he leaves for America has his cousin (Luli Deste) on his arm.

Robinson, who was forty-three, had had his hair dyed to hide the grey that was beginning to appear on his temples. The director, Marion Gering, never even noticed, so busy was he in trying to make the film work. After several weeks and little on film, Robinson was so disgusted with the material that he took it upon himself to have tea with Robert Sherwood. By the end of the afternoon the great writer had agreed to punch up the script, and he eventually shared screen credit with Kandell. *Thunder in the City* was completed, but at double its original $350,000 budget. Robinson wanted to forget about it.

Rather than return to the States immediately, he decided to rest and relax. With Kandell, who was now a close friend, he wandered into an art gallery and ended up buying Renoir's *The Girl with the Red Plume.* Then he went to another gallery and bought a Morisot. In Paris he bought a Gauguin, a Cézanne, another Morisot, another Renoir. Suddenly, he was shipping a worthy art collection back to Beverly Hills.

But he also knew his contract with Warner Bros. was still awaiting in Hollywood. He wrote to Jack Warner explaining he'd be returning in early November and suggesting a movie about the French hero Danton. "During my stay here I have received a few inquiries for my services in America," Robinson wrote. "Having in mind, however, that my first desire is to make my next picture for you I have, for the time being, deferred consideration of those offers until I receive some word from you as to when you would most likely require me." He closed by pleading, "Give me a good one and we'll both be happy."

What Warner had waiting for him was a new contract, one that would guarantee the studio two pictures per year. It was a two-year deal, but there were no properties immediately available.

An offer came from Broadway producer Max Gordon to play Napoleon, Robinson's dream role, in *St. Helena*. But Robinson now didn't want to go back to the stage. He rejected Gordon's offer—as he later learned Muni did too—and instead asked Warner to lend him to Paramount so he could play opposite Marlene Dietrich in *Josephine*. Warner vetoed that but revived *Napoleon*, assigning the project to yet more writers and sending memos to the research department for yet more information. Despite all the years of discussion, the project would never come to fruition.

5

THE ANTI-FASCIST CAUSE

*Name calling will not stop me. I am fighting for those Ameri-
can things that I hold dear.*

—Edward G. Robinson

The political sense that had been reemerging in Robinson for some
time had reached boiling point. During his time in Europe, he had
sensed that, as historians later confirmed, the seeds for World War II had
been planted the day the armistice for World War I was signed. London
had been filled with German and Austrian émigrés, many of them Jewish, part Jewish, or denying they were Jewish. Hitler was a reality in Europe, a growing menace, and Robinson wanted to be doing something
about it.

During June 1936, while Robinson was in Europe, the Hollywood
Anti-Nazi League had been formed, dedicated to convincing the government to oppose Hitler and to find homes and work for refugees. Donald
Ogden Stewart, later blacklisted, was the first chairman. The Most Reverend John J. Cantwell, then archbishop of Los Angeles, was among the
first members, although church pressure forced him to resign three
months later. That summer the League sponsored an address by Prince

Hubertus and Princess Marie Lowenstein, German exiles, at the Wilshire Ebell Theater. They spoke of growing Fascism in their country to a crowd of film colony notables. When they finished their lecture, Frederic March and his wife, Florence Eldridge, stepped forward and joined the League. During the next few years many other prominent liberals would do the same.

Robinson, too, joined in the autumn when he returned to Beverly Hills. It seemed a natural front for fighting Fascism. The League supported Spanish Loyalists, and so did Robinson. Ogden Stewart wrote a radio serial program sponsored by the Guild and Robinson listened to it and urged others to do the same. He allowed his name to be used freely in *Hollywood Now*, the League's weekly paper. He urged studio heads not to give a contract to Hitler propagandist filmmaker Leni Riefenstahl and celebrated when her move to Hollywood was blocked. The same process was used against Mussolini when it was reported Il Duce was coming to Hollywood to visit his son, a producer involved in a short-lived partnership with Hal Roach. Roach said that Mussolini Sr. wanted to learn about movies. The League preached that he wanted to learn how to make propaganda films. Il Duce did not visit. And later Robinson spoke out against MGM's signing of German actress Louisa Ulrich, claiming, as the League said, that she was a close friend of Joseph Goebbels.

Robinson felt good. He was participating. It is difficult in retrospect to believe his later contention that he was not aware there were members of the Communist Party active in the League. Of course he had his suspicions, but like other immigrant Jews he thought of Communism as just another variation of secular humanism. The New York Jews of his youth had covered a wide political spectrum: They had been socialists, Labor Bundists, communists, anarchists, liberals, democrats; the different parties warred, fought, squabbled, but often found themselves ultimately on the same side.

So when Texas Congressman Martin Dies accused the League of being a Communist front, he was attacked by the liberals, and instead Melvyn Douglas, John Ford, and Dorothy Parker were called upon to address meetings. And if Robinson had any suspicion that the League might someday be considered subversive, it was squelched when a German American Bund Convention was picketed in 1937. Carrying placards with League members were people from such diverse groups as the American Legion, the Veterans of Foreign Wars, the California Christian Church Council, AFL, CIO (they were not yet merged), and the American League for Peace and Democracy. In fact, at the League's first anniversary gala in June 1937, the cream of Hollywood turned out at the Ambassador Hotel.

The whole of Hollywood at that time was highly—and occasionally heatedly—politically aware. As early as 1934, Louis B. Mayer had shown his militant conservative stripes by forcing all MGM employees to contribute to a campaign to defeat the Socialist Upton Sinclair for the governorship of California. Three pseudofascist military units—the Hollywood Hussars, the Light Horse Cavalry, and the California Esquadrille—had been founded in 1935 and 1936 and included in their membership such stars as Gary Cooper, Victor McLaglen, and George Brent.

McLaglen told the press that his Light Horse membership totaled one thousand by 1936 and "had offered its services to city, state and federal authorities at any time they might be needed." Speakers at the club's specially designed stadium, which included an auditorium capable of seating seven hundred, told the group of the coming Communist menace and issued instructions on how to Red-bait.

Similarly, Cooper had begun the Hussars as a club whose membership was "limited to American citizens of excellent character and of social and financial standing, who are physically fit, not under 5' 7" in height, and between the ages of 18 and 45." They wore a service uniform similar to those used by the United States Cavalry of post-Civil War Days, and the full dress uniform was modeled on the original Hungarian Hussars. Recruiting slogans for the Hussars talked of starting "a military-social organization with good fellowship and community spirit." Sections included a medical and first-aid detachment, a signal communications troop, a signal photographic section, a motorcycle detachment, a military police and intelligence detachment, and buglers and a mounted band.

The three groups—Brent's California Esquadrille was organized in much the same way—were funded, in part, by William Randolph Hearst (Robinson's boyhood hero) and founded because many in the motion picture industry were becoming increasingly paranoid over a radicalism from abroad seeping into their own community. As the liberals and radicals to the left supported the loyalists in Spain, so the Coopers and Brents supported Franco. Adolphe Menjou went one step further and accepted Adolf Hitler's personal invitation to attend the 1936 Olympics in Germany. Menjou was already compiling his obsessive file on Communists and radicals in the United States and their ventures.

Coupled with his—and Hollywood's—involvement in fledgling causes such as these, Robinson was still under contract to Warner Bros. as an actor. Finally in January 1937 his studio put him to work on a film, *Kid Galahad,* in which he played a shady boxing manager with a hidden heart of gold. Humphrey Bogart was the villain, and Bette Davis was "Fluff," the boxer's moll.

Robinson had originally suggested a young starlet named Jane Wyman for the part, and she was tested, but Jack Warner had insisted on Davis. Robinson protested that she wasn't soft and vulnerable enough—"hard as steel" is how he described her to the bosses. The pair had never warmed to each other. Robinson complained that Davis was not a good actress, perhaps allowing himself a little jealousy (Davis had one thing Robinson lacked—an Academy Award, which she had captured for the mediocre film *Dangerous,* made a year after *Of Human Bondage* had catapulted her into stardom). Davis privately fumed that Robinson would pocket more than $50,000 for the picture and her salary would come to $18,500 (Bogart's was a mere $3,185). Though decades later they would admit respect for each other's talents, their coolness would carry on for the next few years. Davis sang the praises of Paul Muni as an actor, which infuriated Robinson, and later, in 1941, when Davis wrote to Robinson asking for a donation toward a canteen for British émigrés she was organizing, he turned her down, one of the few occasions between 1939 and 1947 he declined to contribute to anything connected with the war effort.

More important to Robinson than the films he made in 1937 was his realization that he enjoyed living in California. Pals Pepe Schildkraut and Sam Jaffe were increasingly on the Coast to do films, and the Robinsons entertained lavishly and often in their showplace home in Beverly Hills. Manny, by this time, was a mischievous four-year-old, who was a trial for the governesses hired to take care of him. Robinson decided a boy needed more room in which to grow, so he purchased a small ranch in Higginsville, in the hills overlooking both Beverly Hills and the San Fernando Valley.

Gladys also wanted the Rexford Drive house turned into a better living environment, and Eddie thought the now large art collection needed its own home. They drew up plans to tear out the badminton court and replace it with a small museumlike structure to house the collection. At the same time the entire interior of the main house would be redone.

Contractors were employed and work was begun while the Robinsons moved to the new ranch in the interim. After a few weeks housing inspectors from Beverly Hills stopped all work, pending approval of the proper building permits. Certain parts of the blueprints were rejected, changes were made, and as the city's involvement caused the process to drag on—and cost more—Gladys became increasingly depressed and solemn, sinking into a dark, brooding mood. The woman who had been walking on air with excitement was now a pale, sad shell. Robinson sent her to a physician for a checkup, and some pills were prescribed, but neither Robinson nor the doctors recognized in her the initial symptoms of what was to come. She was, after all, the "belle of the ball" whenever the pair went out on the town. At one winter party at Basil Rathbone's, the couples were told to come dressed as a famous bride and bridegroom from history. Robinson naturally chose his dream role—Napoleon—with Gladys as Josephine. Although Jack Warner took one look at his star and revived the Napoleon project, the enthusiasm lasted only a few weeks and the character was dead and buried again as far as the studio was concerned.

Again, it seemed, there were no roles for Robinson. Warner bought a property entitled *Casino* about an intellectual spy who uses a circus as his cover, but when Louella Parsons declared it a "pretentious" story in her column, the film was scrapped. Such was her power, but her criticism was not without merit. *Casino* had been designed as a musical, a genre that Warner had consistently rejected for Robinson despite overtures from Busby Berkeley from time to time about using the gangster star as he had employed Cagney.

With no parts in the offing, Robinson took off for a vacation to New York in April. There was little for him to do there except visit with family and friends and revel in playing the movie star. Any feelings about being only a visitor to California were gone, and Robinson turned this trip to New York into a triumphant return. For the benefit of the press, Robinson went to the 45th Street theater where he had played in *Juarez and Maximilian* and pointed to the alley wall where he had—he good-naturedly claimed—once written, "Cheer up, better times are coming," signing it "Edward G. Robinson." Lo and behold, the scribbling was still there, and it earned the movie star a lot of press.

He complained to reporters that "I'm tired of bad-guy roles" and entertained them at dinners. His Warner Bros. press releases of the trip picture him as a tourist trying to absorb as much of New York as he could. One had Robinson going into a fancy restaurant for a thick juicy steak and dessert, then dashing to his favorite deli and topping off the first feast with a corned beef sandwich and a cold beer. Gluttony for the hometown boy made good.

Keeping up the presentation of Robinson as a cultured star, the press agents prompted the reporters into giving a big splash to Igor Stravinsky's declaration that his friend Eddie Robinson was also his favorite movie star. The cultured Robinson—and at least this part was fully accurate—was pictured attending concerts at Carnegie Hall and touring the art galleries in search of a new buy. He did buy more French Impressionists, on which he was now a recognized expert.

On May 13 he agreed to appear on Kate Smith's popular radio show and became so excited about the music that in the last minutes of the show he pushed musical director Jack Miller aside and led the house band in the final chords. "I always wanted to lead a band," he apologized sheepishly after it was over. His popularity with audiences soared.

Yet there was no word from Warner on what his next film role would be, although scripts and treatments had come and gone. Louella Parsons published that Robinson was sought for the Van Gogh part in *Lust for Life*, but it never materialized, even had Robinson wanted to do it.

He needed money, as word from Gladys came that the bills on the redecorating and construction were mounting. Pleading his case to Warner, he returned to the Coast and was sent on loan to MGM for a silly melodrama called *The Last Gangster*. In it he portrays a man who gets out of jail only to find that his wife has remarried and her new husband (Jimmy Stewart) has adopted his son.

More important to Robinson than the film, which he walked through, was the political climate—or lack of it—at MGM. L. B. Mayer had insisted that no one discuss politics with the star, particularly the Sinclair campaign or the New Deal. Director William Wellman and Stewart—whose political consciousness pleased their boss—were told to keep mum. Lionel Stander, who played the real villain, was considered a political radical, and Robinson felt close to him on the set. Stander recalled:

> Eddie was a pro, et cetera, but he was also very jealous. He hated to have anyone taller than himself on a picture. He was very conscious of his height. I'm 6' 1." Wellman had a terrible time moving the cameras to balance us ... I was also a collector of paintings, so as I remember art dominated our conversations off the set. I was always telling him to buy new American artists. If he had taken my advice, I think his art collection would have been worth millions more than it was. Eddie was very cautious in his purchases and was always listening to the dealers. I kept telling him to quit buying that French Impressionist shit. I don't think he ever did buy a young American artist's work.

Louis B. Mayer was a national figure, and his Washington connections were in evidence when he dropped by the *Last Gangster* set one day with J. Edgar Hoover, director of the FBI, and Hoover's assistant, Clyde Tolson.

Hoover was a Robinson fan, and the feeling was mutual. Robinson gave the top G-man a prop gun, and they exchanged notes on crime fighting in the movies versus the real thing. Hoover agreed to send Robinson an autographed picture, after the star gave him one.

When Hoover returned to Washington, he sent letters to his new Hollywood friends, Robinson among them. "It was a distinct pleasure to be able to chat with you and also to visit the set where you were engaged in making a picture," Hoover wrote. "Please let me know when you are again in Washington. I would like very much to see you again and to have the opportunity of personally showing you something of our activities here." It was signed "with kind regards," with an added handwritten note thanking Robinson for the photo taken of the star with Hoover and Tolson.

No matter what America might think of the Hoover legacy today, it is not surprising that Robinson admired him in the 1930s. He stood, at the time, as the symbol of the forces attempting to wipe out organized crime. Robinson knew all too well that gangsters were romanticized—his own popularity was based in part on that appeal—but so was the FBI. Robinson framed the photo taken of himself and Hoover. Young Manny would recall staring at it, trying to imitate Hoover's look just as he would try to imitate his father's snarling appearance as a gangster in film after film. The photographs would have an honored place in the Robinson home for a decade.

After all, Robinson had his own, readily admitted, desire to reform the world, which led him to agree to an offer from Lever Brothers to begin a weekly radio show. CBS premiered *Big Town* on September 27, and it was for many years one of the top shows in the country. Robinson portrayed Steve Wilson, crusading editor of the *Illustrated Press,* assisted by Lorelei Kilbourne, his understanding love interest played first by Claire Trevor, then Ona Munson, then Fran Carlson. Each week Steve Wilson would pit himself against some creeping evil that was threatening Small Town USA. It could be gamblers, or criminals, corrupt officials, or villains holding back on milk supplies in order to raise prices. Robinson was at his finest vocally, with his deep, strong tones filled with both strength and warmth, authority and kindness. America voted it the second-highest-rated radio series for much of the time it was on the air. Only Jack Benny had more listeners.

If the truth be told—and Robinson admitted this—it was not only humanism that convinced him to do the series. Perhaps primarily it was the money. Robinson was allowed to package the show, serving technically as executive producer and hiring the entire staff. For himself, there was a salary gratefully paid by Lever Brothers—which used the show to plug Rinso detergent—of $4,000 per show the first year, $6,000 the second year, $7,000 the third, and so on. Robinson would earn a week's salary from Warner Bros. in but one day on radio. It was income that could buy art by the masters, trips to Europe, furs for Gladys—and eventually would keep Robinson afloat when crusaders of another stripe went after him.

Warner Bros. at first resisted giving approval for Robinson to do *Big Town*, but then relented when Robinson agreed to give them half a day's work on Saturday in exchange for permission to leave the set at noon each Tuesday in order to go on the air that night. Lever Brothers had to agree to plug Warner movies on each show, with the film company supplying the text for the announcer: "You have just heard Edward G. Robinson, Warner Bros. star, and we suggest you see his latest picture [name of film] at your local theater," or "We suggest you look for other forthcoming Warner Bros. pictures such as [name of film]."

Back at the studio, Robinson was making *A Slight Case of Murder*, based upon the stage comedy by Damon Runyon and Howard Lindsay. A relatively easy film for Robinson—he played a bootlegger turned beer baron—it finished one day ahead of schedule at $40,000 under its $469,000 budget. The critics adored the film when it premiered in February 1938. While the studio promoted it as "Edward G. Robinson in Damon Runyon's blazing story of the mobster who murdered and laughed," the critics recognized it as the full-fledged farce it was.

Anyway he looked at it, Robinson realized he was back on top. *A Slight Case of Murder* was a huge box office success; his radio show was doing well; even his family life seemed stable. They had passed a happy Christmas together, although the Goldenberg in Robinson still felt guilt over having a Christmas tree and posing as Santa Claus for Manny's sake.

Christmas 1937 also meant the family was together in the redecorated house on Rexford Drive, which had been designed to be a gallery for the art collection. Robinson always joked that "the art owns us." In the living room hung Corot's *L'Italienne*, Daumier's *Second-Class Coach*, Cézanne's *Black Clock*, plus Van Gogh's *Country Road*, a Seurat, a Géricault, a Pissarro, and Renoirs. In the dining room were four pastels by Dégas and one of his sculpted figures of a ballerina. Elsewhere in the house were even more. Beulah Robinson, Eddie's niece, would recall that among her first recollections of her uncle when her family visited was the image of him taking out his handkerchief and wiping some dust from the frames or straightening them.

The Christmas celebration was significant to Robinson for another reason. His family had been remembered by his new friend, J. Edgar Hoover, who had sent Manny a G-man set, including handcuffs and a miniature fingerprint set. Robinson was pleased, and even more so when he received a letter in the new year from Hoover praising him for his work in *The Last Gangster*:

> I have just returned to my office from viewing it, and I could not refrain from dropping you a note to tell you what a good picture I think it is and what an excellent performance you gave. I think you know that I am somewhat of a Robinson fan and I do think that you have more than sustained the excellent reputation which you have established for being a real artist in the presentation of your characters. The picture also teaches a worthy lesson and carries a powerful message.
>
> I do hope that in the near future, either on this Coast or in the West Coast, it will be possible for us to see each other again, because I would like to renew our acquaintance of last summer.

Robinson responded by asking him to listen to *Big Town*.

Robinson's friends might have thought he had everything he wanted at this point: he was wealthy; even though he was increasingly having arguments with Gladys, on the surface they seemed to be a contented couple;

Manny was growing well, although he had a penchant for getting into trouble (just minor little-boy things at this point); the career was on a steady course. But Robinson was not content. He looked at his studio work and saw a stream of gangster pictures, nothing with the prestige of the parts Muni had been getting, or even Bette Davis. He began to clamor for similar roles, films of historical importance, or biographies. Since at this point Warner had Muni tagged for that slot, Robinson was not being considered for such parts. Yet, his arguments continued, and Warner eventually offered Robinson *The Amazing Dr. Clitterhouse*, the story of a physician-psychiatrist who joins with gangsters in order to study the criminal mind.

Warner was warned against using Robinson by his staff. Cedric Hardwicke had played the role on stage, and they reasoned that Robinson would not succeed in the role because the audience would see him as one of the gangsters, not the "interloper" he was meant to be. In memos they suggested Charles Boyer, Ronald Colman, Melvyn Douglas, Cary Grant, and even Bette Davis. But Warner knew that Robinson had to be placated, and he stuck to his guns.

It was a long film to make—from the end of February until early April—but Robinson relished the role even if only because he was flattered to be playing a part once played by the highbrow Hardwicke. When it premiered during the summer, though, Robinson had to admit his error; critic after critic pointed out that he was miscast, although they agreed he had acted well.

Clitterhouse had not satisfied Robinson's desire for better roles. Instead, he was enraged when he discovered in April that Warner Bros. was planning *Juarez and Maximilian* as Muni's next film. Since Robinson had a clause in his contract promising him a film on the life of Profirio Diaz—Juarez's general—he immediately accused Warner of being on the verge of breaching his contract. In a handwritten letter to Jack, he said:

I read with no little surprise that you intend to do *Juarez and Maximilian* shortly. You will remember at the time we discussed our present contract, that among other suggestions I made for future stories for me, *Juarez and Maximilian* was included. You were so enthusiastic for me to do this particular story that you incorporated it in our contract under the title and reference to the life of Diaz. While your treatment will center about the character of Juarez instead of Diaz, this variation should not have altered your obligation to me since I could just as easily play Juarez as Diaz. I have suffered keen disappointment in the past with other stories I have given you—only to find that they were good enough for others but not for me. Knowing you, Jack, you will do as you please in this matter, but I could not let this occasion go by without letting you know exactly how I feel.

Juarez was made with Muni and Davis, but only after Warners had checked out its legal stand with the Robinson contract. As a result, the character of Diaz was expunged from the Muni picture. And Robinson was packed off to Columbia for *I Am the Law*, in which he portrayed a law professor turned special prosecutor. The critics noted that Robinson's career and characters were getting "tired." And Eddie knew it.

In July, Robinson was sent several screenplays for his approval, including one on the life of Haym Solomon, the Jewish financier who had helped the American cause during the Revolutionary War. While Robinson was mulling over the scripts, he discovered that a writer named Norman Burnstine, who went professionally by the name Norman Burnside, had written to Warner Bros. offering his treatment for a film on the life of Dr. Paul Ehrlich, the German Jew who had discovered the cure for syphilis. Burnstine reasoned that a film on a Jew who had done so much for humanity would do good at a time when anti-Semitism was running rampant in Europe and even in the United States.

"There isn't a man or a woman alive who isn't afraid of syphilis—and let them know that a little kike named Ehrlich tamed the scourge," Burnstine wrote. "And maybe they can persuade their hoodlum friends to keep their fists off Ehrlich's coreligionists—in spite of the political Spanish fly spat out by Coughlin, Winrod, Ford and others."

Not surprisingly, Burnstine had suggested Muni for the role, but Muni had made it a policy never to portray a Jew on the screen. Research into the project was nevertheless started, while Warner and Wallis began to discuss whether Robinson would fit the role.

A disgruntled Robinson meanwhile had decided to take a vacation with Gladys in Mexico, where they went to visit a friend, the artist Diego Rivera. It was a hot August, but they were enjoying themselves when Rivera suggested that they visit a friend of his—Leon Trotsky, who was living in Mexico under tight guard. Eddie and Gladys eagerly agreed. A meeting was set up, and on the appointed day and time the Hollywood couple went to see the great revolutionary. For Robinson, it was a satisfactory and fascinating visit, as Trotsky talked about his childhood in Brooklyn, about the movies, and about the monster Stalin. Robinson offered to have prints of his films sent, and Trotsky was pleased. They left, with Robinson feeling good about the trip.

But on their return, he noticed that Gladys had a completely different impression of the meeting they had just had. She talked about the status of having made the visit, the decor, the security. Robinson was beginning to realize they had grown apart intellectually. It worried him. "She was very competitive with him, which was ridiculous," Aben Kandell, the writer, recalled. "She was swimming in waters that were infinitely too deep for her. Gladys had no idea why Lenin and Trotsky separated and what they really stood for. She came back from Mexico filled with muddled concepts. This was too much for her. But to hear her tell it, she and Trotsky really hit it off . . . She was already beginning to show signs of what you might call a mental stress," Kandell added. "She was trying to put herself on a par with Eddie. She went away often and I began to suspect he was glad to have some peace in the house."

The marriage was beginning to deteriorate, as Eddie and Gladys found they had less and less in common. Gladys would go about her social affairs while Eddie worked at the studio, studied scripts, or broadcast *Big Town*. Manny was left in the care of a governess most of the time, and his behavior showed resentment. He took to imitating his father's voice, first for attention and approval, then to intercept telephone calls for fun. He destroyed his father's cigars and cigarettes. Once, when the family went sailing, he pushed his mother into the water. Home life was beginning to be a trial for Eddie. What had seemed blissful just a year before was now tense and often disturbing.

When he returned to Warner Bros. after the rest, Jack and Hal Wallis were waiting for him. Not only had they chosen him to portray Ehrlich, but they also wanted him to think about playing the lead in *Storm over America,* a film they were planning loosely based on Leon Turrou's *The Nazi Spy Conspiracy in America.* Since Warner's representative in Germany—a Jew—had been murdered under mysterious circumstances in Hitler's country, he thought it was time to stop pussyfooting with diplomacy and say something on the screen about the rising Nazi menace and its front in the United States—the German-American Bund. Robinson, who had been fighting for such a film for several years, could not have been more pleased.

There was a catch or two, though. An independent film company had previously announced a project on Ehrlich, and the legal considerations would take precedence over the script. Robinson was willing to wait. *Storm,* too, needed research and legal attention. For one thing, the Bund had threatened a $500,000 lawsuit if they went ahead with the film. Again, Robinson was willing to wait.

There was also the problem of his contract, which was up for renewal. With two choice films dangling in front of him, Robinson forgot his anger and went into negotiations. The October 3 document was for three years, commencing on January 19, 1939. Robinson agreed to appear in two films each year for the home studio, with a guarantee of $85,000 per picture. He retained the right to make two films each year for other studios "upon such terms as may be satisfactory to the Artist." In other words, no more loan-outs, unless Robinson approved.

Warner Bros. was to send him at least three scripts or treatments every May and September for his approval (although he had already approved *Storm* and *Ehrlich*). Another clause guaranteed him the principal male role in each film, a concession from the studio since all parties were well aware that Robinson was rapidly approaching fifty, a time at which other stars had to move into character roles. Furthermore, no actor could be given better billing or have his or her name in larger type than Robinson. Warners also promised to have a parking space for Robinson and to handle all his fan mail, including the cost of a photograph for each person who wrote. He was to have a "star dressing room" and his own makeup artist and stand-in. All in all, it was a top contract, and Robinson was pleased.

Robinson was not shy about pushing for the roles he thought himself worthy of. After he read a piece in the trade papers that Wallis was preparing a script on the life of Beethoven, he wasted no time in making his feeling on the matter known, jockeying for position against Muni, who also wanted the part.

Just two weeks after he signed the new contract, he wrote to Wallis:

> You know that some years ago I suggested the Beethoven theme, and expressed my keen desire to play this role. During our recent negotiations, which resulted in the present contract, the Beethoven subject came up, and neither you nor Jack interposed any obstacles. Please do not misunderstand the spirit in which I say to you that once again Warner Brothers will probably do what it chooses to do in the matter; but once again I cannot let this chance go by without letting you know how I feel about it. Our relationship has been so warm and understanding over such a long period, that I feel free to write in complete candor.

Robinson continued by imploring, "I want the gamut [of my roles] broadened, but not from conceit or actor's temperament, but in order to do justice to my capacities." Robinson promised to do a script called *Brother Orchid*, about a gangster who retires to a monastery, but not unless he was given pictures that he found more prestigious (*Ehrlich* eventually would be such a film). "I want again to express a strong desire to appear in the international spy ring story you are going to do," Robinson's letter stated, then underlining, "I want to do that for my people." He added, "You mentioned that the story may not be too good, but I see no reason why efforts should not be expended to make it a knock-out story." The letter ended with a plea for a film about Benjamin Franklin, another character Robinson wanted desperately to play.

Wallis replied by promising Robinson the role in *Storm*, which was now retitled *Confessions of a Nazi Spy*. But there were script delays, he said.

But Robinson was not waiting for a film to herald the anti-Nazi movement. The Anti-Nazi League in Hollywood now boasted four thousand members, and with Robinson among the leaders, the group was planning its biggest push ever in December. Since there had been fifty-six signatories of the Declaration of Independence, the League devised a Committee of 56, Hollywood notables who would lead the patriotic activities scheduled for that month. And they agreed that there was not a better spot to launch the Committee than Robinson's home, a move that filled Robinson with pride.

On the night of December 9, the Committee of 56 held its meeting, and Clark M. Eichelberger, director of the League of Nations Association and also director of the American Union for Concerted Peace Efforts, spoke. Then the 56 sat down and signed a "declaration" to President Roosevelt and Congress requesting them "to bring such economic pressure to bear against Germany as would force her to reconsider her aggressive attitude towards other nations." The signatories were a veritable who's who of Hollywood—numbering amongst them Myrna Loy, John Ford, Joan Crawford, Burgess Meredith, Spencer Tracy, Jean Hersholt, Lucille Ball, Don Ameche, Claude Rains, Melvyn Douglas, Rosalind Russell, James Cagney, Gale Sondergaard, Aline MacMahon, Henry Fonda, Pat O'Brien, Jack Warner, Fay Bainter, Priscilla Lane, Donald Crisp, Ben Hecht, Joan Bennett, Dennis O'Keefe, Bette Davis, Groucho Marx, Elliot Nugent, Bruce Cabot, Ann Sheridan, Dick Powell, Tony Martin, Alice Faye, and even the right-wing George Brent, as well as two of Robinson's least-favorite fellow actors—Paul Muni and Miriam Hopkins.

The Committee of 56 and the League immediately joined in with a planned December 14 broadcast on NBC's radio network to honor Rededication Day, the anniversary of the signing of the Bill of Rights. Robinson was among those who would participate by reading short plays directed by Frank Capra. Even the conservative W. R. Wilkerson in his *Trade Views* column in *The Hollywood Reporter,* of which he was founder-publisher, praised the efforts of the League. "From time to time," he wrote, "misinformed sources have gone on record with the opinion that this part of California is the habitat of various persons antagonistic to American ideals . . . the broadcast should punch home the fact that it [Hollywood] is willing and able to render patriotic service when the need arises. Certainly that time is now."

On December 21 the Committee announced that its members would narrate film clips of Nazi atrocities and make filmed pleas for American action against Germany—clips that would be shown in the theaters. The Committee specifically asked for an embargo of goods to Germany and arranged for petitions saying just that to be available outside the theaters when the patrons were leaving. Irving Reis of Paramount wrote the text, and Robinson was glad to help, along with Douglas, Fonda, Cagney, Muni, and others.

The fact that all America was not behind the movement was hammered home in letters that Robinson received. One, from a man in Chicago, came right to the point: "Every Christian in this country will recognize you for what you really are. A cheap, big-mouthed ignorant Jew lacking in a sense of public decency and decorum." The writer added, "We all have been conscious of the methods by which Jews attempt to control business, finance and other avenues of business."

Besides the reaction of Americans who had read about the Anti-Nazi League movement, the FBI also became aware of Robinson's activities and at this point began a file on the star that would expand for well over a decade. The FBI report was particularly interested in what the Communist publication the *Daily Worker* had to say about the meeting, and about one other personality, Melvyn Douglas.

Douglas's words were linked to Robinson. Douglas had said, "The time has come for the power of publicity of the film industry to join in a mighty protest against German oppression." The FBI report noted, "Some of the signers were the same old crowd of movie celebrities who were so enamored of the 'Loyalist' reds of Spain, a majority of whom were not Spaniards but were the riff-raff Bolsheviks of all nations who had flocked to Spain, led by the GPU agents of Moscow. Douglas publicly declared that he expected between twenty and thirty million signatures of theatregoers. This adventure died as quickly as it was accouched."

While it is true that the League never saw its petition goal realized, the FBI failed to mention that among the 56 were conservatives such as George Brent, Miriam Hopkins, Bruce Cabot, and Jack Warner, and apolitical types such as Joan Crawford. The FBI was eager to point out that Robinson and Douglas were big boosters of the Democratic Party and Roosevelt.

Robinson left for New York right after Christmas to spend New Year with his family, but a telegram from Wallis just after the first of the year sent him rushing back to Hollywood. The studio had decided to proceed immediately on *Confessions*, thanks in no small measure to Herman Lissauer, the head of research, who had taken it upon himself to champion the project. Lissauer sent memos to Warner and Wallis—shown to Robinson—urging them to make the film. The memos detailed anti-Semitic actions taken by the German-American Bund.

"Bund is spreading propaganda that Jewish firms are discharging gentiles to make way for Jewish refugees from Germany—Macy's took out an ad in New York to deny this," Lissauer wrote. "There may be a way to contradict this in the story." He also furnished pamphlets that the Bund put out: "Nazi instructions for Our Friends Overseas" and "Handbook for Foreign Germans." Robinson read them for research, but for Warner it meant there could be no more delays. Construction began on the necessary eighty-three sets. Paul Lukas, who was shooting a picture for Hal Roach, was signed to play the Bund leader, and though this choice created more delays, by the first week in February he was ready. Marlene Dietrich, who was a German vehemently opposed to Hitler, made a last-minute pitch to play the spy-hairdresser, but Paramount would not let her go. Robinson began work on February 13. Francis Lederer, who played the title role, was already a week into his work by then.

Immediately after filming commenced, trouble began for all concerned. Jack and Ann Warner were the first to receive death threats, and each principal member of the cast had his life threatened thereafter. Warner hired armed guards for himself. Robinson received crank phone calls and changed his telephone number but continued receiving them. His home became a regular stop on the police patrol.

The German government promised to make a film exposing American corruption if work on *Confessions* continued. German officials in the United States protested to the State Department, but Warner stood firm. And, Wallis, too, put as much effort into *Confessions* as he had put into any film in his entire career, as did all those involved. Robinson went through the script by Milton Krims and John Wexley and made dialogue suggestions. Anatole Litvak, the director, well known for his lateness on the set, and for his demands for many more takes than were necessary, changed his habits after a few days on *Confessions*. It was a strictly closed set, which fueled the excitement. All Hollywood buzzed about the film, about Warner's bodyguards, about the German officials who were storming into Warner's office to protest. As a result, the community eagerly awaited the product.

In *Confessions* Robinson's character, although heroic, does not appear until after the first hour and has less screen time than Lederer, Lukas, and George Sanders (the last borrowed from Fox to play the spy's contact). But it is Robinson's character—named Ed Renard, but based on Leon Turrou—who ferrets out the Nazis and the Bund members involved in a spy ring that stretches from the United States to Scotland to Germany, all involved in stealing American military secrets. Robinson's work in the film took only a few weeks and was finished by the beginning of March. Wallis timidly approached him with the suggestion that, in keeping with the docudrama style of the film, the studio wanted to forgo star credits in advertising and in opening titles. Much to Wallis's pleasure, Robinson—whose contract guaranteed him star billing—said, in writing, "You can bill me any way you want." He did receive top billing, but under the title, and gave the studio additional permission to leave his name off the advertising. His face was enough to draw an audience.

With filming completed, Robinson was in exceptionally high spirits and decided to celebrate by throwing a birthday party for Manny, the likes of which even Beverly Hills had never seen before. Manny would be six and had been giving his parents problems. He was continuing his mischievous and sometimes destructive ways despite their efforts to calm him down (on one outing to the Hillcrest Country Club, he had rifled the lockers). He was beginning to be a trial, and Robinson vowed to spend more time with him, hoping it would straighten the child out. The birthday party would be the first step.

It was to be given at the Higginsville ranch, and Harry Warner— Manny's godfather—was enlisted to help provide the props. He sent over a Black Maria and small jail, all in unison with the cops-and-robbers motif so appropriate for the child of Edward G. Robinson. Jack Haley Jr. was one of the youngsters invited to the party, which has become legendary, and remembered it well:

Manny and I didn't go to the same school or hang around in the same neighborhood, but in those days the kids of stars were great avenues to create publicity. Occasionally, Manny would be at my parties and I would go to his. I have a vivid recollection of that party, because it was the most outrageous event for children I ever saw in my stay in the Hollywood Garden.

First, you have to realize how the invitations came. A policeman came to the door of your home and asked to see you. You came to the door with your governess, shaking, wondering what they were getting you for this time. The policeman served you with a "warrant" to appear at Manny's party.

The next week you were picked up and put into a paddy wagon with all the other celebrity kids and taken to the ranch house in the hills. I've never seen anything like that party. They had sharpshooter exhibitions; they had a train going around the entire grounds that you sat in. There was a corral with horses . . . There was a police show—they were big in those days. There was a big tent outfitted like a western saloon; a huge oak bar with brass rails. They only served ice cream, but every flavor imaginable.

After awhile I hooked up with Gary Crosby and his kid brothers. We had a reputation for being inordinately mischievous. But Manny was a real heavyweight. He proved it that day. He saw us and came over saying, "C'mon with me. I want to show you something." We followed him and he went behind the bar and peed into the ice cream while the attendant wasn't watching. We were stunned. The nurse caught him, but they couldn't punish him in front of his other guests. To this day Gary and I talk about it and admit we've never been more astonished by anything.

"Of my generation Manny was one of the most tragic figures," Haley said finally. "You sensed he was emotionally disturbed even then."

The story of Manny's behavior trickled back to the studio and throughout Hollywood, though even the most notorious of the gossip columnists wouldn't dare print a word. Irving Fein, who managed both Jack Benny and George Burns during his career, was at the time head of photographers at Warners. "I remember the photographer came back to the studio and talked on and on about what a menace that kid was," Fein said. "He said Manny was throwing ice cream all over the place. He got good shots, but was visibly shaken."

Eddie and Gladys, humiliated over Manny's behavior, set about trying to be more strict with him. For a while, he calmed down.

A few weeks after the party—on April 21—*Confessions* had its premiere. Only a handful of the audience realized the drama that was unfolding around them: Police were on the roof to guard against bombs being planted in the theater; plainclothes detectives sat among the star-studded crowd, while more police roamed like security guards throughout the theater. There were no incidents. The only explosion was from the crowd itself giving a standing ovation when the film ended. A sample headline used for a review was "Nazi Spy Film Will Shock You by Its Frankness," and Robinson, eager to give interviews, told the press, "the film is tame compared with the truth." *Confessions* went on to have huge success at the domestic box office, although internationally the film was banned in Germany and many other European countries, including Yugoslavia and neutral Sweden. The German ambassador in Washington denounced the film, calling it "pernicious propaganda poisoning German-American relations." But Robinson, Warner, and Wallis had the last laugh when the $500,000 lawsuit filed by the Bund had to be dropped. Its leader, Fritz Kuhn, had been jailed for pocketing the organization's funds.

Confessions appeared in 1939, perhaps Hollywood's most glorious year, considering the competing products: *Gone with the Wind, Stagecoach, The Wizard of Oz, Mr. Smith Goes to Washington, Wuthering Heights,* and others. *Confessions* received no Academy Award nominations but did set a standard for political films in Hollywood during the next two years. It was also one of the few Hollywood films of its time to play down the stars in favor of its story. Its style was copied after World War II during Hollywood's film noir and docudrama period. *Confessions* remained one of Robinson's favorite films, although it was his next picture for Warners that would always top his personal list.

6

HOLLYWOOD'S MOST IMPRESSIVE ACTOR

Listen, sister, just remember that Little Caesar is now a solid citizen.

—Edward G. Robinson

That film was *Dr. Ehrlich's Magic Bullet*, which now had the go-ahead from Warner after the legal problems had been ironed out. Since Muni had dropped out, the role was handed to Robinson, his first chance at a film biography—considered the prestige motion picture. Ehrlich's discovery—the cure for syphilis—had been negated by Hitler, who declared that "a scientific discovery by a Jew is worthless," and his party had set out to destroy all records of Ehrlich's work. In the same spirit as *Confessions*, Wallis set out to do the film, but there were problems. The first draft of the script by its originator, Norman Burnside, was weak, and the project had been turned over to Heinz Herald, who in turn had presented a version that Wallis and Warner found too clinical. This was 1939, and the studio would have to be very careful about how it handled venereal disease and sex hygiene if the film was to pass muster with the Motion Picture Code. The script was handed to John Huston to rewrite, while Robinson sat at home, wondering what his next move should be.

He decided he needed to do something and under the terms of his new contract accepted an offer at MGM to star in *Blackmail,* the story of a man sent to jail for a crime he did not commit, who escaped and under a new identity started a thriving business. It was not a success. When the film premiered in September, Bosley Crowther of the *New York Times* wrote, "What a sad thing it is to see this distinguished inhabitant of the Rogue's Gallery, this Napoleon of crime, this indomitably amoral spirit who belongs with the Borgias, feebly trying to go straight in *Blackmail.*"

Robinson was not around to read the reviews, though. Annoyed because there were still delays with *Ehrlich,* he had taken Gladys and Manny to Europe, where he had shopped for paintings, posed for a portrait by Jean Edouard Vuillard, the great French artist, and tried in general to relax. It was not possible. Europe was in turmoil. Because of the political climate and the release of *Confessions,* Robinson had to have a police escort during much of his stay. Refugees from Germany and Austria poured into France with tales of torture and horror. The Robinsons were warned that Germany was poised to go to war, and France would surely be involved. The family fled to Le Havre, where Robinson thought he had tickets for a passage on the *Athenia* in late September. Much to their dismay, there had been an error in booking, and no such tickets existed. They were forced to wait in a hotel while the *Athenia* set sail without them. A day later they managed to get on the *America,* although in order for them to do so, the captain gave his quarters to Eddie and Gladys, and Manny and his governess took a nurse's cabin. As the *America* was leaving the harbor, news came that the *Athenia* had been attacked and sunk by a German U-boat, one of the first passenger ships to suffer such a fate. The Robinsons' elation was quickly turned to gloom when they heard that Sara Roosevelt, the president's mother, was aboard. The Robinsons had nothing to do for the entire trip back to New York but hold their breath, praying that the U-boats would pass them by. Robinson made notes about the stories they had heard from the refugees and became more determined than ever to become involved in the Hollywood Anti-Nazi League and other such activities.

Instead, he discovered that the activities he had been participating in had all but fallen apart. The Communist Party, which had been anti-Hitler, switched its position once Germany and Stalin's Soviet Union had signed a nonaggression pact in August. Suddenly, Hitler was, to the party faithful, no longer an enemy. The organization changed its name to the Hollywood League for Democratic Action and began to denounce "the war to lead America to war." Robinson was outraged by the switch, now fully aware that there had been at least some Communists active in the League. He resigned his membership and turned his interest to the Polish Relief Fund, offering his house for a fund-raising party that would help those in the country under attack from both Germany and the Soviet Union. He argued extensively with those former political associates who rationalized Stalin's attack on Poland by saying he was trying to create "a protective front." Robinson would have nothing to do with the Communist Party line. His party for Polish Relief cost his own bank account several thousand dollars and raised $20,000.

Politics and the discussions of war were set aside at the end of October when Robinson finally got his starting date for *Dr. Ehrlich's Magic Bullet.* He was ready. He had spent many hours with Ehrlich's daughter, son-in-law, and grandson, who had visited Los Angeles, and he had done extensive research. There were many similarities between Robinson and Ehrlich: Ehrlich smoked twenty-five strong cigars each day, as did Robinson; both men found it difficult to refuse requests for loans of money; Ehrlich, like Robinson, always defended his coreligionists, had an interest in Israel (Palestine then), and refused to convert although his career was always hampered by his insistence on remaining a Jew.

A good portion of the $765,000 budget on the film was for makeup, and the artists were quick to see similarities in appearance between Robinson and Ehrlich. The result is that Robinson not only does not look like the gangsters he had been playing for a decade, he comes close enough to Ehrlich that even the doctor's daughter was fooled when she saw a still of the actor. Since this was an important film for Warner Bros., the studio hired James Wong Howe as cinematographer, joining William

Dieterle as director. Flora Robson was chosen for Hedi, Ehrlich's wife, but a few days before filming began, the role went instead to the diminutive Ruth Gordon, whose height pleased Robinson. It was a rare film role for her.

Filming the picture was grueling, not because the part was physically demanding, but because the heavy makeup made it necessary for Robinson to be at the studio before 7:00 A.M. for a two-hour session. When he was consistently late on set for his 9:00 A.M. call, the makeup session began even earlier.

In addition, there were delays. Scenes had to be reshot again and again. One sequence focuses on a dinner party in which Ehrlich scandalizes polite society by announcing that he is researching the disease. The hostess, a rich philanthropic woman portrayed by Maria Ouspenskaya, risks scandal by offering Ehrlich the money he needs for research. Ouspenskaya had been an acting teacher and, late in her life, had become one of the most sought-after character actresses in Hollywood. But she was old, and nervous in front of the cameras, and the production notes record the scenes with her, which were to have been completed in less than one week, took much longer. As a result the film ran behind schedule and inched more over budget each day.

Ehrlich was filled with sentiment, as most of the biographical films of that period were. The studio had also gone to great lengths not to be blatant about the good doctor's ethnic heritage. The only real Jewishness was saved for the death scene, when Ehrlich invokes another leader of his people, Moses, intoning the latter's death sequence from the Pentateuch: "And Moses went up from the plains in the mountain that is over Jericho. And the Lord showed him all the land. And the Lord said unto him this is the land which I have promised unto thy people. I have caused thee to see it with thy eyes, but thou shalt not go hither. So Moses the servant of the Lord died there in Moab according to the word of the Lord." But, in the final version even this was cut.

When it was completed on December 8, Robinson was in high spirits. He told Hedda Hopper, "Playing Ehrlich was the easiest acting job I ever did because he was so simple, a great figure struggling with terrific problems. These gangsters are twice as hard to do. They're shallow, nothing to them."

Robinson saved his more emotional moments for his short speech at the traditional end-of-film "wrap" party. This film had been his big professional chance, his opportunity to bury the gangster characters in which he had been consistently cast. "Now we can catch up on the hours of lost sleep," he told the cast and crew. "I can even get acquainted with my family again, and who knows, perhaps I can even get that roughneck son of mine to address me as 'Doctor' or 'Sir' instead of 'Hey, you mug.'" His face turned serious as he continued: "One thing I sincerely hope this picture will accomplish—something that even the G-men haven't been able to do—and that is the final arrest and execution of that Edward G. Robinson Public Enemy Number One—Little Caesar. I'm not going to highbrow you, but I think it's about time I reformed and changed my machine-gun bullets and mug roles for Magic Bullets and roles as different and as important as Dr. Ehrlich."

With *Ehrlich* completed, Robinson told the press he wanted his next part to be either Benjamin Franklin or the lead in *The Forty Days of Musa Degh*, about Armenian refugees. He knew, though, that he had promised Warner he'd do *Brother Orchid*, and to give him strength for what would not be an enjoyable film, he took Gladys and her daughter, Jeanne, to New York for relaxation, then to Washington, D.C., where he met with Franklin D. Roosevelt.

Manny, left behind both because of the school term and because his school performance was poor, buried his resentment and tried to make amends by writing to them. "Dear mummie and daddy," he scrawled, with his governess, Augustine Cole standing by him. "i received your wire. i am fine but i miss the dearest mummie and the best daddy in the world, a million hugs to you both and jeannie. your son, manny XXXXOO!"

Robinson was back in town for the *Ehrlich* premiere, and it was the triumph he had hoped, although he had to put up with statements in the press such as, "Is Edward G. Robinson going to be another Muni?"

The film opened in late February, and by early March it was breaking box office records, the highest-grossing film till then for two straight weeks. It eventually trebled the Warner Bros. investment, but biographical films were no longer the rage in Hollywood by the time the Academy of Motion Picture Arts and Sciences gave out its Oscars for 1940. Not only was Robinson not nominated, but not one aspect of the film earned a nomination.

He rested and did his *Big Town* broadcasts until March, when *Brother Orchid* went into production, complete with ten thousand fake flowers for the garden scenes. The tale of a gangster who decides to leave the rackets and accidentally ends up hiding out in a monastery, only to find he likes the life there, *Orchid* took one month to complete. Although it eventually earned solid notices for Robinson and a good financial return for Warners, Robinson hardly smiled the entire time it was filming. His real interest was the film that was to be his reward for *Ehrlich—A Dispatch from Reuters*, the story of the news agency and its creator.

He was so excited about *Reuters* that he agreed to go into production just days after *Orchid* had completed its final production work. It was a chance to do another biographical film, another prestige offering. It was also another role that Muni had rejected—again, Reuter was born Jewish, and Muni refused to portray Jews on the screen. By this point Muni's rejection was a technicality, though, as he left the studio in 1940.

As in *Ehrlich*, the heavy makeup made it an uncomfortable part to play, and the similarities between Robinson and Reuter were not so pronounced as those between Robinson and Ehrlich. Some of Robinson's scenes in the picture are not with people but with cooing carrier pigeons, and the audience found these scenes nonsensical when the film was released—Little Caesar with birds? Plus, costar Eddie Albert had problems with a hoarse throat on and off throughout production, holding up work several times.

When *Reuters* was released in December, the market had fallen out of biographies. The audiences had little interest, and the film was a financial failure. More disturbing to Robinson were his weak reviews, and the fact that Warners was once again sending him gangster and tough-guy roles. He refused the role of Mad Dog Earle in *High Sierra*, if only because it had been offered to Muni first.

Meanwhile, though, when *Reuters* completed production in June, Robinson took a vacation, informing the studio that he had no intention of working until after the middle of September at the earliest. While the film was being edited, Warner was less than pleased with what he saw. Robinson was beginning to show his age. The studio head worried that he could no longer procure the "principal roles" Robinson's contract dictated and told his associates that Robinson might become a liability. While Robinson was away, on July 26, Warner sent a memo to his production chiefs and legal advisers asking what it would take to get the studio out of Robinson's contract, which still had a year and a half to run. Hollywood had always had a youth complex, and Warner was afraid. The days when an older man—a George Arliss, a Wallace Beery—could carry a film were ending. He was told that canceling Robinson's contract would cost more than it was worth, and besides, Robinson had approved the script for *The Sea Wolf*, a popular Jack London story that the studio executives thought could be successful.

Robinson had no idea that his career had been debated by his bosses when he returned to the Burbank Studios in the autumn to film *The Sea Wolf*, which he had decided to do despite the fact that it was, once again, a role that Muni had rejected. Robinson had several reasons for the choice. The story on which it is based, by Jack London, had been a personal favorite when he was a young boy spending his afternoons in the Astor Place Library. Also, he thought that the film was inadvertently an allegory for what was happening in Nazi Germany. Wolf Larsen, his character, is the skipper of a mysterious ship, a cruel, heartless, slave-driving man who is, in many ways, the personification of evil. Eventually the heroes—John Garfield, Alexander Knox, and Ruth Hussey—escape from the ship (*The Ghost*) in a small boat, but after drifting endlessly at sea they come upon *The Ghost* again. It is sinking, and Wolf is determined that they sink with him. Only when Alexander Knox sacrifices himself and agrees to stay with Wolf do the other two have a chance to escape.

Filming was essentially uneventful, except that Wallis sent several memos to associate producer Henry Blanke and director Michael Curtiz reminding them to watch Robinson's accent. Perhaps it was the memory of those younger days reading the story, but Wallis insisted that the Robinson he saw in the rushes had regressed into a New York accent. Robinson respected John Garfield greatly—they both had the same background, New York Jewish and Theater Guild—and Robinson took a sort of paternalistic interest in the younger actor. Although Robinson was always intense while working on a film, he found Garfield even more so and attempted to calm Garfield down. They were not to meet again, until the blacklisting began.

While *Sea Wolf* was filming, Robinson reestablished himself on the political scene in Hollywood. Unaware of his Jewish origins, Mary Pickford had sent Robinson a leaflet that he interpreted as anti-Semitic, and rightly so. It stated that Jews were going to be voting as a bloc for Democratic candidates, including Roosevelt, of course. Since Robinson was on the local committee to reelect the president, he took no time in responding to Pickford's letter and leaflet. "It is false," he wrote, "in fact misleading in purpose and seeks to destroy, if not nullify, the liberty of conscience in the exercise of the freedom of suffrage, by threat and coercive ultimatum . . . I can only believe that your endorsement of the circular was unwitting and made in the excitement of the political campaign."

The year now passed without incident, though Robinson periodically would ask those he was visiting to keep their radio on so he could hear news of the war in Europe. With no prestige films coming his way from Warner Bros., he agreed to appear in *Manpower*, in which he would star with Marlene Dietrich and George Raft, the latter another perennial Warner Bros. tough guy with whom Robinson had worked little up till now.

Robinson hardly knew Dietrich either, although they had almost starred together in *Josephine* and Dietrich had made a pitch to join him in *Confessions*. Now past her prime as a glamour queen, but still very much a star, she invited Robinson to her house to get acquainted before filming began in late March. Robinson was nervous about the meeting as he had always assumed Dietrich to be cold and unreachable. But he discovered, as they sipped wine and chatted, that she was anything but. Dietrich off set was quite the hausfrau—she really did her own cooking and much of her own cleaning but didn't advertise it in publicity releases as other stars tried. She was a lover of Impressionist painting, as Robinson was. Most importantly, she was as vehemently against Hitler as anyone in Hollywood and had been responsible for sponsoring dozens of refugees from the German, Austrian, and Hungarian film industries.

Robinson developed a schoolboy crush on her, but Dietrich (rumored to be having an affair with Jean Gabin) was still married and was much too professional to get involved with her leading man. Dietrich had also taken time to become better acquainted with Raft, and he too was smitten. He had less in common with Dietrich, though, and, in fact, little in common with Robinson: Raft was a heavy drinker, a gambler, and practically illiterate.

From the outset the *Manpower* set—on Stage 11 of the Burbank Studios—was uneasy. Both Raft and Robinson had revealed, in part, their feelings for Dietrich after a report from Hedda Hopper suggested that Ann Sheridan might replace Marlene. Both male stars were furious and stormed to the front office only to be told the report was incorrect.

Robinson was once more riding high at the studio, since *The Sea Wolf* had just opened and was a big hit. Raft's fortunes had been slipping and his gambling had got him into financial trouble. He was, from the first day, difficult.

Manpower is the story of two power company linemen—Hank (Robinson) and Johnny (Raft). Best buddies, they nonetheless both become involved with the same dame, Fay, who had previously been in jail. Hank marries her because he feels she has had a raw deal from life, but Fay secretly loves Johnny. The friends fight when Hank finds out the truth, and Hank works recklessly and falls to his death, leaving Johnny and Fay to start a new life together. It was an unashamed tearjerker.

As was often the way, the death scene was one of the first to be filmed. Raft objected immediately: The script as written had him holding Robinson's arm in pouring rain to keep his buddy from falling, only to lose his grip and watch Hank fall to his death. After heated arguments the scene was changed to have Hank grasping a rope that breaks. Thus, Raft thought the audience would not find him weak. It had not been an easy scene to shoot. More than 800,000 gallons of water was used during filming to simulate rain. Robinson himself lost eight pounds in eight days while the filming of the rain scenes was in progress. Raft wanted the bosses to realize he was a star and stayed at home for a few days, claiming illness. Robinson retaliated as warring stars tended to do—he took April 12 off, insisting he had hurt his knee, and the studio heads rushed to pamper his ego. Raft was enraged, thinking he was being overlooked.

On April 18, Robinson and Raft were rehearsing a scene when Raft suggested to director Raoul Walsh that a particular line of Robinson's was wrong for his character and should not be spoken. Robinson asserted that the line seemed fine to him and Raft should worry about his own. "Look, George," he said. "You may think the line does not make any sense, but I have to speak it and it is all right with me." Raft was enraged and let loose a volley of obscenities that shocked cast and crew—an anger that had been building up every day as he and Robinson vied for the affections of Dietrich. Robinson was humiliated by the language and stormed off the set. Wallis was called to the scene, all too aware of these delays eating into the $600,000 budget. The day was lost for filming, but the two men's egos were placated, and they reappeared on set the next day, shaking hands and joking. Dietrich remained silent throughout.

All was well until noon on Saturday, April 26, when Robinson and Raft were shooting a scene in which one of their drinking buddies makes a snide remark about Fay, and Johnny has to keep his pal Hank from getting into a fight. Instead of just brushing Robinson away, Raft overdid it, roughhousing his fellow actor and pushing him around the set. Robinson wheeled around and screamed, "What the hell is all this?" to which Raft replied with some more choice obscenities. Robinson stormed off, then confronted Raft. "George, you're a fool for carrying on in such an unprofessional manner," Robinson was reported to have said. "I came here to do my work, not indulge in anything of this nature. It seems impossible for me to continue." Raft saw red and punched Little Caesar in the side. Character actors Ward Bond and Alan Hale, both large men, immediately jumped in to break up the two actors, and it took director Walsh's added strength to calm them down. Robinson, tears in his eyes, again walked off the set, and production halted until late Monday morning.

This time Wallis would not take matters sitting down. With Robinson's approval, he had the studio file charges against Raft with the Screen Actors Guild (SAG). It wasn't just for Robinson's sake. The budget had rocketed to $825,000. But when the film was released in July, it was a big hit, and with Robinson's permission the charges were dropped. Dietrich walked away amused, and Robinson and Raft did not speak to each other for fifteen years. Still, they each had a gold watch inscribed with a message from Dietrich as a souvenir of their time together.

Perhaps Robinson had won the battle, but neither he nor Raft was popular in the front office. Robinson continued to fight about story ideas and scripts, and few suitable projects were forthcoming. A particular argument centered around a project called *The Night Before Christmas*, based on the less-than-successful play by Laura and S. J. Perelman. Gladys Robinson had seen it in New York and convinced Eddie that it was a suitable vehicle for him. Warner Bros. had paid $30,000 for the rights, but when Robinson thought it over, he decided it was a rather flimsy story. Wallis felt betrayed.

"These people absolutely flabbergast me," Wallis wrote in a memo to production chief Roy Obringer. "Now Eddie tells you that he wants to think it over a little and wants approval of the script, which is not at all in accordance with our understanding . . . Is it going to be impossible for anyone to talk to these people and to take their word for these things?" the memo continued. "If so, I would like to know about it and I will save myself a lot of telephone calls and a lot of aggravation. This is a hell of a time for him to start making conditions."

As Wallis and Jack Warner bitched about their star's actions and Warner again brought up the possibility of dropping Robinson from the studio, the star went back over to MGM to film *Unholy Partners*, a twisted and forgettable tale of a crusading tabloid editor (Robinson) who takes on the racketeers and dies heroically. It was a film that Robinson liked to forget about, one he agreed to do only out of loyalty to its director, Mervyn LeRoy.

Robinson returned to his home studio in the late fall to film what was now called *Larceny, Inc.*, about a small-time hood who, planning to crack the vault, buys a luggage shop next to a bank, only to discover that the straight life isn't so bad. Jane Wyman, whom Robinson had wanted for *Kid Galahad*, was the female lead as his adopted daughter.

Warner Bros. and Robinson knew right at the outset that it had limited appeal; the script by Everett Freeman and Edwin Gilbert did not excite the producers. Still, though the film failed at the box office, it has had frequent runs on television in the 1970s and 1980s, particularly around Christmas. At the time of its release, though—in April 1942 (an odd release date for a film that has a plot revolving around the December holiday)—*Larceny* was a financial flop and the studio was not pleased. It would be Robinson's last film under his contract.

He had not taken a fee for doing *Larceny*. Instead, Robinson had arranged for Warner Bros. to donate $100,000 to the USO. Robinson was convinced that the United States would soon be at war. The Soviet Union had been attacked by the Nazis in June 1941—despite the nonaggression pact—and because of his hatred of the German cause, Robinson was willing to step forward and give support to the Russians, and for that matter, to any country at war with the Nazis.

It was this early support for the Russian cause, not his greater support for the USO and American effort, nor his aid to the allies, that interested the FBI. The Bureau took full note that Mr. and Mrs. Robinson were among the sponsors of a concert promoting the Russian Benefit Committee at the Shrine Auditorium on December 3, 1941. He'd also sponsor a similar concert for Russian War Relief on December 31. Robinson reasoned that Nazi Germany was the enemy.

The full involvement of the Robinsons in the war effort commenced after Pearl Harbor brought America into the war. However, for Gladys, the war brought out the manic-depressive tendencies that her husband, family, and friends had been trying to keep at bay for years. She reacted to the events at Pearl Harbor by suing Eddie for divorce. He was served papers in their home and, not knowing what to make of it, called the lawyer she had hired. The lawyer was proceeding slowly with the paperwork but agreed that his client needed professional care. After much persuasion, Gladys was sent to Las Encinas in Pasadena for shock treatments. She returned home somewhat better, but for the remainder of their marriage there would be highs and lows. "She was a manic-depressive," Sam Jaffe recalled. "I hate to use the word, it's just a tag. When she was high, Eddie was like Jesus Christ. When she was not, he could do no right. I was with Eddie when he took her to an analyst. She had a light electric treatment. It was a miracle. After the first treatment she was home again. But it was no cure."

Niece Beulah Robinson had, through the years, also become close to her aunt, although in 1941 she was still a young girl. During the 1940s she would make several extended visits to her family in Beverly Hills. Gladys became an important figure in her life, helping her learn about fashion and style, and convincing her that her own last name—Goldberg, which her father, Willie, had shortened from Goldenberg—would not do if she wanted to find a job in the fashion industry. Beulah said about Gladys: "We all had our innings with her. She could like you but despite that, because of the illness, you could fight. It wasn't her fault. You'd realize that despite the pain she was causing you it was not something she wanted. She was exciting to be with. We traveled together. We went to New Orleans. We went across country by train. She had a lot to do with shaping my life."

Eddie and Gladys, now at least stable together, threw themselves into the war effort the best way they could. Their home was opened to the USO, and thousands of soldiers on their way to the Pacific front came through for refreshments and a look at the famous art collection. Gladys also hosted teas for a variety of war effort groups—the USO, Russian War Relief, Desert Battalion. There were always visitors.

His age rendered Robinson ineligible for service in the armed forces, but Robinson wanted to do his part. During 1942 his work in films consisted merely of a quick role in *Tales of Manhattan* at 20th Century Fox. He broadcast the last of his *Big Town* radio shows on July 2, since sponsor Lever Brothers would not let him tackle issues connected with the war effort, and Robinson decided that the story of an editor fighting corruption on the home front was no longer applicable to events around the globe. Robinson decided to donate all of the money earned in 1942—except for enough to pay his taxes—to war funds, particularly the USO and war bonds. His work for these groups earned him a commendation from the American Legion presented to him on a *Big Town* broadcast.

Robinson's donations ledger for the year is a lengthy list—China War Relief; War Service, Inc.; Hollywood Canteen; Medical Aid to Russia ($500); American Flying Service Foundation. There are also dozens of USO-related expenses for parties, food, butler services, and transportation.

Still, he wanted to do more. Frank Capra's film unit—making war documentaries—did not need him. It was Robert Sherwood, with whom he had become friendly while filming *Thunder in the City*, who came through with an appointment of sorts. Sherwood contacted Robinson at the end of the summer and asked him if he would go to Europe to work for the Office of War Information. Robinson was on a boat in the autumn.

In Europe his duties were twofold—to entertain the troops and to read patriotic and propaganda broadcasts over the radio. The first duty was an education for him. He wanted to step out in front of the masses of green-clothed servicemen and tell them how proud he was to be an American because of their work. He tried that speech, but it failed. The men did not want to hear Edward G. Robinson, American; they wanted Little Caesar. Since an actor always wants to please his audience, Robinson wised up quickly. "Pipe down, you mugs, or I'll let you have it," became his rallying cry. "Whaddaya hear from the mob? Don't worry about a thing. I told 'em you'd take care of that Shicklgruber gang." There was stunning applause, but Robinson was heartsick. All the years of improving himself culturally, of fighting for roles like Dr. Ehrlich, and he was still Little Caesar. But still, he knew this was no time for such self-indulgent feelings.

His work on radio was just as personally rewarding. Broadcasting on the BBC, Robinson made dozens of statements to the war-torn British and propaganda messages in German to the enemy, which he later discovered were heard by thousands of German citizens. An irony was that Robinson tried to hide his Yiddish accent when speaking German, only to be told to be more guttural. What came through was a touch of Emanuel Goldenberg.

The return from Europe was noted by the FBI, which had an agent on the pier when the SS *Queen Elizabeth* docked on November 13. Robinson had no idea that his movements were now being monitored, or that his war work would later give the Bureau a chance to theorize that he could have become acquainted with espionage agents.

What Robinson did find was that Warner Bros., with whom he still had a contract, had no suitable projects for him. Instead, the executives—in tandem—were making a conscious and subtle effort to rid themselves of the fifty-year-old actor whose contract demanded "principal roles." A memo dated December 14, 1942, details the script ideas and treatments that were to be sent to Robinson and makes it clear that they were chosen to be rejected.

On the list are *A Beast with Five Fingers*, a horror movie on the list of B pictures that even with Robinson's salary would only require a $350,000 budget (half that of his current films). There was also *The Good Die Poor*, a tired story about a newspaper editor who takes over a local radio station. Robinson had played this role too many times, and the memo even notes, "Feel certain he would pass this up." The list continued with weak fare until the last suggested subject—*The Treasure of the Sierra Madre*. The memo notes that Walter Huston was penciled in for the part of the old man, but that it could go to Robinson. Still, it was not a principal role, and Robinson would indeed turn it down. Huston went on to win an Academy Award for best supporting actor for that role when the film was made with Humphrey Bogart in the lead.

While he battled Warners for a decent script, Robinson busied himself with his work for the war effort. In April he agreed to be a sponsor for the American Committee for the Protection of the Foreign Born, which he believed was set up to help refugees. Since the Soviet Union was now an ally, he participated in the congress of the National Council for American-Soviet Friendship and allowed his name to be used as a sponsor. There was, surely, other work—for the USO and for government-sanctioned groups—but he was beginning to associate himself with a list of groups that would later turn out to be his downfall.

In fact, the FBI file that was by now gaining some thickness took little note of his work for the American war effort. Any connection with the Soviets, which the Bureau had perceived as an eventual enemy, was duly noted. On June 14, 1943, a United Nations in America dinner was held at the Hotel Biltmore in New York City, sponsored by the American Committee for the Protection of the Foreign Born. The FBI report on the meeting states that it "was participated in by the International Workers Order . . . and at this affair renowned persons of different political shadings paid tribute to everyday Americans, negro and white, native and foreign born. There appeared a picture of Edward G. Robinson, which bore the caption 'Edward G. Robinson, Movie Actor, Rumanian born, Praised Uncle Sam's Concern for All.'"

To Robinson the dinner, and his sponsorship of the Committee, was only a small part of his life. Still seeking film work, if only to pay his taxes, he went to Columbia for *Destroyer*, his venture into war movies. He portrayed a middle-aged perfectionist in charge of a group of sailors who becomes a hero by manning a gun during a sea battle with the Japanese. The critics recognized *Destroyer* for the piece of propaganda fluff it was, but Robinson was unconcerned. Instead, he went back to Universal for the first time in more than a decade and received top billing for *Flesh and Fantasy*, in which he appeared in one of three one-act plays produced by Charles Boyer and directed by Julien Duvivier (brought to America one step ahead of the Nazi invasion of France).

The contract squabbles with Warner Bros. had now turned into a full-fledged war. The studio sent off terse letters to both Robinson and his agent, Frank W. Vincent, criticizing him for rejecting stories. He retaliated by writing directly to Jack Warner in a three-page letter:

> Here we are in a fix again . . . During these last several years I thought we had grown up and could treat each other with consideration and understanding. Four years ago I was persuaded to enter into a contract with you against my will, merely because I did not want to face a situation such as confronts us now—battling over the approval of stories. I remember you saying at the time, "Eddie, I wouldn't think of signing a contract like this if it were not for my knowledge and experiences in our dealings with you these past years."
>
> At times I agreed to do stories which my better judgment opposed, but because Warner Bros. were certain and definite that they were proper vehicles for both of us, and I deferred my opinion to theirs. One glaring example was *Larceny, Inc.* I confess it was originally I who presented the story to Warner Bros. but when it was submitted to Hal Wallis, it was not my intention to play it.
>
> What I am getting at is this, Jack—over many years of our association (I am probably the oldest player on your lot), we have had some quarrels and differences. Six years ago you almost convinced me that I was "poison" at the box-office, but we both held on, and here are the pictures that followed: *Bullets or Ballots, Kid Galahad, The Amazing Dr. Clitterhouse, Confessions of a Nazi Spy, Dr. Ehrlich, Brother Orchid, Sea Wolf, Reuters, Manpower.*
>
> These were splendid vehicles . . . Many of the above stories you worked on for two years to get into proper shape. Do you think, Jack, that if anyone else had played *Larceny, Inc.* or *Reuters* that the box-office results would have been any better? It isn't conceit which prompts me to doubt it.

He went on to praise Warner's record, but chided him:

> You waited until the final days to submit stories for my approval, which was not our practice before this, and merely as a gesture for what you thought was fulfilling your obligations under our agreement. You sent me two stories which I had previously rejected, and another one so ridiculous as to become laughable.

If it is your intention to drop the contract, then let us settle our differences amicably. Jack, I have as much dignity, pride and self-respect as you have, and I do not feel that such attitude of avoidance was justified, for it hardly reflects the spirit under which we started business together, and have been functioning through all these years . . . You have splendid material which you can offer me—why don't you do it?

Robinson signed the letter, "With warm regards, believe me, Eddie," but it was too late for a reconciliation. Warner was well aware that Robinson was the oldest contract player he had and proper vehicles were thin, while Robinson's contract called for high salaries. It took a few months for the paperwork to be completed, but on August 6, Robinson was released from his thirteen-year association with the studio. He was paid $50,000 for the two films left to go on his contract. More important, he was now a freelancer, without the protection of a studio. And because Warner had let it be known he had dropped Little Caesar, Robinson's career was in trouble. Too many producers turned away, thinking he was a has-been.

Ironically, while the contract discussions were going on, Robinson had mended his differences with Paul Muni, with whom he had quietly feuded for years. Muni had landed many of the roles at Warner Bros. that Robinson had craved, and a good deal of his insistence on better roles was to rival Muni for prestige parts. But in March, while the letters were flying back and forth between Robinson and the studio, Muni, Frank Sinatra, Ralph Bellamy, George Jessel, John Garfield, Luther and Stella Adler, Jacob Ben-Ami, and fifty Orthodox rabbis joined with Robinson in New York's Madison Square Garden for *We Shall Never Die*, a memorial to the Jews already known to have been executed by the Nazis. It featured the music of Kurt Weill, the words of Ben Hecht, and Robinson and Muni standing before forty thousand people reading the history of the Jewish people. They realized they were on the same side and would visit each other occasionally in the years to come. It had taken the realization that they were both through with Warner Bros. to bring them together.

Without the studio behind him, Robinson set about to salvage his career. He went back to Fox to work in *Tampico*, a love story centered on the war. Robinson was again cast as the captain of a tanker, one who marries a mysterious woman believed to be a Nazi spy. Only after his ship is sunk and he has left the woman does he realize that it was his first mate— portrayed by Victor McLaglen—who was the spy.

Robinson was aware that he was on uncharted ground, a man without the power of a studio. He knew that McLaglen was the head of a neomilitary group in Hollywood, and he suspected the Irish actor of being pro-Nazi, if only because the Nazis were fighting the British. Because of his status, he kept his mouth shut, at least on the set.

Off the set it was a different matter, and the FBI seems now to have always been lurking, an agent with notebook in hand. When half a dozen Russian dignitaries visited Los Angeles in August, Robinson showed them his art collection, as he had done not only for everyone of importance in Hollywood and Washington, D.C., but for literally thousands of GIs as well. The FBI did not make that distinction but filed a report stating that Robinson had been one of those designated to greet the visitors— who of course, but the file does not note, were allies at the time.

In September, Robinson spoke alongside two Russian Jews—Lieutenant Colonel Itzik Feffer and Professor Solomon Michaels—at the Shrine Auditorium. The visitors were representatives of the Jewish Anti-Fascist Committee of the USSR. The FBI file shows that Robinson "brought down the house by speaking at length in English, Yiddish and Russian," and was quoted as saying, "The entire American people and the peoples of the Soviet Union have joined together in their hatred of Hitlerism. Let us resolve to remain together in love of humanity." In October his name appeared in the souvenir journal of the tenth-anniversary banquet of the American Committee for the Protection of the Foreign Born, and in November on a pamphlet saluting the tenth anniversary of American-Soviet Relations.

All that he did in public did not erase the problems that Robinson was experiencing at home. In early 1944 Gladys had a relapse of her mental problems and again sued him for divorce. She was taken to a clinic for treatment, but the process was expensive. He needed to make films for the cash, if nothing else. He agreed to Columbia's offer for *Mr. Winkle Goes to War*, a silly yarn about a forty-four-year-old man who is drafted and becomes a war hero. Not only was he miscast—as a meek man who would rather sit alone in his shop than be with his wife or among people—but his wife was played by Ruth Warrick, one of the tallest actresses in Hollywood. She practically had to play their scenes together on her knees. Robinson didn't have to wait for the reviews for this one to know he was in serious career trouble.

He was fifty; the paunch was beginning to show, and although his hair was dyed, his age showed in his face. For more than a dozen years since *Little Caesar*, he had not taken a supporting role. The time had come to change his outlook, and he knew it.

Billy Wilder saved the day. Wilder, an émigré from Austria, had known Robinson slightly through mutual friends from Europe, through their joint love of art, and through political involvements. He thought Robinson perfect for the part of Barton Keyes in *Double Indemnity*, which he was preparing for Paramount. Based on the novel by James M. Cain, the film loosely told the true tale of a woman and her lover who had killed the woman's husband for the insurance. Robinson would play the insurance company's claims manager, while Barbara Stanwyck would play the woman, and Fred MacMurray was cast as the insurance agent who kills the husband for the love of the woman.

It meant third billing. Even more, it was designed to be MacMurray's film. He had heretofore played in light comedies and with *Double Indemnity* sought a new image. MacMurray was in virtually every scene, while Robinson would have but a few choice segments. Robinson took the role anyway, and he appears on the screen with the snarling, energetic power he displayed in *Little Caesar*. Although his height was a problem for Wilder, who didn't want Robinson's stature minimized, no camera angles could contain Robinson's interpretation of Barton Keyes. He dominated every frame he was in. The film also touched on a theme never before explored in Hollywood—that of the filial love between two men unrelated by blood.

Robinson's work was completed in a few weeks, and with Gladys showing signs of improvement, he set off for Europe, visiting the Normandy beaches just days after the D-Day invasion. He was one of the first celebrities ashore. While in Europe he would make a film for the British Royal Air Force and again broadcast for the Office of War Information. His contacts with officials from many countries—including the Soviet Union—would later be used by the FBI as a possible indication of collusion with espionage agents.

He was back by the end of July and took to spending afternoons at the Hillcrest Country Club while he awaited film work. One of the few non-comedians to be allowed to sit at the "Roundtable" at the club, he became friendly with Jack Benny, George Burns, the Marx Brothers, the Ritz Brothers, George Jessel, and Al Jolson, all of whom had started their careers in vaudeville. It was a daily scene of high comedy, quick dialogue, and a competitive spirit. Although Robinson laughed easily, he remained quiet during most of the repartee, not able to compete with comedians for attention. "Yeah, he sat at the Roundtable, but he didn't talk much," George Burns recalled, still a fixture at the club in the 1980s. "The smart one was Jessel, but come to think of it, with Jessel we always listened trying to figure out what he was saying."

Spending time with comedians served other purposes. By laughing, Robinson could forget his career problems and his troubles at home. His life with Gladys was a constant squabble, and Manny had been bouncing from school to school—including a stab at a military academy; Manny's grades were poor, and there were continuous reports of disciplinary action. But his comedian friends also helped in that they knew failure as much as, or more than, anyone else in the business. They could laugh about the quiet spells and the bad reviews as easily as they could glow with success. Robinson needed a little of that attitude to buoy him up.

It came in handy in early August when *Mr. Winkle Goes to War* was released. The reviews were frightful. "He swaggers through most of the sequences, not quite sure whether he is Little Caesar or a timid bookkeeper," one critic wrote. Another found it impossible to accept Robinson as "a very mouse of a man, hen-pecked beyond endurance." The film failed miserably, and Robinson feared his career would go down with it. He played gin rummy at the club to try to forget his troubles. When *Double Indemnity* was released a month later, though, his anxiety turned to relief. Many of the critics said he had stolen the film. The fine-tuned detective drama went on to earn seven Academy Award nominations, including Best Picture, Best Actress, Best Screenplay, Best Director, although it won no awards (and Robinson failed once again to attract even a nomination).

But even after *Indemnity* was released, no work came his way immediately, so he busied himself with politics. Since Roosevelt was again running for reelection, he joined the Hollywood Democratic Committee, serving on its executive board and having his name listed along with Jesse Lasky, Emmett Lavery, Talbot Jennings, Sol Lesser, and J. K. Wallace. Robinson and Melvyn Douglas, also a committee member, had purchased Roosevelt's felt hat in an auction the year before and now donated it back to the candidate so he could once again campaign with the symbol. He also joined the National Citizens' Political Action Committee (NCPAC), which was organized in July 1944 in part by the Congress of Industrial Organizations (CIO) to lure independent voters toward FDR in November. Again, he was joined on the membership list by a stream of well-known and respected liberals.

Even his involvement with so-called liberals was thus noted in FBI files. The Bureau recorded that in September 1944 the *Labor Herald*, a publication of the CIO in California, listed Robinson as an "outstanding liberal" and mentioned that many NCPAC meetings had taken place in his home. Similarly, Robinson's attacks on Thomas E. Dewey, Republican candidate for president, earned mention, despite the fact that these had been made by a loyal and active member of the Democratic Party.

The image Robinson gave the press at the time was one of serene home lover. "Tough Guy Turns Farmer" one interview was headlined. Robinson had delighted in taking the reporter to the ranch, where they had chatted amidst "the chickens and the butter churns." He talked of crowing roosters and pigs that had escaped their pens and eaten a neighbor's petunias. An open field would become a helicopter pad after the war, Robinson said he had promised Manny. And, with a wink, Robinson said the ranch also doubled as a place to come with his gin-rummy-playing partners. "Listen, sister," he told the reporter, "just remember that Little Caesar is now a solid citizen."

As 1944 came to an end, Robinson worked on an RKO film, *The Woman in the Window*, which he agreed to do in order to work with the great German film director Fritz Lang (forced to come to Hollywood because he was partly of Jewish descent). Robinson portrayed a professor of psychology who becomes embroiled in murder and crime, only to awake to discover it was all just a dream. While the work was routine, events on the set began to trouble him. Raymond Massey and Joan Bennett, his two costars, were both members of the conservative faction in Hollywood, and they involved the cast and crew in off-camera discussions about prevailing Communist influences in Hollywood. It was their impression, as it was of other members of the company, that something had to be done lest the Communists take over the industry. Since the war was still in progress and the Soviets were still allies of America, Robinson at first took the other side—that he knew of no ranking Communists and that Russia still needed support. His words were received with glares, and Robinson found himself retreating to his dressing room. What he had accomplished was not political discussion, but having himself branded as a "fellow traveler." It was a small hint of what was to come.

Yet, Robinson would have rejected any suggestion that his liberalism would work against him in just a few years. This was America, the country for which he had stood on a soapbox long before he had even been in a theater. And, even in his early fifties, he retained the same idealism he had had as a youth. In November 1944 he sent a telegram to an American-Soviet Friendship Rally in New York, proclaiming, "In time to come the recognition of the Soviet Union by the United States will be remembered as the beginning of an era which brought savagery, ignorance and hunger to an end. It will be remembered as the first step taken toward new horizons of a world where security and culture are meant for the happiness of all people everywhere." After all, it had been his president, Franklin Delano Roosevelt, and his party, the Democrats, who had taken that first step. The FBI didn't care. It recorded the telegram in the file.

Robinson spoke at the Red Army Day dinner in New York in February 1945, saluting Stalin and Roosevelt, who, the country knew well, had met in friendship. The FBI didn't see it that way. The Bureau's files included Robinson's toast in Russian and English to victory, Stalin, Roosevelt, the Red Army, the American army, and George Washington.

As he was not a member of the Communist Party, Robinson had no way of knowing that the party had dissolved in 1944. He had heard of a new group that was of the opposite persuasion. The Motion Picture Alliance for the Preservation of American Ideals (MPA) had been formed in February 1944 as the brainchild of director Sam Wood, obsessed with the notion that Roosevelt was heading the country into Communism and that Hollywood was overrun with Reds. Joined by other directors such as Norman Taurog, Clarence Brown, King Vidor, Victor Fleming, and actors Gary Cooper, Robert Taylor, Adolphe Menjou, John Wayne, Ward Bond, and columnist Hedda Hopper, Wood had proclaimed, "In our special field of motion pictures, we resent the growing impression that this industry is made up of, and dominated by, Communists, radicals and crackpots . . . We pledge to fight, with every means at our organized command, any effort of any group or individual, to divert the loyalty of the screen from the free America that gave it birth." The MPA offered Martin Dies, who had first investigated Red influences in Hollywood, $50,000 to head its organization. MPA members wrote letters to congressional conservatives suggesting that an investigation of communists in Hollywood be launched.

Wood and his ilk had begun to equate Roosevelt's New Deal with Communism, and it was the FDR liberalism that actually took the brunt of their wrath. They attacked the federal welfare programs as socialistic; they asserted that the rise of unionism—and its mass acceptance by America in the 1930s—was proof that the left wing was organizing the proletariat against free enterprise. Since Robinson was an outspoken FDR supporter in Hollywood, he was more than suspect. He had to be a target, along with many other liberals and supporters of trade unionism.

Hollywood was about to go through its most trying episode with labor unions. Although the motion picture crews and the writers and the actors had been unionized since the 1930s, Robinson was content to merely be a member of the Screen Actors Guild and had not participated actively in his union, nor in the struggles of other unions. There is no record to show Robinson in the forefront of the attacks on Willie Bioff when, as head of International Alliance of Theatrical Stage Employees (IATSE), Bioff was indicted in the early 1940s for conspiracy and extortion (convicted in 1941). That he had milked the studios for hundreds of thousands of dollars did not seem to trouble Robinson, as it did Lionel Stander, one of the stars who exposed the corruption.

IATSE, or IA, had since the late 1930s been in dispute with the Conference of Studio Unions (CSU), run by a former boxer named Herbert Sorrell. An arrogant man, he was friendly with liberal and left-wing factions in town and was rumored—probably erroneously—to have been a member or former member of the Communist Party. The dispute was more than just between the two unions; it was also between the not yet merged American Federation of Labor (AFL), which supported IATSE, and the CIO, which supported CSU. Sorrell had earned approval from the liberal factions by proposing in the early 1940s that all unions—the Screen Writers Guild and Screen Actors Guild included—join together. Its proposed constitution suggested that when one member union went out on strike the other unions honor that strike and, in essence, shut down the industry. It was not a suggestion that appealed to the studio bosses, who had at least made peace with IATSE, but it gained the interest of much of the community at large.

In May 1945, two months after a man named Roy M. Brewer had arrived in Hollywood to lead IATSE, things came to a head, with part of CSU going on strike. A vehement conservative, Brewer had already joined forces with the Motion Picture Alliance for the Preservation of American

Ideals, a group that had consistently been seeking to excise left-wing and liberal thinkers from the motion picture capital. Brewer was soon to be called "strawboss of the purge," and his presence turned the strike, a mere labor confrontation, into something far more political, a situation that would now attract national—and federal—attention and force members of the community—Robinson included—to take sides.

Robinson's activity on the Hollywood Democratic Committee had been a matter of public record. When the election of 1944 ended, the group decided to broaden its horizons and changed its name to the Hollywood Independent Citizens Committee of the Arts, Sciences and Professions (HICCASP), boasting twenty-seven hundred members. Robinson was a member of the executive board along with such liberals as Olivia de Havilland, John Garfield, Ira Gershwin, Sheridan Gibney, Johnny Green, Miriam Hopkins, Emmet Lavery, Lewis Milestone, and Orson Welles. Also on the board were a number of individuals who might have been considered more radical in their outlook, but Robinson would have no reason to suspect that they were members of the Communist Party or former members—Henry Blankford, Sidney Buchman, Edward Dmytryk, John Howard Lawson, William Pomerance, Robert Rossen, and Frank Tuttle. The goals of the group were clear—to retain the humanistic approach to politics that had grown nationwide during the New Deal days. It was a haven for those who had been early to attack the approaching war in Europe. It was not meant to be a front for Communist Party politics.

Another HICCASP member was a Warner Bros. B-picture player with whom Robinson had had limited contact, but who had earned a status in Hollywood greater than his success in motion pictures would have otherwise allowed. Ronald Reagan had arrived in Hollywood and been put under contract in 1937. A month later he was named to the board of SAG, because the guild needed to fill its quota of young contract players. Reagan never left his union work, except while he was in the armed forces. In 1941 Louella Parsons, who had come from the same hometown as the young former radio announcer, took Ronnie on a tour with her along with other contract players for whom she foretold stardom. Jane Wyman was one of the starlets, and she married Reagan soon afterward. It was when Wyman was filming *Larceny, Inc.* with Robinson that the two men had had their earlier contact.

Reagan's union work was not entirely altruism. Others had used it to advance their status in the industry, as a tool to work their way up the ladder. Before and during the war, Reagan had been active in the so-called liberal organizations, if only because they were the places to be. He had once been voted the star with the best physique by female fans, and his easy manner made him popular with liberals—and, he would contend later, Communists. After World War II, he joined HICCASP, but as the right-wing element began to topple the Left's influence, Reagan would become their tool as well.

It was Roy Brewer who had the leading position in the efforts by the Hollywood Right to assert that they perceived their troubles to be induced by Communists. By spring 1945, Brewer's IATSE was handing out leaflets claiming that the strike was that in name only, that in reality it "must be a result of a long-range program instituted many years ago by a certain political party for one reason: To Take Over and Control Organized Labor in the Motion Picture Industry." Brewer described it as "a political strike" and charged Sorrell with being "sympathetic to the communistic idea."

The harangue continued as the strike continued. Every effort to link Sorrell to the Communists was made. When a National Labor Relations Board (NLRB) election was held in May, ballot after ballot was challenged, making it impossible to decide who would have jurisdiction—IA or CSU. Picketing of the studios grew to mass proportions. In October, after a summer of strife, tear gas and fire hoses were used to break up a picket line at Warner Bros.—and the industry realized it had gone too far. By the end of October all were back to work, with the AFL planning thirty days of negotiations. The strike was over.

Robinson had stayed clear of the dispute, except perhaps for discussions on the set or at parties. He had, during that period, made one more trip to Europe to visit the victorious troops. There, just weeks after VE Day, while touring a cemetery in France, he spent the afternoon with a soldier named Tom Dowling, and so moved was the actor by the soldier's story that he sent Dowling a Christmas card each year for the rest of his life.

He had also found time in the spring to film *Our Vines Have Tender Grapes* for MGM, in a role that Wallace Beery had rejected. It was a tale of America, a slice of life as seen through the eyes of a seven-year-old girl, a member of a Norwegian farm community in Wisconsin. Robinson portrayed the father and patriarch, with a suitable accent and soiled farmer's clothes. The film was episodes in the girl's life and was written by Dalton Trumbo. For Robinson, it was a relief to be with a writer on the set with whom he could speak openly about politics. Trumbo was to the left of Robinson, but they both shared similar desires for America—that the principles fought for overseas, freedom and an end to racism, would be realized in America. Their friendship, which before filming had been merely a longtime acquaintance, blossomed—a union that was noticed by many of the wrong eyes.

Later in the year Robinson was back at Universal filming *Scarlet Street*, the monotonous tale of a cashier who becomes embroiled in romance with a "fallen woman," played by Joan Bennett. Fritz Lang again directed. The film was of little interest to Robinson, who counted the days until it was over. But it was a film with touches that aroused the interest of the censors and had the effect of adding a new sexual facet to Little Caesar. The censors protested a scene in which Robinson paints Bennett's toenails as she lounges in a negligee. The New York Board of Censors in particular disliked the scene in which Robinson's character—Christopher Cross—climbs a telephone pole to hear the high-voltage hum of the electric chair to which a man he has framed for the murder of Bennett has been condemned. And the censors insisted that six of the seven ice-pick stabs employed by Cross to kill Kitty be cut from the final prints. The cuts were made, but not before Universal had mustered enough press coverage to guarantee the film a good box office.

There were also problems with Manny in 1945. Robinson, who had pushed Manny continually, had to accept reports that his son was performing at a substandard level. During the summer Manny was sent to the University of California at Los Angeles Clinical School for remedial work in mathematics and other subjects, "to improve to the 8th grade level." Reports from the school indicate that "Edward had an average achievement level of 6th grade and was attempting 8th grade work. His spelling and reading were good, but his mathematics and information in literature, Social Studies and Science were retarded."

The impressions and recommendations upset Robinson. "He has learned to cover up his deficiencies and be fearful of any failure that might be reported to and bring censure from his father whom he respects and admires," the teacher wrote. "He is defensive and much of his tendency to show off, demand attention to himself, and exhibit difficulties of behavior, would disappear if he could be completely up to grade in his school subjects, successful in his school work and happy and well adjusted in his own age group."

Robinson was heartsick. He knew there had been a breach between himself and his only son. He knew he hadn't communicated, completely or properly, the mental troubles the boy's mother was experiencing. At age twelve, Manny had already been in trouble for drinking and for misusing the family ranch at Higginsville. Robinson yearned to make up with the boy, but there was an emotional barrier. He and Manny only communicated with difficulty, and the boy's relationship with his mother had deteriorated even further.

The Rexford Drive household had now become an expanded one. Friend Sam Jaffe was living on the third floor of the house whenever he was in California for film work—which was frequent. Sam fulfilled Robinson's need for comradeship—lacking in a man without a studio and in a husband whose wife had a separate bedroom and barely communicated, busying herself with community activities instead. There was also still the art collection, visited by many Hollywood greats, with Jaffe or any other friend available pressed into service as curator. Greta Garbo came, as did

Dorothy Parker. Beulah Robinson—nicknamed "Boo" by Manny—
remembers the time she answered the door, covered in charcoal dust from
her own art work, to Cary Grant.

If Robinson's position among the social set in Hollywood was firm, his
status with the studios had further begun to falter. At first Robinson
thought it was his age, but it became evident to him that as the Cold War
began to take shape in early 1946, his political point of view—nothing
more than that of a liberal Democrat—could be working against him. Hollywood, like the rest of the country, was becoming split between the liberal factions, who sought to retain the spirit of the New Deal, and the conservative factions, represented by the Motion Picture Alliance for the
Preservation of American Ideals, which at last had its chance to attack
Communist influences, and to be heard.

Robinson, still believing that in America all points of view were welcomed and that his patriotism would not be questioned, despite the MPA,
lent his name to a full-page advertisement in the *New York Times* on
March 14, 1946, under the title "Citizens United to Abolish the Wood-
Rankin Committee," which had been formed by the House of Representatives as a permanent House Committee on Un-American Activities. The
FBI did not let this signing go unnoticed. Nor would the Committee in a
short time.

HICCASP was by then affiliated with the national Independent Citizens Committee for the Arts, Sciences and Professions (ICCASP) and
had more than three thousand members—Reagan still among them. John
Crowell was chairman; Bette Davis, Dore Schary, John B. Hayes, and
Joseph Szigetti, vice chairmen; Danny Kaye, treasurer; and E. Y. Harburg,
secretary. Robinson still thought of the committee as a forum for perpet-
uating the New Deal and electing Democratic or liberal politicians. Nothing more.

Early in the year he was back at RKO to do a film on a subject in which
he desperately believed—the fight against anti-Semitism. *The Stranger*
was one of the first postwar Hollywood films to tackle the subject of prejudice. This would become a genre in itself, as the country—briefly—

craved to fight racism in America as its soldiers had overseas, and films such as *Gentleman's Agreement, Crossfire,* and *Pinky* won accolades.

It was also a chance to work with Orson Welles as both actor and director, and with Loretta Young, his costar in *The Hatchet Man* in 1932. Robinson portrayed a character not unlike Renard in *Confessions of a Nazi Spy.* He played an inspector with the Commission for War Crimes, following Konrad Meinike, an escaped Nazi official, to a small town in Connecticut in hopes of tracing the notorious German leader Franz Kindler (Welles). Kindler is posing as Charles Rankin, a college professor, and is engaged to Young. Robinson pretends to be an antique collector and discovers Rankin's identity. The Nazi runs from the authorities, only to fall from the clock tower in the town square, impaling himself on the sword of a warrior, one of the hands on the huge clock.

When it was released in July, *The Stranger* failed to excite the critics or the audiences. They found it stilted and contrived, with Robinson's notices no better than those of the wunderkind Welles.

By that time Robinson had had a few personal trials of his own. In March it was Manny's birthday, and the thirteen-year-old had, much to Robinson's delight and Gladys's acceptance, decided to be bar mitzvahed. The youth's decision was motivated by several feelings: He thought it would win his father's approval, and he also knew that his Jewish friends had received many gifts at their bar mitzvahs.

Among the guests that March at Temple Emanu-El in Beverly Hills were Mr. and Mrs. Harry Warner, Manny's godparents. Warner was thoroughly impressed, both by Manny and the proceedings, so taken that he decided to produce a brotherhood movie that would contain a service from a Catholic church, one from a Protestant church, and Manny's bar mitzvah as the Jewish representation.

For Manny, the news he was to be before cameras was his big chance. He had for several years been insisting that he wanted to become an actor like his dad. Robinson reluctantly agreed, but a few weeks after the ceremony, Gladys again took ill, the letdown after the big event. She resumed the divorce threats, and Robinson sent her to Menninger's Clinic for treatment.

With those family troubles at the back of his mind, Manny went before the cameras in late April to perform his bar mitzvah for a potential audience of millions. Warner had sunk $10,000 into the effort, and within days a print was sent to the house for Manny. He loved watching himself and would spend hours in the family screening room running the short film again and again, as he had done with his father's films. Robinson was less impressed. To him, the child came over as a ham, as exploited, and considering Gladys's condition, it seemed too heart-wrenching a moment to allow the film to be used. It would turn the public eye on the family, at a time when they wouldn't welcome it. Robinson asked Harry Warner to drop the project, which Warner did; the film was released to church and civic groups, but never to a mass audience in theaters.

Manny was bitterly disappointed and could not understand his father's logic. He retaliated by behaving badly, drinking and locking himself in his room. It took the combined efforts of Robinson and houseguest Sam Jaffe to pull the lad together, but the breach between father and son widened for some time. Manny felt betrayed.

Hollywood, itself, was again plagued by union dissension. The 1945 strike had settled nothing, and the IATSE and CSU continued to battle. Roy Brewer had become a powerful figure in town—one to be reckoned with both for his leadership of IA and for the prominent position he held with the Motion Picture Alliance. That the Alliance was, as many right-wing organizations tend to be, anti-union and pro-studio, should have made his labor position suspect. It began to do so with the liberal community, which although outwardly neutral had begun to look on Sorrell's CSU with a favorable eye.

Robinson's loyalties were divided. On the one hand he tried to remain neutral, on the other hand he didn't know what to make of either leader. Brewer was conservative, which he detested, but was also active in Democratic Party politics, while Sorrell was rumored to be a Communist. Sorrell did his cause little good in May when, backed into a corner, he called another strike when Brewer and the Teamsters attempted to create a machinists union affiliated with the AFL, overstepping the nonaffiliated machinists who were loyal to Sorrell. The National Labor Relations Board stepped in to settle matters, but Sorrell lost strength. He called another strike, but the producers squelched the territory issues by granting concessions to workers aligned with both unions.

Brewer saw this as an opportunity to play his trump card. In July, Sorrell was called before the Los Angeles Central Labor Council on charges of being a Communist. Assisting Brewer in the preparation of documents against Sorrell was Ed Gibbons, a vehement anti-Communist, who had written the leaflets that asserted CSU Communist influences in 1945. While Brewer was going after Sorrell, Gibbons was collecting a file on the Hollywood community that he would use a few years later when he became the co-owner of *Alert*, an anti-Communist publication that would become a tool of the blacklisting. Anyone who so much as muttered a word of support for Sorrell would find himself on Gibbons's later lists. Robinson stood forth at an HICCASP meeting and suggested that some group move in to forge a compromise between the warring unions. Gibbons put that information in his little black book.

Sorrell's trial turned out to be indecisive. No one ever proved him to be a Communist, but the issue of so-called Red infiltration in the industry became the major topic throughout Hollywood and around the swimming pools of Beverly Hills. Most liberals, Robinson included, did not want to wage war on the left-wing or radical elements, still assuming their numbers and influence were small, and still abiding by the free speech principle of the First Amendment. Robinson shrugged when Dalton Trumbo, his friend and the writer of *Our Vines Have Tender Grapes*, was mentioned as being a Commie. Trumbo had been the first editor of *The Screenwriter*, a magazine published by the Screen Writers Guild. An anti-Communist writer, Richard Macaulay, had submitted an article attacking a piece by Alvah Bessie, one of the few Hollywood residents who had fought for Loyalist Spain. *The Screenwriter* had refused to publish the rebuttal, and Macaulay insinuated around town that the staff must be Red. Robinson did himself no good by defending his friend Trumbo.

The debate found its way into HICCASP, where Ronald Reagan, Olivia de Havilland, Dore Schary, and Johnny Green tried to get the organization to accept a motion condemning Communism. Reagan was particularly vocal. As an attractive actor with a solid military record and good at speaking in public, he had become a favorite of the liberal and Left elements looking for suitable figures to state their positions. But Reagan had no strong political convictions. As Hollywood began to take sides on the labor issues, and the finger began to be pointed at alleged Communists, his mentor, George Murphy, warned Reagan that in the struggle to come he would find himself on the wrong side of the studio heads if he continued to be part of groups that didn't support Brewer and the IA. Reagan was ambitious. Having been relegated to B pictures before the war, he yearned to be in the front line. He was also moving up the hierarchy in SAG, which was led by the conservative Murphy and the equally conservative Robert Montgomery. He chose their course, no doubt partly as a career move. When HICCASP refused to condemn Communism, he was one of the first—and the most vocal—to leave. He openly criticized and detailed the comments of those who stayed.

Robinson was one of those who stayed for a while longer. Although he feared the organization was losing some of its original purpose, it was his belief that those with different opinions should meet on common ground to work out their differences in the traditional American forum. He carried that ideology into his assessment of the union troubles in the industry.

This ideology put him on the losing side in the labor struggles. By the end of the summer, the IATSE and CSU were again at war. The Carpenters' Union, which was backed by the CSU, thought it had jurisdiction over the set erection jobs, but Brewer had promised the studio heads that the IA would not honor any picket lines called for by the CSU and that his union would supply replacements for any striking CSU members. Buoyed by this, the studios refused to hear the Carpenters' demands, and a strike was called. This time, though, the Teamsters ferried IA and scab labor across the picket lines, where violence broke out daily and the police made daily arrests. All CSU members were discharged, and accusations of Communist involvement were bandied back and forth by the warring sides. SAG's leaders—Reagan, Murphy,

Montgomery, and Edward Arnold—were by this time among those claiming Communist involvement in all facets of the industry. Although their union was ostensibly neutral in the IA-CSU matter, they themselves favored the cause of the producers, who in turn were obviously siding with Brewer and the IA.

In September, a SAG delegation consisting of Reagan, Murphy, Arnold, Montgomery, Dick Powell, Walter Pidgeon, Jane Wyman, Alexis Smith, Robert Taylor, and Gene Kelly went to the AFL convention in Chicago hoping to get the parent union to participate in a settlement. The AFL heads would not even see them. The delegation returned to Los Angeles to face their own union, which was now split into camps along with the rest of the town. Many among its members accused the leadership of tilting toward the producers' point of view and defecting from neutrality. Robinson was among that group.

A few days later SAG held a membership meeting at the Legion Fight Stadium to discuss the matter. Outside the stadium, CSU members picketed, chanting, "Don't wreck our union." Inside, "bodyguards" roamed the aisles with bicycle chains in their hands, which they tapped against the side of the chairs whenever the debate became too volatile. The packed house heard Reagan, Murphy, and the ultraconservative Adolphe Menjou discuss the results of the trip to Chicago, as well as the threat of Communist infiltration in the industry. Reports from those in attendance, such as the liberal Alexander Knox, say that Reagan "spoke very fast" and was on "an anti-Communist crusade."

What the liberal faction wanted was not to join with the CSU, but to mediate from a point of neutrality. Katharine Hepburn, Robinson, Paul Henreid, and Knox each took a turn at the podium, making a plea to accept a resolution from the Interfaith Religious Council calling for conciliatory arbitration. The idea, in Robinson's mind, was to get all sides involved talking to each other. He didn't realize that the situation had gone beyond the control of any liberal group. It was in the hands of the reactionaries, one of whom—Menjou—was making extensive notes on every liberal he spotted making a statement.

The bodyguards triggered the conservative element of the crowd to shout Knox, the last of the four "liberal" speakers, off the podium. The meeting ended with the conservative element in firm control of the union, an element whose leadership was friendly to the producers. A triumphant Roy Brewer walked up to a select few of the liberal actors after the meeting—Knox and Robinson among them—and promised to "run them out of town."

Robinson was shaken by the events. There were now actors in town with whom he could hardly exchange a word. Reagan gained sympathy for himself and his cause by advertising that he had been forced to seek police protection for his home and family because of death threats. Actors were calling each other "fascist" and "Commie."

In this name-calling, Robinson uneasily found himself in the second category. Newspapers around the country, among them the *New York World-Telegram*, published articles about prominent people in all walks of life whose names were associated with Communist fronts. In the *World-Telegram* article, Robinson and John Garfield were said to have their names involved in eighty-one such organizations. The smear had started. Whether Menjou was giving information to FBI informants—or Reagan, for that matter—is speculation. But everything Robinson had ever said in the context was coming back to haunt him, twisted and misinterpreted.

An incident that took place at this time made the breach with Reagan complete. Robinson had continued his afternoon vigil at the Hillcrest, finding it one place where his politics were not put to a constant test. Despite its membership roster, which included a who's who of the studios, the Hillcrest had retained its humanist outlook. Membership was based on the candidate's record of charitable donations, and much of the club's leadership sided with the common man. It was an atmosphere of which Robinson approved. Reagan was not a member of the club, partly because he was not Jewish, and partly because he may not have had the capital to make suitable donations to charity. But he was given honorary membership status because of his position in the industry and allowed to use the restaurant and other facilities—at least for a short period after the war.

"Before the governor's race in 1966 I was visiting with Reagan at his home in Pacific Palisades," recalled John Babcock, who was then a reporter and later a successful broadcast news producer. "Nancy was there. It was relaxed and we were chatting while I asked him questions. He brought up the issue of anti-Semitism. He said that allegations of anti-Semitism against him were ridiculous. I was surprised by the topic. I told him that I hadn't heard of any such accusations. He told me I would. 'Well, I'm not,' he continued, and I was surprised that he wanted to speak so openly on the subject. 'My agent is Jewish,' he told me. 'I'm close to the Jewish community.'" He explained to Babcock that the anti-Semitic charges went back to the months of the labor strife.

Reagan told me that during the labor dispute, after he had taken a position some of his Jewish friends turned on him. One evening he was taking some friends to dinner at the Hillcrest. He didn't say who the friends were. Presumably Jane [Wyman] was with the party. Apparently when he got to the restaurant, the maitre d' stopped him at the door. The first time he had ever been stopped. The man asked his name. Now, Reagan was certainly recognizable to anyone in Hollywood, and so was Jane Wyman. But the man asked him his name anyway. Reagan said he was tremendously embarrassed since he had guests, but he gave the man his name. He was told that his name was not on the honorary list. "I was mortified and humiliated," Reagan told me.

I guess they went somewhere else for dinner, but when he got home Reagan told me, "I called my good friend Eddie Robinson and said, 'Eddie, what in the hell happened at the Hillcrest?' Eddie said he'd check it out. He called back and said there had been a change in the policy of honorary memberships and there was nothing he could do. Nothing he could do. That's what they told Eddie, but I always thought it was directed against me."

Babcock summed up his impression, "In the mid-sixties he was still angry at the Hillcrest. It still stuck in his craw."

Reagan had called Robinson because he thought Eddie had influence at the club. Robinson was not one to meddle in proscribed affairs and pull strings. He did nothing to help Reagan in the matter. Perhaps Robinson, too, was seething at Reagan's performance at SAG. Whatever the reason, he had slighted Reagan, an old acquaintance who was now on the opposite side politically.

Worse, the studios began to look upon Robinson as an enemy, and the flow of scripts to him evaporated. The Motion Picture Alliance had become stronger because of hostilities throughout the town, and he had been labeled on the wrong side of the issues. From Louis B. Mayer, Jack Warner, and other moguls sympathetic to the Alliance, there were no offers.

Still, Robinson continued what he thought was merely the political activities of a liberal who wanted to be involved. In September 1946 he sent greetings to the Veterans of the Abraham Lincoln Brigade on the occasion of its national convention. The FBI wrote that his telegram declared, "Today it is not enough just being a liberal. One must be militantly anti-Fascist and in so doing, hail the valorous deeds of those who first saw the threat of Fascism in Spain and courageously fought against it."

On October 1, he was listed in an article in the *New York Daily News* as a Communist sympathizer, so named by Matthew Woll, vice president of the AFL. The *News* had lifted the attack from an editorial in the trade union publication *American Photo Engraver*. The FBI put this in the record. Robinson shuddered and, of course, denied the accusation. But the country had not yet reached the point—which it would in just a few months—where accusations of Communist involvement and denials of such accusations made headlines.

With no work, and Gladys ill, his only enjoyment was his afternoons at the Hillcrest and his bantering with the comedians at the Roundtable. He also became friendly with the writers, producers, and other well-placed executives who frequented the club. He had lunch a few times with Sol Lesser, former studio executive turned independent producer. Lesser had the rights to a film property entitled *The Red House*, written by Delmer Daves from the novel by George Agnew. Lesser proposed that Robinson star and join him in forming a company that would produce the film.

United Artists would finance and distribute the result. Daves was set to direct, and Robinson readily agreed.

There were problems with the script from the outset. *The Red House* was a horror film, about a demented man (Robinson) who went to all lengths to keep his adopted daughter and her suitor away from the red edifice that was the scene of his secret torture (he had murdered the daughter's parents there years earlier). Filming was on location in the San Joachim Valley, and it was not going well. Daves, desperate to make the film work, got Lesser and Robinson to agree to bring in writer Albert Maltz to bring punch to the script.

Robinson and Maltz had met only briefly in their days in Hollywood when the writer arrived on the set. Maltz had written the text for *Moscow Strikes Back,* a 1942 propaganda documentary about the Russian allies, which Robinson had narrated. They had exchanged greetings at rehearsals but had had no social contact. Maltz said:

> I don't think Robinson even recalled having met me in 1942 when I arrived on the set. As far as he was concerned I was there to do emergency work on the film. I had been called in by Daves. We had a pleasant time in our off hours. We'd have dinner, maybe take a walk. Our conversations were almost always about the scenery or the script. He was very smart, very astute about scripts and writing. I don't recall discussing politics at all. We'd have our dinner or our walk and then I'd go back to work. That was our contact at the time.

Robinson had not seen the need to discuss the political situation in Hollywood with Maltz. He had not yet realized the extent to which Reagan, Murphy, Montgomery, and organizations such as the Motion Picture Alliance were hungry for the blood of radicals and liberals. The CSU-IA struggle was petering out, although it would not finally be over until 1949. But, in 1947, CSU members began crossing the picket lines holding IA membership cards, and slowly the conflict had been reduced to activity only at B studio lots—Nassour, Monogram, and Eagle-Lion. The cries that the CSU was Communist-inspired had reached Congress, and a resurrected House Committee on Un-American Activities, led by J. Parnell Thomas (R-N.J.), chairman, was itching for its chance at the headlines that investigations of the movie capital would bring. Unionism, as such, had been broken in Hollywood thanks to the defeat of the CSU. The IA—and Brewer—were firmly in the producers' corner. The next step had to be to silence the Left.

Yet, while Robinson was aware that there were no scripts coming his way, he had not become wiser to the trends in Hollywood. His continued membership in HICCASP, which had opposed Brewer and the IA, put his name on the wrong "lists." And he did not leave the organizations of which he was a part; instead, he became a sponsor of the Progressive Citizens of America at their February 11, 1947, meeting. The PCA had been formed in 1946, and even liberal historians of the period admit its membership included Communists, as well as fellow travelers and others like Robinson—liberals who wanted to make a difference.

He had joined because the PCA, like HICCASP, outwardly said it supported and would endorse Democratic candidates for office. Robinson also joined for the same reasons he had joined the Anti-Nazi League: The organization sought to end reactionary thought and, Robinson hoped, prejudice and the usual array of evils as perceived by liberals. It also became one of the last bastions for fighting the congressional committee that would come to be known as HUAC (although the initials do not conform with House Committee on Un-American Activities).

A month later—in March—*Red House* opened to decent reviews and a moderately strong box office. From a cost of about $850,000, it would gross twice that amount and pull in a profit exceeding $100,000. Robinson could still attract ticket buyers. But the studios didn't see it that way, and no further scripts were sent to him.

There is no way to know whether the studio heads knew that the FBI was by this time listing Robinson as a suspected member of the Communist Party, not just a sympathizer. An informant told the Bureau's New York agents in April that Robinson "was a member of the CP and had always been very cooperative." The report concluded, "It should be noted that the above source is highly reliable." The informant's name has never been discovered.

At the same time, the FBI was investigating charges that the American Youth for Democracy organization was fostering Communism on college campuses. "The specter of Communism stalks our college campuses," a source was quoted as saying. Edward G. Robinson was on the list of organization sponsors.

In early spring, Robinson, who by now was aware that his politics could be one reason for his lack of work, was invited by the *Chicago Herald-American* to be part of a May 19 program for "I Am an American" Day. Robinson was eager to attend as he saw the event as a chance to prove his patriotism. He accepted, only to find the invitation rescinded. The newspaper told him that it had erred; he was not "acceptable." Any doubts he might have had about the coming purge evaporated. He knew what the paper meant.

Against the advice of friends and advisers, Robinson decided to take action. He sent a telegram to the man whose company owned the *Herald-American*, William Randolph Hearst. This was the same Hearst who had inspired young Emanuel Goldenberg to take an active interest in politics. Robinson planned to remind him of that. The telegram asked Hearst to recall that campaign in 1909, playing on the sentiment of Robinson's first automobile ride in a Hearst campaign vehicle. Robinson detailed both his and Gladys's activities during the war and told Hearst, "I am sure there is not a great deal of difference between us in our regard for the principles of Americanism." The next day he was back on the list of those who would be speaking at "I Am an American" Day. Robinson was no speechwriter, so he turned to one of the last writers he had contact with—Albert Maltz. Maltz had written for a wide array of publications, had written books, and was known to have an ability to spin prose for such occasions. Still, Maltz insists that he had not discussed politics with Robinson up to this point. "He asked me to write the speech," Maltz recalled. "He told me what he wanted to say. It was stuff I found agreeable. I wrote it basically using the thoughts he had in his mind." The speech was highly patriotic, but relevant to Robinson's situation. "Wars have a way of stirring up the juices of hatred," he told the crowd. "And sometimes after the enemy has been defeated, the juices continue to flow and they stimulate intolerance even towards our brothers. But I think Americans will reject intolerance."

Appearing on the podium that May 19 with Robinson were Cardinal Strich, archbishop of Chicago, and General Kenney, commander of the Strategic Air Command. There were other show business figures—Dale Evans, Joe E. Brown, Bebe Daniels, Ben Lyons—but none had Robinson's imposing delivery. The day after the event the *Herald-American* printed his speech in total. He was a hit. The headlines dulled the murmurs about his radical involvements. His name was crossed off the Hollywood lists of those who should not work.

Robinson was exuberant, and indeed his agent began receiving inquiries for his services. But Hollywood was in the midst of a crisis. President Harry Truman had let it be known he expected the community—as the country's ambassador to the world—to be part of the fight against Soviet aggression and Communism throughout the world. Hollywood was told to help foster positive images of America. Although films such as *Crossfire* and *Gentleman's Agreement*, which dealt with anti-Semitism, were in various stages of production, the moguls reneged on their earlier decision to replace the romance, gangster, and glamour films of the 1930s with product that had more substance.

Washington made certain that Hollywood knew it meant business. Robinson and others were not aware that the FBI was investigating their coworkers, friends, and neighbors. J. Parnell Thomas criticized the industry for not rallying to his cry for hearings to determine the extent of so-called Communist Party influence and infiltration in Hollywood. The joke making the rounds at the Hillcrest and other places Robinson frequented was that for every actual Communist in a cell there were two FBI members.

But HUAC and Thomas were deadly serious about investigating the motion picture industry, and Thomas brought his staff to the Biltmore Hotel in downtown Los Angeles at the end of May to press his point. To his suite came a steady flow of Red baiters, including Wood and Menjou, as well as sympathetic leaders such as Reagan.

Thomas's main targets were suspect writers, but anything he did in Hollywood got him big headlines and more power for the task he had entrusted to his committee. Surely Robinson's name must have been included in the conversations.

But his work was slow, because the studio heads were not yet ready to come around. The moguls agreed to endorse an open investigation of Hollywood by HUAC, but they were not ready to let HUAC dictate hiring practices, preferring to have their own lists. Eddie Mannix, one of the top executives at MGM, insisted he would not join a witch hunt "as long as I am able to protect the material on the screen" from Communists and subversives.

Thomas left after a few weeks, but his influence in Hollywood did not. His representatives were frequent visitors to the studios. Studio heads became more and more nervous about whom they hired, even if they weren't ready to fire anyone. The agents and informers mixed with the Hollywood right wing, jotting down the latest accusation, the latest innuendo. Too much of it found its way into the national press. Robinson's name was in the headlines again, but unlike in Chicago, it was because his patriotism was being questioned.

On August 31, the *New York Times* headlined a story "Civil Rights Groups Called Red Front" and noted that Robinson was on the "Initiating Committee" of the Civil Rights Congress, now called a Red organization. In its own investigation, *Newsweek* discovered Robinson to be "persistently found in Communist fronts."

Robinson tried to ignore what was coming. He had been signed by Universal to appear in *All My Sons*, based on the play by Arthur Miller. In it he would play Joe Keller, a seemingly solid American who during World War II had been tried and acquitted for manufacturing defective airplane parts the use of which had caused twenty-one deaths. In the course of the ninety-four-minute film, Keller's son, portrayed by Burt Lancaster, discovers that his father was guilty and only escaped conviction because of a legal technicality. Worse yet, Joe's other son caused his own airplane death in the aftermath of the disgrace. The son is horrified and disowns Joe Keller. Robinson dies, but by his own hand, in suicide.

It was Robinson's practice to shut out the world when he was preparing for a film. The work came first, even before the paintings. After Labor Day, with script in hand, he retreated to his study to learn his lines, disregarding the political horrors that were coming to a boil in Hollywood. There were costume fittings, story meetings—Robinson always wanted script changes—meetings with director Irving Reis. Production would begin by the end of the month. Besides, in his mind he had done no wrong and felt that vindication—if it came to that—would be easy. Robinson did not recognize what was happening around him, nor how he would be—almost fatally—tied into the events of the next decade.

7

HUAC BURSTS
THE BUBBLE

The Great Chief died and everybody's guts died with him.

—Edward G. Robinson on FDR and blacklisting

The world around Robinson—and for that matter Jack Warner,
Ronald Reagan, Roy Brewer, and the rest of the industry—was not
the same in October 1947 as it had been just a few years earlier. Hollywood had never been stronger as a community than it was during World
War II, with stars and extras alike joining in the victory effort. Any other
concerns were put to the back of the community's mind, just as in the rest
of the country. Stars still put their feet in immortalizing cement at Grauman's Chinese Theater, yet the 1940s had been free of the sex and drug
scandals of the 1920s and 1930s, the fodder the fans loved. Stars looking
for a night out on the town still might go to Mocambo's or Ciro's, but
during the day or the evening they could be seen eating ice cream at Wil
Wright's or trying out new nightspots. The Beverly Hills Hotel, the symbol of wealth in that city, had fallen on hard times from which it would
not recover until a new wing was added in 1949. Hollywood Boulevard
was quickly losing its luster, as was the Miracle Mile district of Wilshire
Boulevard, while more "name" merchants chose a Beverly Hills address.

The studios themselves found they were no longer the keepers of their own destiny. Monetary needs had forced them to seek help from banks and larger corporations based in New York. The New York barons often called the shots. And something new called "television" was on the horizon. KTLA, the first commercial station west of the Mississippi, had opened its doors in January 1947, at the same Sunset Boulevard studios where Jack Warner had his offices when Robinson signed his golden contract.

Robinson need only read the casting notices in the trade papers to know that his career was on shaky ground and would have to find a new direction. Former gangster-movie star George Raft was now making decidedly B-rated pictures. Not one Cagney film was released in 1947, and Charles Laughton—who like Robinson was a "nonpretty" character actor/superstar—also had no releases in 1947. Robinson's old rival Muni was gone completely. He would make but two more films in his lifetime. Only Humphrey Bogart was doing well, now a bigger star (thanks to *Casablanca* and *The Maltese Falcon*) than Robinson would ever have imagined.

At Rexford Drive, the paintings still hung in their places, but the servicemen who had crowded into the house for relaxation during the war were back with their families, or in graves somewhere in the Pacific. Manny was bouncing from school to school, always a problem: There were monthly incidents, it seemed. Gladys would, in 1947, again sue Eddie for divorce and again wind up in a sanatorium.

The mood in the country at large was one of cold war. The Soviets controlled a significant portion of Eastern Europe, and Vienna and Greece had barely been saved from Russian domination. Former heroes such as Winston Churchill had fostered the undeclared war of nerves and rhetoric. Henry Wallace had been fired from the cabinet for advocating accommodation with the Soviets.

More significantly, President Harry Truman—Roosevelt's handpicked successor—had broken the progression of the New Deal, although it could even be argued that FDR himself had been moving away from it when he died. But Truman instituted a loyalty investigation of federal employees and left no doubt that he expected Hollywood to join in the presentation of America as the bastion of democracy to a changing outside world. "Join" may not even be the proper word. Hollywood motion pictures were the *image* of the United States outside the borders. The community had to be clean.

The Truman Doctrine was one of intervention—usually outwardly economic—to negate the Communist parties in Europe and those that were flexing their muscles abroad. America had to be a proper example to the world. From the spring of 1947 to well into 1948, a New York federal grand jury was sending subpoenas to dozens of current and past government employees accused or suspected of being Communist Party members.

Since J. Parnell Thomas, chairman of the House Committee on Un-American Activities, and his staff had visited Hollywood, there was no question but that an investigation into the pasts of film employees was inevitable. Hollywood could resist no longer. Not even the power of the moguls could keep Washington away. By September the community knew who HUAC's targets would be—eighteen writers and directors and one actor, Larry Parks. Eventually only ten of these would be subpoenaed for the October hearings—the Hollywood Ten—but the liberals in Hollywood knew this was time for action. Writer Philip Dunne, directors William Wyler and John Huston, and actor Alexander Knox met in a Mexican restaurant across the street from Paramount and formed the Committee for the First Amendment (CFA), under the principle that "any investigation into the political beliefs of the individual is contrary to the basic principles of our democracy. Any attempt to curb freedom of expression and to set arbitrary standards of Americanism is in itself disloyal to both the spirit and the letter of the Constitution." Among the early members were Humphrey Bogart, Lauren Bacall, Norman Corwin, Henry Fonda, Ava Gardner, Paulette Goddard, Benny Goodman, Van Heflin, Katharine Hepburn, John Houseman, Myrna Loy, Burgess Meredith, Gregory Peck, Barry Sullivan, Cornel Wilde, and Billy Wilder.

The group planned to battle HUAC every day in Washington, D.C., and to steal headlines. They were careful not to take as a member anyone who could be even remotely connected with Communism. In fact, they declared themselves to be anti-Communist in every statement, every publicity release.

The Right was building its own headlines. For years, Billy Wilkerson, the publisher of *The Hollywood Reporter*, had been hammering away at the community to do something about the Reds in its midst. Now he, too, took the forefront to let his beliefs be known. In his September 22 Trade Views column, the heart of the bible of the industry, Wilkerson stated that Hollywood had replaced New York as the "center of Communist activity." He urged the studios to fire any and all writers suspected of being Red. "There had better be an early washout or we'll face trouble," he penned.

By early October Robinson was too busy working on *All My Sons* to be involved in the Committee, although early meetings took place at the home of Ira Gershwin, one of his oldest friends in the industry. Robinson hardly had time to read the newspapers, which were beginning to feature the debate that was raging in the film capital. In the press, big Hollywood names—Frederic March, Judy Garland, Frank Sinatra—charged that HUAC had no legal right to hold hearings, that a congressional committee can only be called for the purpose of gathering information for legislation. There was no particular legislation pending. And a new term was being bandied about—"premature antifascist"—used to denote someone who got involved in the right popular or humanistic causes before the bulk of Hollywood did. It was used to define Robinson.

HUAC opened its hearings on October 20, 1947, to full national coverage, both in the papers and with national radio networks. Louis B. Mayer and Jack Warner were friendly witnesses called on the first day. Warner said he had fired eleven writers because they were Communists, among them Robinson's friend, Dalton Trumbo. Mayer said he'd fire writers too and agreed that the Communist Party should be outlawed if it were legal. Producer-director Sam Wood of the MPA took the stand and among the directors he named was Frank Tuttle, whose home Robinson had often visited.

The trade papers gave the hearings full coverage. On the same day as the hearings, the Memphis, Tennessee, Censor Board had banned the reissued *The Little Rascals* comedies because the shorts featured a "Negro" child in school with white children. This, too, earned some trade coverage—a mere six lines in a box alongside the coverage of the hearings in *The Hollywood Reporter*.

Among those testifying the next day was Adolphe Menjou. His testimony would spell trouble for Robinson, and Menjou presented himself to the Committee as not just an actor with more than twenty years' experience in Hollywood, but as a lay expert on Communist infiltration in America. Menjou looked dapper as always, affecting the style and manner of dress that had made him a star in the 1920s and carried him through character roles in the 1930s and 1940s. One of his first acts was to praise the MPA, which, he said, "had prevented an enormous amount of sly, subtle un-American class-struggle propaganda from going into pictures." As for his fellow actors, he noted that there were "a great many people who act an awful lot like Communists," actors who could take a role and "under the proper circumstances, by a look, by an inflection, by a change in the voice" make a role subversive. He declined to specify which actors he was referring to.

But he wasted no time in branding two organizations top-ranking Red fronts—HICCASP and the Progressive Citizens of America; Robinson was a member of both. He went after Herbert Sorrell, offering the Committee a photostat of Sorrell's Communist Party membership card, which listed the labor leader as Herb Stewart. It was his next statement that damaged Robinson. Menjou had been present at the September 1946 meeting in which Robinson had spoken for neutrality on the CSU-IA question. Menjou would not forgive him for what he considered to be siding with Reds. Puffing on one cigarette after another, Menjou told HUAC:

> I attended a meeting of the entire membership of the Screen Actors Guild. The meeting was called in order to try to settle the strike. Now, the board of directors of the Screen Actors Guild had exerted all of their efforts to settle this strike in every way possible. I think a magnificent job was done by the board of directors, particularly Mr. Reagan, the president. After long, long deliberations and trips to Chicago and everywhere else, they finally came to the conclusion that it was a jurisdictional strike and could have been settled, but Mr. Sorrell did not want to settle it. That was the conclusion made. This meeting was called by a group of 350 people. Mr. Reagan spoke for, I think, more than an hour and a half, explaining the position and the work and the labors that he had gone through to try to determine who was right and who was wrong, because there was an effort to call all the actors out on strike, which would have thrown some 30,000 people out of work. Now then, that particular evening the opposition wanted to be heard. Mr. Sorrell spoke. Following Mr. Sorrell appeared Mr. Edward G. Robinson, Mr. Cronyn, Mr. Alexander Knox, and Mr. Paul Henreid. They all admitted what a wonderful job Mr. Reagan had done, but they wanted the strike settled on Mr. Sorrell's side, which in my opinion, would have meant more trouble, more chaos, and no solution to the trouble, excepting that the unions would have been under the complete domination of the Communist Party. I think sanity prevailed. There was a motion presented by myself that the membership stand by its duly elected board of directors, which was majority voted, and the meeting was over.

Menjou had succeeded in linking Robinson to the CSU, distorting the facts slightly—Robinson had been for discussions between the CSU and IA sanctioned by religious groups. He continued by telling HUAC, "I am a witch-hunter if the witches are Communists. I am a Red-baiter. I make no bones about it whatsoever." He found the producers to be "as fine a group of men as I have ever met." Menjou told the committee their work was justified. As for his own future, Menjou said he was considering moving to Texas, because "I think the Texans would kill them [the Communists] on sight."

The testimony was featured in the Hollywood trade papers the next day, although Robinson's name was not printed as part of Menjou's testimony. *The Hollywood Reporter* mentioned that the HUAC hearings were making headlines in the British press. It was big news that America was cleaning up Hollywood's Commies, and Little Caesar was among them, as far as HUAC and, now, the international press was concerned.

Howard Rushmore, who had been the film critic for the *Daily Worker* in the 1930s and now worked for the Hearst chain, was on hand in the Committee room the next day. Rushmore was an admitted Communist Party member, although he had been in the party only from 1936 to 1939, before most of the so-called fronts had even been established. Under questioning, he dealt Robinson the worst blow so far. The Communist Party loved Robinson, in Rushmore's estimation. Both Robinson and Charles Chaplin were "sacred cows" who, according to *Daily Worker* editorial policy, were always entitled to favorable reviews. Why Robinson had received such treatment was not made clear, but Rushmore noted that "for ten years he had been joining Communist fronts and he's still doing it." Those statements made the newspapers the next day. Some even headlined the news that Robinson was a Red favorite. It meant more trouble.

Reagan, Gary Cooper, Robert Montgomery, and George Murphy were in front of the Committee on the 23rd, as was director Leo McCarey (who, just months earlier, had announced openly that he would not cast Katharine Hepburn in any film because she had made a campaign speech for Henry A. Wallace). Cooper disputed reports coming from Italy that he was a Communist, and instead, he noted that he had rejected many scripts because he found them subversive. His involvement with the Hollywood Hussars was never mentioned (his agent had persuaded him out of the organization a few years before).

McCarey's testimony had all the drama a director would want. At one key moment, he noted that two films he had made had not made "a ruble" in the Soviet Union. The films were *Bells of St. Mary's* and *Going My Way*. McCarey reasoned that they had been rejected by the Russians because "There was a character in them they didn't like." "Bing Crosby?" he was asked. "God," was his response.

Reagan took the stand looking as "preppy" as possible, in a tan gabardine suit, with blue knitted tie and a white shirt. Despite the intellectual-looking tortoiseshell glasses that he wore, the women in the hearing room recognized him as the man they had once voted the best physique in Hollywood. There was an appropriate vocal swoon from the crowd, so noted by the *New York Times*. He was by this time president of SAG, since Robert Montgomery had resigned a few months earlier to pursue directing interests. Reagan named no names, but he made sure his position was known. He would aid the Committee in any way possible.

"Well, sir, ninety-nine per cent of us are pretty well aware of what is going on, and I think, within the bounds of our democratic rights and never once stepping over the rights of democracy, we have done a pretty good job in our business of keeping those people's activities curtailed." He was a follower of Thomas Jefferson's principle, "if all the American people knew all of the facts they will never make a mistake." Reagan added that the Communists' tactics were "fifth column." He had pledged the aid of SAG in cleaning up the mess in California.

The Hollywood papers made full use of the story the next day, and on the facing page was a full-page ad paid for by the Committee for the First Amendment. There were more than one hundred names listed in four columns following Article I of the Bill of Rights. "We are arranging for radio broadcasts and other steps to protest at the conduct of the Washington hearings," the ad stated. "If you wish to volunteer to help us or to contribute money, please wire: Bill of Rights, care of Western Union, Beverly Hills, Calif."

The name of Edward G. Robinson was not among those who had signed the advertisement, because he was making a film. Gladys Robinson was a signatory, though, along with Bogart, Bacall, Fonda, Eddie Cantor, John Houseman, Walter Huston—who had recently completed the role in *Treasure of the Sierra Madre* originally intended for Robinson—and his son John, who had done rewrites on *Dr. Ehrlich* and was now preparing a film that would be Robinson's last really great role.

There were other newspaper advertisements during the next few days. One headlined itself "Memo to a Bunch of Suckers" and told the community that supporters of the Hollywood Ten or of any rights they might have were playing into the hands of the Reds. "Sign their petitions! Lend them your names and prestige! Pay their expenses! Vote for them in your guilds and unions! Front for them! Stooge for them! Give them the shelter of the constitution—so they can roll it up and stuff it down your throats when the moment pleases them." There were no names attached to this statement, just "(Contributed by a group of Americans in the motion-picture industry, from all crafts and unions, who believe in the preservation of the entire constitution of the United States of America.)"

The Committee for the First Amendment sent its selected group to HUAC to protest about the hearings on October 27, expecting there to be witnesses sympathetic to their cause. The papers back home knew better. Monday the 27th would be the start of the testimony by the alleged Communists—John Henry Lawson, Alvah Bessie, and Dalton Trumbo. It was also noted that the hearings on the previous Friday had not been well attended by spectators, since the witnesses were names not then generally known—Lela Rogers (Ginger's mother), Walt Disney, and Oliver Carlson, a self-professed former Commie, an author-teacher who would make a career out of finding Communists under beds for the next few years.

Despite their star-studded membership, the CFA came away from the hearings looking foolish. Instead of finding sympathetic witnesses, they had found themselves sitting in support of Lawson. While they did, certainly, refute HUAC's right to question Lawson, their presence behind a man whose time before the Committee was less than pleasant, and who was labeled a Red, did not put Bogie, Bacall, and the rest in a good public relations position.

The first HUAC hearings ended on October 30, but it was an issue that would not die. In his Trade Views column of November 3, Billy Wilkerson indicated that letters had "poured into this desk, and almost every other channel of motion-picture reporting, from ticket buyers, criticizing the activities" of the First Amendment forces. He reasoned that "Hollywood did *not* come out of the hearings victorious" and that "the adverse press against us added up to a stinging defeat." The column at the end of the week hammered home the same thought. The liberals, he said, were playing into the hands of the Communists and would channel their liberalism "to boost the industry that has boosted you."

Hollywood is, like any other industry, supremely concerned with its public image. The powers in Hollywood felt that the industry had, indeed, been dealt a blow in Washington, rightly or wrongly. The publicity surrounding the Hollywood Ten case was not beneficial, and pressure was coming from the financial heads in New York now controlling the industry to do something about it. They wanted something that would show the public that Hollywood was as interested in fighting the Cold War as was the rest of the country. On November 24, fifty members of the various organizations to which the producers and financiers subscribed met at the Waldorf-Astoria Hotel in New York to discuss the situation. After two days of deliberation, a statement, known later as the Waldorf Declaration, was released. Its tenor would put Robinson and other activists like him on the wrong side of the coin along with the Hollywood 19 and so-called Communists.

Succinctly, the Declaration said that the industry would not employ any member of the Hollywood Ten until "he is acquitted or has purged himself of contempt and declares under oath that he is not a Communist." But the statement did not stop there. The producers said, "We will not knowingly employ a Communist or a member of any party or group that advocates the overthrow of the Government of the United States by force or by illegal or unconstitutional methods." They added that "There is a risk of creating an atmosphere of fear" and invited all Hollywood guilds "to work with us to eliminate any subversives; to pro-

Emanuel Goldenberg's bar mitzvah photo, 1906. (Courtesy of the author)

In the Navy, 1916. Note that EGR is already hooked on cigars. (Courtesy of the author)

On stage in The Kibitzer, *which he also cowrote, 1929. (Courtesy of the author)*

Five Star Final, *1931. (Warner Bros. / USC Special Collections)*

Typical tough-guy pose: EGR shows Ben Weldon who's boss in Kid Galahad. *(Warner Bros. / USC Special Collections)*

Dancing lessons with choreographer Eddie Larkin for I Am the Law, *1938. (Columbia Pictures / M.B. Paul)*

EGR, Manny, and Gladys at the infamous sixth-birthday party for Manny, 1939.

Promotional shot: EGR in makeup for Dr. Ehrlich's Magic Bullet, *with photo of the real Dr. Paul Ehrlich, 1940.*

With Manpower *stars George Raft and Marlene Dietrich. A love triangle on and off the set caused Raft to physically assault EGR, 1941. (Warner Bros. / USC Special Collections)*

Destroyer, *1943. (Columbia Pictures / St. Hilaire)*

Backstage on the Destroyer set with director William Seiter, script supervisor Dorothy Cummings, and costar Edgar Buchanan, 1943. (Columbia Pictures)

"I'll take care of this Schiklgruber gang!" Entertaining the troops, 1944. (Photo courtesy of Photofest)

Marching against right-wing activist Gerald L. K. Smith, 1945. (Courtesy of the author)

Howard Brown aka the deadly Johnny Rocco in Key Largo, *1948. (Warner Bros. /
USC Special Collections)*

As Dathan in The Ten Commandments, *1956. (Paramount Pictures)*

With David Wayne and Tim O'Connor on TV in The Devil and Daniel Webster, *1960. (NBC)*

With George Hamilton and Dahlia Lavi at the wrap party for Two Weeks in Another Town, *1962. (MGM)*

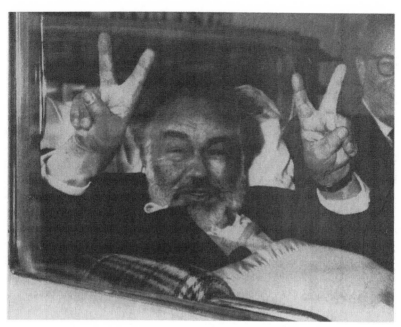

Entering a London hospital after suffering a heart attack in Kenya, 1962. (UPI)

With Jane, 1963. (Courtesy of the author)

Good Neighbor Sam *with Neil Hamilton, 1965. (Columbia Pictures)*

Fund-raising for Israel with former Miss America Bess Myerson, 1967. (Courtesy of the author)

In London, on an art-buying spree, EGR displays purchases, 1971. (Courtesy of the author)

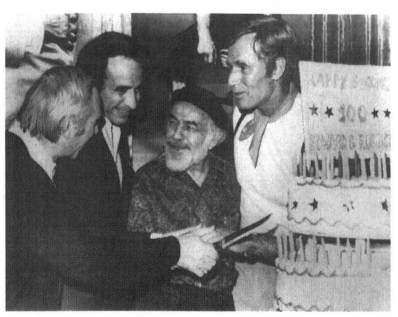

Celebrating the end of production of his 101st movie with Soylent Green director Richard Fleischer, studio executive Daniel Melnick, and star Charlton Heston, 1972. (AP)

Painting of EGR with his mother, by EGR. (UP1)

tect the innocent." Among those in attendance at the meetings were Nick and Joe Schenck, Spyrous Skouras, Warner, Mayer, Barney Balaban of Paramount, and RKO's Dore Schary, who had previously been counted among the liberals on the issue. At one stroke the producers had not only allowed, but almost *advocated*, blacklisting and loyalty oaths. The lists that had been talked about in whispers were now forced out of the bottom drawers of desks. The blacklisting and graylisting had begun.

Perhaps Robinson remained unaware of all this. Although he had not been active in the CFA while filming *All My Sons*, he quickly put his name on subsequent advertisements when filming was completed on December 5. He knew there had been nothing wrong in what he had done politically, so had nothing to fear, and besides, he went from filming *Sons* to *Key Largo* almost immediately. There wasn't time to worry. As far as he was concerned, thanks to his performance at the "I Am an American" Day rally, his name would be counted among the patriotic. If there was any other problem, he could take care of it.

The signals were all there for Robinson to note. In a two-column front-page editorial, on December 2, Billy Wilkerson implored the industry, "Let's Go to the Movies." He hammered away his point that films were there to entertain and they would remain that way. "We think our major production battle has been won," he wrote. "We are ridding ourselves of those who have spread discontent, because their leaders wanted to ruin our business because our business, with its happy entertainment, was ruining their cause of Communism." Inside the same issue, on page four, a story headlined "Red Action Mulled at Writer, Director, Producer, Huddles" ran next to the editorial. "The industry's new Commie ban, how to apply it, and what to do about it, occasioned a producer huddle yesterday and Writer and Director board meetings that ran far into the night," the article stated. Even the American Civil Liberties Union seemed powerless to change the coming policy. Its director, Roger Baldwin, was quoted in the article as saying, "We do not question the industry's right to suspend employees cited for contempt of Congress until they are acquitted or purged of the charges. To deny employment to men in positions where their views may influence the content of pictures is reasonable. To deny it in other positions is not."

On December 11 Robinson was home, resting after the end of production on *Sons* and learning his lines for *Key Largo*. The trade papers carried a story that must have touched home. Charles Chaplin, who had been named with him by Howard Rushmore, was leaving Hollywood. The man who had helped form United Artists declared that "Hollywood is dying" and that it was standardizing its films. Chaplin acknowledged that a few cranks had been calling him a Communist, and that he had decided to move to Europe. In his Trade Views column the same day, Wilkerson said good riddance.

Six days later, in another page-one editorial entitled "A Molotov among Us," Wilkerson reported on the latest meeting of the Screen Writers Guild in which Dalton Trumbo had attacked his accusers in the industry. Wilkerson declared in bold type, "Something must be done about these people! It must be done immediately!" He added, "There are several ways of doing it" but did not elaborate. He didn't need to.

Robinson was implicated again and again, and all too often on a national basis. On November 24, his old friend Helen Gahagan Douglas, wife of Melvyn Douglas and a representative to Congress from California, demanded on the House floor to hear a list of films thought to be subversive before the government continued its attacks on Hollywood. Where was the menace? The response she received was blatantly anti-Semitic, and not censured. John Rankin, Democrat from Mississippi, took the floor to counterattack the petitions from Hollywood against what HUAC was doing:

Here is a petition condemning the Committee. I am going to read some of the names on that petition. One is June Havoc. Her real name is June Hovick. Another is Danny Kaye, and we found out his real name is David Daniel Kaminsky . . . another one is Eddie Cantor, whose real name is Edward Iskowitz. There is one who calls himself Edward Robinson. His real name is Emanuel Goldenberg. There is another here who calls himself Melvyn Douglas, whose real name is Melvyn Hesselberg.

But not everyone was losing in the dynamics of the political fronts. In her December 2 column, Louella Parsons had nothing but praise for Ronald Reagan's activities and conduct. "You can be sure that Jack Warner, who is fighting communism in Hollywood along with other producers, is giving Ronnie the break he deserves," she wrote. (Actually, although Reagan was no longer playing second leads, he was still making B pictures.) But at the Screen Actors Guild, he was now undisputed top dog. At the HUAC hearings he had been a lame-duck president filling out the term of Robert Montgomery. A month later he had been elected to his first full term, the first of six, five of which would be during the blacklisting period.

Robinson was fully aware of these events and certainly discussed them with friends, but his work always came first and work now meant *Key Largo*. It was a film that would involve long hours, with production lasting from December 1947 through March 1948, ending more than twenty days over schedule. Now a classic, it is the story of an embittered former army officer (ironically played on stage by Muni) named Frank McCloud, a good vehicle for Bogart. McCloud has come to a run-down Florida Keys hotel run by James Temple (Lionel Barrymore) and his daughter-in-law (Bacall). Temple's deceased son had been McCloud's buddy. Staying in the hotel is a sadistic gangster named Johnny Rocco, whose luck with the law may have run out, but who still has the power and financial resources to get to Cuba and then to Europe, when the time is right. Meanwhile, he has taken over the hotel with his entourage. The story follows McCloud's renewal of the life spirit and his eventual killing of Rocco.

The set was a pleasant place to be. Portraying Rocco's dame was Claire Trevor, Robinson's sidekick from the *Big Town* radio broadcasts. Lauren Bacall would have tea for the stars in her dressing room most days, where Robinson would delight the assembled with stories, often told with a thick Yiddish accent. Although Bogart was now a bigger star than Robinson, he made Robinson feel it was still the other way around, knocking on his dressing-room door and calling the older man to the set each morning. Bogart had even agreed that Robinson's name could be listed 50 percent above his on the credits and in advertisements for the film, although Bogart's name positioning to the left of the screen and in the cast titles could technically give him top billing. That the film was from Warner Bros., a lot that Robinson had not been near for more than five years, made the making of the picture all that much sweeter emotionally.

The first sight the audience has of Johnny Rocco is the gangster naked in his bathtub, a cigar in his mouth, and firearms around him. It is a powerful image. Through the course of the film, Rocco browbeats James Temple (Barrymore), who is crippled and uses a wheelchair; he humiliates Gaye (Trevor) by making her sing in order to have a drink; and he causes the death of innocent Indians, whom Rocco had accused of killing a sheriff's deputy (a deed he himself had committed). Bogart, too, suffers, being physically beaten by Rocco, but in the end Rocco is left alone, begging for his life from Bogart.

Politically, the set was—at first—a haven for Robinson as well. Bogart, Bacall, and Huston, the director, were all members of the Committee for the First Amendment, as was producer Jerry Wald (although Huston would not allow him on the set). Yet, as the filming progressed, the militant liberalism of all involved began to wane. Hollywood conservatives were not standing for it.

The anti-Communist crusade in Hollywood did not stand still while *Key Largo* was being filmed. On January 2, Billy Wilkerson resumed his watchdog stance, claiming in his Trade Views column that individuals who had testified before HUAC as friendly witnesses were being kept out of employment by key-placed Commies. He listed no names, and one is hard-pressed to figure out who he meant, considering that Menjou, Reagan, and McCarey all worked in 1947 and 1948. Wilkerson insisted "there are still a lot of Commies on our studio payrolls." The same issue featured a page-one article, "Congress's Schedule Clear of Industry Legislation in 1948," stating that for the first time in many years there were no bills before either house that affected Hollywood directly.

On January 6, about fourteen hundred people filled Hollywood Post 43 of the American Legion to honor the "Friendly 21," witnesses such as Reagan, Disney, Cooper, Murphy, Menjou, and the others who had testified the past October. *The Hollywood Reporter* covered the event, and in his Trade Views of the next day, Wilkerson published the congressionally sanctioned definition of a Communist organization, the first part being "hatred of God and all forms of religion." Communists in the industry, he reported, "are now getting blown up themselves."

A two-paragraph article on January 27 said that lawsuits initiated by Adrian Scott, Edward Dmytryk, Lester Cole, and Ring Lardner Jr.—all members of the Hollywood 19 and the latter three in contempt of HUAC—would be going to federal court. The Trade Views of the day condemned the Actors Laboratory, insisting that "its primary function apparently is to draw young actors and actresses into the orbit of Communist front organizations." Several of the Hollywood 19 and others who were already blacklisted—including Gale Sondergaard, the Academy Award-winning actress—were listed in Wilkerson's latest attack.

Wilkerson was in high spirits in his Trade Views of January 30. The "pinkos" had been complaining that there was a blacklist against them, he reported. "But there is nothing they can do about it." Wilkerson pointed out that there was no way for a writer to "prove he is being denied employment because of his political beliefs," adding, "The industry is entitled to this laugh. It's been used, tricked, swindled, lied to, and dangerously hurt by these law-users. But times have changed. This time it's a case of 'man bites dog' . . . and that's news."

Robinson read these diatribes on the set of *Key Largo*, as did his colleagues and the rest of the Committee for the First Amendment members. Although the founders of the CFA had gone to great lengths to make sure there were no suspect members, the Red-baiters were having a field day with the list of CFA-advertisement signers. (Eventually, as many as eighty-four of those who signed the advertisements would have trouble finding work or have no work at all.) As the attacks continued, the enthusiasm of the CFA members vanished. Ed Sullivan warned his old pal Bogie that the country was beginning to see him as Red because of his politics. Bogart's reaction was to tell interviewer Lillian Ross, "Roosevelt was a good politician. He could handle those babies in Washington, but they're too smart for guys like me. Hell, I'm no politician. That's what I mean when I said our Washington trip was a mistake."

Off the set, Robinson's file was growing at the FBI, and the government investigators for HUAC were hearing about it. The Los Angeles Division of the Bureau had received an anonymous letter stating:

A remark dropped to me by a gentleman of Red leanings who thinks I am of that ilk. The information is that Edward Robinson who was born with a strictly Russian name holds secret meetings at his palatial home and is attended by Reds of the upper strata. As a front they are supposed to inspect his gallery of paintings. These visitors are actors, writers, and members of the motion-picture industry. Robinson is recognised as one of our great character actors. I think it is a good idea to investigate these meetings, and perhaps it might develop into something worthwhile.

The letter was signed "An American." The Bureau did a fingerprint check and a handwriting analysis but was unable to determine who sent the note.

When *Largo* filming was completed in March, the militancy that the cast had shared in December was gone. The CFA was dead. Bogart had published an article in that month's *Photoplay* announcing, "I'm no Communist." They made him a "dope," Bogart insisted, as he succeeded in removing all possible Red taint from his reputation. Robinson was not so lucky, and he felt Bogie had betrayed him. He was even more alone now, and while he had never been all that close to Bogart, there would now never be truly warm contact between them again. Bogart had backed down.

Robinson did not have the same opportunity, even had he wanted it at this juncture. The FBI would not allow it. The Bureau was well aware that Gladys was planning to leave for Europe in early April (to attend an exhibition of her paintings). For the Bureau, this was a chance to do additional investigations to see if the Robinsons had espionage contacts. "Review of Los Angeles files reflects definite possibility Edward G. Robinson and wife, Gladys Lloyd Robinson, involved in Russian espionage activities," a memo stated. "Robinson reported to be a member of the CP [Communist Party]. He is a known associate of various CP members and the sponsor of many Communist dominated and CP front organizations. Los Angeles office received anonymous letter advising that Robinson was using his paintings as a cover for Communist meetings."

Robinson was not fully aware of the "case" being built against him, but the month of aggravation caused by the innuendos in the press was salvaged by his reviews for *All My Sons*, which were excellent. The film was not a box office blockbuster, but for Robinson, the decision to take the part had paid off.

He took only a few months of rest. Gladys was in Europe, Sam Jaffe was in residence on Rexford Drive. Robinson spent his time painting in his studio and preparing for his next film, again with top billing. Entitled *Night Has a Thousand Eyes*, Robinson played a professional mentalist who predicts the deaths of his vaudeville partner, his partner's wife, his partner's daughter, and eventually his own. When it was released in October it was a financial washout. But his July notices for *Key Largo* were good enough to keep him on top, or so he thought.

And despite the heat of HUAC, Robinson still found causes he believed were necessary to endorse. On August 2, he lent his name to the American Council for a Democratic Greece, along with Albert Einstein, Arthur Garfield Hays of the ACLU, and W. E. B. DuBois. And the pressures of HUAC had still not altered Robinson's sense of friendship and decency, his belief in what America stood for. Dalton Trumbo wrote to him from prison begging for money, as his family was about penniless. Robinson lent him $2,500, not realizing it was one more sin on an ever growing list.

He also found time to make his first trip to Israel, which impressed him greatly. When he returned in October, he asked Albert Maltz to write him a speech, which Robinson delivered at Israeli bond fund-raisers across the country.

At the end of the year there was yet another film role waiting—the pressures of the Red hunt had not quite destroyed his career. It was *House of Strangers* at 20th Century Fox, in which he played another Italian-Sicilian despot, this one a usurer. The film really belonged to the young lovers, portrayed by Susan Hayward and Richard Conte, but Robinson had top billing and, as usual, his dynamism stole the show. Fox held the film's release over until 1949 in order to display it at the Cannes Film Festival that spring. It was a good move. For his work as Gino Monetti, Robinson earned an award as best character actor, the only major trophy he would earn during his lifetime for his work on the screen. It was an award that should have been his crowning achievement—but his world collapsed around him instead.

Hollywood was now fully involved in the fight against the Communist menace, and a film entitled just that—*The Red Menace*—had been produced. But the rest of the country had been seized with the fears of Reds as well. In Washington, Alger Hiss was on trial. So was an obscure former analyst for the Department of Justice. Her name was Judith Coplon, and she had been arrested on March 4 along with her Soviet lover, Valentin A. Gubitchev, for allegedly stealing FBI data slips, intending to give them to the Russians. She had acquired, it seems, lists of known Communists in America. The government prosecutors wanted to have only particular slips read into the record and even balked at that because the material might be sensitive.

The defense attorneys had other ideas, though, and on June 8 her attorneys read into the record extensive FBI files that they considered necessary in order to judge the extent of the material Coplon had allegedly stolen, and to judge whether it was vital to national security. It could mean a difference in the length of her jail sentence if she was convicted. The objection by the prosecution was overruled.

The headlines the next day did not make clear just how the reports tied in with the Coplon case. Instead, they heralded that "Movie Stars Called Red at Coplon Trial." The *New York Times* made it the lead story, although previous articles on the trial had been relegated to inside pages. Among the names revealed by the "FBI Confidential Informant ND 402" were Frederic March, Canada Lee, Florence Eldridge, Dorothy Parker, Donald Ogden Stewart, Albert Maltz, Alvah Bessie, Dalton Trumbo—and Edward G. Robinson.

It was March, not Robinson, who took the brunt of the attacks. He was called an "outstanding Communist Party fellow traveler." Robinson, along with March, John Garfield, Melvyn Douglas, and Paul Muni, was cited for having been praised by publications—many of them foreign—connected to the Soviet-dominated Comintern. Robinson wasted no time in denying any involvement. "I am not now, nor have I ever been a member of the Communist Party," he said in a statement to the press. "Nor have I been remotely connected with the party. These rantings, accusations, smearing and character assassinations can only emanate from sick, diseased minds of people who rush to the press with indictments of good citizens."

Since they were both named, Albert Maltz contacted Robinson and asked him to join a protest against the release of the reports. Robinson refused. He told Maltz he would contact his old friend J. Edgar Hoover instead. He sent Hoover a telegram, but his only response was a formal postcard. Hoover, his "friend," had been keeping a record on him. His attorneys instead investigated the possibility of Robinson's flying to Washington and appearing at the trial to refute the charges in the report. It was decided this was not appropriate.

But Robinson's reaction did not go overlooked by Billy Wilkerson. Using the report released at the trial as fodder for what he had been saying all along—that Hollywood was filled with Reds—he printed on June 13 that Robinson was about to grab a plane and have a showdown with Hoover. Robinson dashed off a letter to Wilkerson that very morning, which was published in the Trade Views column the next day.

"I have become sick and tired of the insinuations and innuendos which from time to time have been cast upon my worthiness as an American citizen," Robinson wrote, repeating that he was not a Communist and never had been. "I have been a member of organizations during the war years which were formed for worthy purposes—the preservation of our American way of life," he continued.

What hurt him more was that the country was beginning to notice. On June 8, the very day his name was read into the record at the Coplon trial, there was an attack from another force—the right-wing Christians. Gerald L. K. Smith took aim at Robinson at a meeting of the Christian Nationalist Crusade attended by 750 people at the Embassy Auditorium in downtown Los Angeles. Robinson had, in 1945, marched in protest at a Smith rally. "Eddie Cantor and Edward G. Robinson are Communists," Smith blasted to the crowd. "Robinson's real name is Emanuel Goldenberg. Robinson is one of Stalin's main agents in Hollywood. Frederic March is part of the Stalin machine in Hollywood. Edward G. Robinson should be put in a Federal penitentiary. I'm not big, but I've been fighting the right people down through the years."

Certainly Smith's tirade was filled with racism. A few minutes later he railed, "Please the Jews—that's where the money is. If you have anything at all to sell to a Jew, just start out by cussing me and they'll buy it. I know people who've made a business out of it." But it was a speech he was making across the nation, one that was going to be heard by thousands of potential theater ticket buyers. However sickened the Jewish moguls might be by what Smith was saying, they were also afraid to go near the men he was smearing.

Adding to it all, Robinson had problems at home again. Gladys had been overcome by the pressures of the HUAC hearings, and their subsequent effects on her household, and had had another breakdown. The pattern was the same as always: She sued Eddie for divorce, and he put her into Menninger's for treatment. But this time, he didn't get to her in time, and Gladys had a chance to tell the press of her plans. Besides fending off the myriad questions on his political activities, Robinson now had to discuss his home situation.

There were no script offers from any of the studios, and no help pending from Washington "friends." The only work Robinson had had all year was a cameo as himself in *It's a Great Feeling* from Warner Bros., which ironically also featured Ronald Reagan in a similar cameo (the only time they appeared in the same movie).

He seemed in good graces at his old studio, so he called Jack Warner and set up a breakfast meeting, hoping for some help with the situation, to get back on the lists that would put him to work. It was a warm summer day when they met. Robinson decided to play the meeting calmly. He tried to be soft-spoken, crack a few Yiddish jokes, to start with talk about old times. Warner was not interested in small talk. He raved on about his theory of Communism, which was that "Communists are cracked." He told Robinson that it was important that the Jews in the industry wash their hands of anyone or anything that was the least bit pink. Warner told Robinson of how the Jewish moguls had risen from the bottom to where they were today. Robinson didn't say a word. He nervously folded his napkin into smaller and smaller pieces.

Finally, Warner got to the point. He offered his Little Caesar no immediate aid but did say he'd contact a few friends who had influence with the FBI, such as the writer George Sokolsky. And he suggested that Robinson talk to the president of his union, Ronnie Reagan, which Robinson thought a surprising suggestion since Warner and Reagan were about to part company. Warner left the meeting as soon as he had finished the last sip of his coffee. Robinson went home feeling ill. Warner went right to his office, smiling and mentioning to an aide that it had been a successful meeting.

All Robinson received from his union leaders—Reagan included—was the cold shoulder and a reminder of what Bogie had done to relieve himself of the Red taint. Robinson, at this point, not only refused to write an article about being duped by Communists, he was in no position to purge himself. The California state version of HUAC had published their list of "known" Communists, and he was on it. There could be no public restitution at this time.

Hollywood was too hot for him, but he still had friends. Gregory Ratoff had gone to London to make a film for Columbia, and he invited Robinson to Britain to take the leading role. Gladys had just come back from Menninger's and was temporarily recovered. Manny had dropped out of high school. The time seemed right to take the family on another trip to Europe.

Ratoff's film was not a success. Called *Operation X* in Europe and *My Daughter Joy* in America, it was the story of a ruthless businessman (Robinson) who plots to marry his daughter to a Middle Eastern sultan in order to gain control of an ingredient, called "X," with which he can rule the world. The daughter loves a journalist. In order to give the daughter some happiness, her mother reveals to Robinson that Georgette is not really his daughter. The news destroys his spirit and dooms the project. He will not rule the world. The one saving grace about *Operation* for the Robinsons was that it was shot all over Europe, so they had another tour of the Continent on Columbia.

While in Rome, they bumped into Elia Kazan, an old friend, who took an interest in Manny's desire to pursue an acting career. When the Robinson's returned to Beverly Hills that fall, Manny went to New York to study at the Neighborhood Playhouse. Kazan had arranged it all. Robinson was hesitant. Manny was a mature sixteen, but still a minor. Kazan's family agreed to watch over the teenager and dole out his allowance. Manny would stay at a hotel. Sam Jaffe, who was back in New York, also promised to make himself available. Eddie really had little choice. Neither he nor Gladys was able to deal with their rebellious son—who had found his way into the liquor cabinet once too often, who had hosted parties with underage girls at the family ranch. Manny was beyond Robinson's control. In New York he would have to stand on his own feet, and Eddie reasoned the experience would do him good.

Although HUAC had not scheduled any more hearings and the Hollywood Ten were either behind bars or on their way there, the issue of

Reds in the movie capital would not die. People like Billy Wilkerson would not let it die. On October 13 he accused the Communists in the industry of being responsible for the failure of any studio to make a film about Cardinal Mindszenty of Hungary, who was rotting in a Soviet prison. Wilkerson said it was because the Communists charged the cardinal with hating Jews, or, put another way, it was the Jews in the industry who were keeping the film from being made.

A month later, the so-called right wing retained their control of the Screen Writers Guild in the union elections. Anyone suspected of Left sympathies was not welcome in the hierarchy.

Arguments throughout town on the new hiring practices were prevalent. Sam Wood, who had founded the Motion Picture Alliance, died of a heart attack following a heated discussion with Margaret Sullavan over his refusal to hire blacklisted writers.

Robinson passed Christmas that year back in Hollywood with no employment and no offers. He could no longer move freely to Europe, because when his passport expired he was not allowed to renew it. The early months of 1950 were taken up by two activities—painting in his studio to retain his sanity, and using any means possible to secure a chance to clear himself before HUAC. He also went to great efforts to have his name expunged from the rosters of the offending progressive organizations to which he had so proudly belonged. In April he wrote to HICCASP asking that his name be removed from the membership list.

No one in Hollywood seemed willing or able to help him. Again he went to Ronald Reagan and George Murphy asking for their aid. Reagan refused outright. Robinson told Murphy that the speech he had made in 1946 urging the start of a dialogue between the IATSE and the CSU was written for him. Robinson insisted that he hadn't known what he was saying—but Murphy could offer no assistance.

But Robinson was not ready to completely lose his pride. When Red-baiting writer Victor Lasky offered him a twenty-six-page "confession" of his Communist and fellow-traveler activities, Robinson angrily declined to sign. Instead, he tried another step and sought the advice of the B'nai

Brith's Anti-Defamation League. They were sympathetic and offered to use their channels to try to get Robinson his all-important hearing.

Liberal activities were out of the question for him now. So, in many cases, was charity. On June 1, Albert Maltz sent him a three-page hand-written letter asking for contributions for a fund to help the families of the Hollywood Ten, since the breadwinners were either in jail or bankrupt from legal fees. "Several of the families are utterly destitute," Maltz pleaded. "They have no resources, no place to turn, no relatives upon whom to lean." Robinson refused to contribute. Cleo Trumbo, wife of Dalton, wrote to him on August 17, asking for a character reference so that Trumbo could be paroled. Robinson declined, for his own preservation, to provide such a letter. He would have no further pleas from the Hollywood Ten.

In June a book had been published that had further damaged Robinson. The soft cover bore the picture of a microphone entrapped by a red hand on its cover. The text would make it the bible of the graylist. The book was *Red Channels*, and it immediately found its place in the consciousness of advertisers and TV and radio casting offices and other such agencies. Robinson was but one of 151 people, and his "contribution" filled the bottom of page 122 and most of page 123. He was identified as an "actor—screen, radio" and listed as a member of ten suspect organizations, among them the American Committee for the Foreign Born, the Civil Rights Congress, the Progressive Citizens of America, the American Committee for Yugoslav Relief, and HICCASP. He was also said to be a sponsor of a Soviet Russia Today dinner.

Since Robinson had not yet worked in television, *Red Channels* did not have a visible effect on his employment, as it did on others in New York. But he had no chance of working on radio after the book was published. He attempted to join in protests with others who were listed, even sending a telegram to a September meeting of the American Federation of Radio Artists and SAG in New York in support of Jean Muir, who had already lost her job. Yet, essentially, he decided to move on his own.

"His position and mine were completely different," Lionel Stander recalled. "I thought there was a danger for the country in helping the Committee or becoming involved. HUAC was part of a conspiracy to impose censorship. Robinson was scared green. He was afraid for his security. He thought he could deal with them. He thought he could get himself off the list. He capitulated."

Robinson thought his world was caving in. Manny was in New York but had become involved with a model several years his senior. Gladys would come and go to Europe, unable to offer any support because of her own mental problems. Friend Sam Jaffe had been working on *The Asphalt Jungle* in Los Angeles and helped, but his own problems with the graylist were beginning. Niece Beulah Robinson visited Los Angeles and brightened her uncle's life, but she was too young to fully understand what was happening.

And his union was doing all it could do to aid the right wing. On September 17, the Screen Actors Guild mailed a press release proclaiming its enlistment in the Crusade for Freedom: "The following telegram was sent: 'Dear General Clay: The more than 8,000 members of the Screen Actors Guild are proud to enlist in the Crusade for Freedom and to take an active part in the battle for men's minds now being waged around the world. We offer you our complete support in this great counter-offensive against Communist lies and treachery. Please call on us.'" It was signed, "Sincerely, Board of Directors, Screen Actors Guild, by Ronald Reagan, president."

Morris Ernst, a friend of Robinson and a partner in the New York law firm of Greenbaum, Wolff and Ernst, was able finally to help. Through contacts, particularly Sam Yorty, a California congressman, Ernst arranged for Robinson to have a hearing in executive session with HUAC's staff—the congressmen themselves being unavailable since the campaign for re-election was in full swing. There were serious preparations for Robinson, and here the Anti-Defamation League became invaluable.

Joseph Roos, who had once been a story assistant to Jesse Lasky, was in 1950 director of community relations for the League and unofficial head of public relations for the Jewish community. He always had a good rapport with Robinson and had called upon the actor many times for fund-raisers and radio shows. Robinson had refused him only when studio work interceded. "I spent time with Robinson briefing him," Roos said, still active in 1982. "We went through his checkbook stubs compiling a list of all contributions he had made since 1938. I was able to help him show that he gave to many things that were either nonpolitical or anti-Communist. And that his contributions to groups that were now suspect were made from his honest-to-goodness commitment to freedom . . . For example, there was the Anti-Nazi League," Roos continued. "Everyone was in it. Yes, there were leftists, but also people who were right of center. I found that Archbishop Cantwell was on the Board of Directors. I had Robinson develop that line."

It was not an easy time, but Roos was able to stand the brunt of Robinson's anger. "He was short-tempered, impatient. I had never seen him that way. I lectured him about not losing his patience when he got his chance before the Committee in Washington. He listened, but I can only describe the situation by saying there was vinegar in his stomach. The man had given tirelessly of himself to causes he held dear and now he was paying for it. And they were making him answer for it."

Roos also arranged for Robinson to make several Voice of America broadcasts in New York before his Washington appearance. He arranged for the *New Leader* to do an article on Robinson's record and the unfairness of *Red Channels*.

As Robinson prepared for his trip east, Hollywood was fighting to decide just how to protect its image and punish its liberal bad seeds. On October 2 the Screen Directors Guild sent non-Communist affidavits to its members, although the consequences for those who did not sign was not explained. A war raged between the Motion Picture Industry Council, the Motion Picture Alliance, and the talent guilds over just how strong the loyalty oaths requested by the studio should be. An early draft was very specific about what the good Hollywood people should say: that they are

Americans; that Stalin is responsible for the war in Korea; and that Marxism, Leninism, and Stalinism lead to totalitarianism. The Alliance wanted something much stronger. Many writers and actors thought the concept of a loyalty oath was un-American, but few would step forward to say so. The Industry Council favored oaths.

Robinson left for New York just as the fighting was reaching a peak in the trade reports. On October 23 he played the role of Molotov, the Soviet leader, in a Voice of America broadcast, the essence of which is evident in the last line, when the character says, "America is the stumbling block . . . but I think we can handle her. In fact, the more earnestly she tries for a just peace, the more we can show her blocking the road to peace; the more she arms to defend nations against aggression, the more of a warmonger we can make her." Robinson was helping to fight the Cold War.

Two days later he made another Voice of America broadcast, this one in Rumanian to his former countrymen. Robinson reminded his listeners that he was one of the few actors in America of Rumanian descent, then said, "The Communist rulers aim at cutting Rumania's ties with the Western world, of enslaving the soul and the culture of the Rumanian people, exactly as they have done with its political and economic institutions."

Meanwhile, Morris Ernst wrote to J. Edgar Hoover asking that the FBI record on Robinson be cleared of any taint. Ernst, who was not Robinson's attorney and helped him only as a friend, reminded Hoover of Robinson's good deeds, the major contributions to worthy causes. There was no response from Hoover prior to Robinson's scheduled appearance before the HUAC executive staff.

Ernst wrote to Robinson at the Hotel Gotham in New York telling him not to worry about the Committee, that he had done nothing to be ashamed of. He said that a meeting with Hoover would not be possible—or feasible—and that Robinson should offer himself to the army as a potential entertainer for the troops in Korea. Ernst also promised to continue his efforts to get Robinson's name out of *Red Channels*.

The events had, understandably, created unbearable anxiety in Robinson. His hair began to thin noticeably, and the gray was evident, the black dye gone. There was no sleep, no fun with his family in New York, no obligatory tours of the art galleries on Madison Avenue. There was only fear.

At noon on Friday, October 27, Robinson had his first appearance before HUAC, in executive session before the Committee's staff with attorney Raymond Bell. Conservatively dressed in a dark suit, Robinson entered room 226 of the Old House Office Building looking nothing like Little Caesar: The spunk had been replaced by nervousness; the snarl had temporarily given way to a respectful tone. His hair was combed back, his eyes hidden by dark glasses (one of the rare times he wore them in public).

The hearing, which was chaired by Louis J. Russell, the senior investigator, began by giving Robinson a chance to state his case. Unlike the Hollywood Ten, Robinson would have a full opportunity to make any statements he thought pertinent. There was much he wanted the Committee to be aware of. He introduced into the record his response to *Red Channels*, and it took seven full pages in the published account of the hearing. The statement detailed his social and political activities, insisted he knew not of Communist involvement in such organizations as the Progressive Committee of America and HICCASP, and insisted that he only lent his name and his time to pro-Russian activities during World War II because Russia was an ally of the United States. He stressed that he aided only that alliance and the Russian people, not the Soviet government. Robinson followed by entering into the record a list of the contributions he had made from December 1938 through to December 1949. Filling fourteen pages in the published report, Robinson hoped to emphasize his philanthropy in general, not his occasional contributions to suspect organizations.

He denied published associations with several suspect groups—the Abraham Lincoln Brigade (Americans who went to fight for Loyalist Spain), the Volunteers for Liberty, the National Conference to Win the

Peace, and others. Instead, he entered into the record letters received from several suspect organizations asking for his support and his response to the organizations: In each case he had declined to participate but had sent them his warmest greetings. It was these greetings, Robinson contended, that had been misused as support and sponsorship. He further insisted he had never seen a copy of the *Daily Worker* in his life.

Russell went through organization after organization: The Council on American Soviet Friendship; the Committee for a Democratic Far Eastern Policy; the American Committee for the Protection of the Foreign Born. Robinson denied participation in the first two and said the latter had used his name without his knowledge.

The interrogation continued with a query about the Hollywood Democratic Committee, which they claimed listed Robinson as a candidate for the executive board, according to the ballot of July 26, 1944. Robinson held his breath and bit his lip for a brief moment. What they wanted to hear were details of his involvement in Roosevelt's campaign for reelection. That, too, was now a crime. He responded that the committees to which he had belonged, including HICCASP, were not fronts, but open groups working for FDR. There was a burst of energy and emotion in his voice as Robinson answered this question:

> Mr. Robinson: I was and I still am a great admirer of the late Chief Executive. My own viewpoint on international affairs was in general agreement with that of FDR . . . Extremely conscious of the responsibilities of citizenship, including the right and obligation to vote, I participated actively and through contributions in political campaigns. In 1940 when the Communists opposed FDR and maligned him as a warmonger, I served on the advisory committee of and contributed to the Hollywood for Roosevelt Committee, headed by Pat O'Brien.

He continued with a history of HICCASP, the prominent liberals who had participated, including James Roosevelt. He detailed other groups to which he had subscribed, all organized for Roosevelt and the New Deal, including the National Citizens Political Action Committee.

The staff listened without expression or emotion. Robinson had had his say. Now it was time to get to the meat of the hearing. Was Robinson a Communist? Investigator Courtney E. Owens started the questioning. He read into the record the material from the Judith Coplon trial that had implicated Robinson. Then he asked the questions that Robinson had been waiting for.

> Mr. Owens: Mr. Robinson, in your experience in Hollywood, have you ever been approached or talked to about Communism, or becoming a Communist?
>
> Mr. Robinson: In all my experiences in Hollywood or any place, in all my life, I have never been approached by anybody to join the Communist Party, nor have I heard anyone propagate any Communistic ideas in my presence. I have never had anyone come to me and say, "I'm a Communist."
>
> Mr. Owens: Do you know any Communists?
>
> Mr. Robinson: No, I don't know of any Communists among my friends or acquaintances.
>
> Mr. Owens: And you have never attended a meeting of any kind that you had reason to believe Communists were sponsoring or were attending?
>
> Mr. Robinson: I never attended a meeting that had Communistic sponsorship.
>
> Mr. Owens: Are you acquainted with Paul Robeson?
>
> Mr. Robinson: Yes.
>
> Mr. Owens: Do you have any knowledge regarding his Communist party affiliation or his Communist-front affiliations?
>
> Mr. Robinson: No. I only know what I read about that.

The same question was asked about Dorothy Parker, about Donald Ogden Stewart, who had begun the Anti-Nazi League, and about Ruth McKinney. Robinson insisted he did not know of any Communist involvements they might have had. Then he was asked if he knew Albert Maltz. Robinson mentioned Maltz's writing for *The Red House* but denied personal knowledge as to his alleged Communist affiliations.

The staff wanted to know about his participation in the Committee for the First Amendment. Robinson said he had joined and contributed money because he himself thought a subpoena was on the way. He believed in "freedom of speech, freedom of thought, freedom of expression" and had participated because the accusations against him had been unjust. He had assumed there were unjust accusations against others. But Robinson had changed his mind: "After the men were investigated, or in the process of investigation, after I listened to two or three broadcasts and the way the whole thing was being conducted as far as the men were concerned, I completely lost my sympathy, because I realized I might have been one of the twenty-three taken in by the kind of pattern they used in defending themselves."

The formal questions over, Russell gave Robinson a chance to enter into the record any information that would support his character. Robinson wasted no time in presenting information about his participation in the "I Am an American" Day rally in Chicago, the telegram he had received from Hearst confirming his participation in the rally, and about the Voice of America broadcasts he had done just hours before his appearance at the hearing. He had the texts of the broadcasts entered into the record, with Russell's approval.

His last remarks were clear: "I am prepared to submit myself for further examination at any time to establish unequivocally that I am not now and never have been a member of the Communist Party or any subversive group or a fellow-traveler. I find, and always have found, Communism repugnant to my beliefs. I will fight it as an individual and as an artist, whenever and wherever possible, just as I have always fought tyranny."

Russell ended the hearing by entering into the record that Robinson's name had not appeared on the list of Communist Party members given to the Committee. The meeting was officially concluded at 2:20 P.M. As he left the room, Robinson allowed himself a deep breath and a quiet smile. He had gone through the first test, however agonizing. There was a sense of hope in his conversations with family and friends during the next few days. The chances of the Committee itself seeing him and, hopefully, clearing him, were good, it seemed. Things might be looking up.

After testifying, Robinson went to see Karl Baarslag, head of the American Legion, hoping for support from that quarter. His reception was only cordial. And back in Hollywood on that October 27 few were paying attention to Little Caesar's performance in Washington. Most of Robinson's acquaintances were at Temple Israel, where twenty thousand people attended the funeral of Al Jolson. Robinson would have been there, too, had he been able.

8

LITTLE CAESAR VS. HUAC

Either snap my neck or set me free. If you snap my neck I will
still say I believe in America.

—Edward G. Robinson

One of the first things Robinson did when he returned to Rexford Drive following his testimony was to send a transcript of the hearing to J. Edgar Hoover. He reiterated that he was not a Communist or a fellow traveler and offered to confront any accuser whose name Hoover might have in the records.

Hoover responded in an extremely formal letter dated November 8, completely lacking the personal notes of the 1930s correspondence. He told Robinson, "I believe you have misconceived the true role of the Federal Bureau of Investigation as a strictly investigative agency. We have always maintained that our organization is a fact-finding agency." He further refused Robinson the chance to face any accuser or discover the contents of his FBI file. There would be no more contact between the two men.

Hollywood still shunned Robinson, and he sat at Rexford Drive awaiting a more important call—his chance to appear before HUAC, and not just its investigators. His new attorney—Michael Halperin of the firm of Wilzin and Halperin in New York, who would act for him through the whole ordeal—sent him constant memos, each with the same message. HUAC was procrastinating in setting a date for Robinson's hearing.

Finally, with only a few days' notice, Robinson was summoned before a subcommittee of HUAC on Thursday, December 22, in the same room 226 of the Old House Office Building. With Halperin, he was in the room at 10:40 A.M. that day, seated before the same investigators he had seen in October, as well as Congressmen Francis E. Walter and Harold H. Velde. By his own request, Robinson was to testify under oath. Taking the oath was the first order of business. Then the questioning began.

The first few minutes were spent reviewing—by Louis Russell and Robinson—the events of October. Robinson again stated that he had never attended a Communist Party meeting, "or anything that smacked of communism."

> Mr. Russell: Have you ever volunteered your services as an agent to the Soviet Government or to anyone attached to the Soviet Government?
>
> Mr. Robinson: Never.
>
> Mr. Russell: Mr. Robinson, have you ever made a statement to the effect that you did not care whether or not the Soviet Government took over the United States as long as you would be permitted to keep your art collection?
>
> Mr. Robinson: This is a vicious lie.

Robinson repeated over and over again that nothing was more important to him than his good name and his Americanism. He told the Committee of Gladys's heritage—a family that went all the way back to Valley Forge—and that Manny was eighteen and about to go into the army. He asserted that anyone who was besmirching his name should be brought under oath to repeat his accusations.

The questioning continued along a similar vein, with the sweat beading on Robinson's forehead and Halperin trying to keep him cool. The expressions on his accusers' faces never faltered. Robinson felt the need to apologize for being emotional.

Mr. Robinson: Because I think I have not only been a good citizen, I think I have been an extraordinarily good citizen, and I value this above everything else. I think I may have taken money under false pretenses in my own business, and I may not have been as good a husband or father or friend as I should have been, but I know my Americanism is unblemished and fine and wonderful, and I am proud of it, and I don't feel it is conceit on my part to say this, and I stand on my record or fall on it.

Mr. Walter: I think it might be well for this committee to direct its attention to the charges that have been leveled against many artists. If there are in the theatrical business those who are trying to spread Communist doctrines, we should know it. If there are others who have been charged with that sort of activity and are innocent, that fact should be established as well. The first of the year I shall suggest that this committee direct its attention to ascertaining the truth or falsity of these charges.

Mr. Robinson: I hope that is what you will do. Either snap my neck or set me free. If you snap my neck I will still say that I believe in America.

Mr. Velde: Do you know of any Communist activities in the movie industry?

Mr. Robinson: Not that I know of. I have heard it spoken of, and unquestionably there must be some of that going on. I don't see how Hollywood could be exclusive in that respect. But personally I don't know of such activities.

Robinson did not realize that, at this juncture, HUAC was itching to get Hollywood back on the stand, to start its hearings anew. The witch hunting was actually just beginning, as Robinson sat innocently wiping his brow, and begging for forgiveness for crimes he could not even detail. Russell appeared to be on his side. He told the congressmen, "I have a list of Communists and suspected Communists in Hollywood, and Mr. Robinson's name does not appear on that list. I have in my possession certain registration cards of members of the Communist Party who are now, or who have resided in Hollywood. I have none for Mr. Robinson."

The congressmen did not respond to Russell, so with Halperin's nudging, Robinson took the chance to mention again the further Voice of

America broadcasts. Besides the work prior to his hearing in October, he had just done two broadcasts in Italian a week before this testimony. He also told the Committee that he would go to Korea if the military situation there permitted.

Walter thanked him for his testimony and Robinson was excused. The ordeal had lasted a little over an hour. Robinson thought he was cleared. Russell had said it plainly; no investigation had turned up the slightest hint of Robinson's involvement in Communist affairs in Hollywood. There was no record of a party card, of a party meeting, of a party statement. Robinson was a New Deal man, he had insisted. Perhaps that, in the Republican-dominated Congress, was his main crime.

"This Robinson hearing was a good thing," Walter told the press. "The time has arrived when we should find out what influences have been at work in Hollywood, who was responsible for the charges of Communism, and who is not a Red. I think we should offer everybody who has even been accused an opportunity to come before us and clear his reputation of these charges. I favor a full and complete investigation of the charges and rumors." Despite that, clearance from Hollywood still did not come, and now there was the possibility of an even bigger investigation.

The day after Christmas, Robinson's press agent released a statement announcing that Robinson had been cleared by the Committee. The two-page press release contained quotation after quotation from the beleaguered star insisting he was no Red. On the same day, Louella Parsons wrote in her national column, "Now that Eddie Robinson has been completely cleared of those Communist charges by Uncle Sam himself, it's time the whispering stopped." A few days later Walter Winchell wrote a similar statement in his column, and Robinson fired off a telegram telling the most famous gossip broadcaster in America, "You have helped to make it a happier New Year for me."

On December 29, after advice from counsel, he wrote to HUAC, adding a statement to his testimony. Robinson said that he had never volunteered his services to any Soviet agent. While in London during the war he had had a brief conversation with a Russian official about making a goodwill trip to Eastern Europe: Nothing ever came of it, but Robinson wanted HUAC to know he was coming completely clean. This later fact was added to his testimony.

Now, indeed, Robinson thought himself cleared of all rumors and innuendos. Although there was still no official word from HUAC, Robinson assumed their clean bill of health was on the way. He spent New Year's Eve with family and friends celebrating, but in his mind at all times was the supposition that he'd be going back to work soon.

HUAC released an evaluation of the Robinson hearings on January 10, but their assessment was far more tepid than Robinson would have wanted. He was cleared of all suspicions of being a Communist or fellow traveler, but the Committee members also started telling the press that all suspected Reds should have an equal chance to clear themselves. Yet, what HUAC said about Robinson still did not do the trick. There were no offers, and he was still shunned by the studio heads and right-wingers in Hollywood. Apparently, he was not fully cleared in *their* minds. His agents—Bert Allenberg and Abe Lastfogel of the William Morris Agency—tried to get someone in town to give him work, but there were no takers.

Robinson took matters into his own hands and on January 23 mailed letters and copies of his testimony to the moguls—including Jack Warner, L. B. Mayer, Sam Goldwyn, and Darryl Zanuck. The letter to Warner is representative:

Because you have always been militant and forthright in your own views of Americanism, and have put the quality of Americanism above many other considerations in your estimate of those whom you deal with, I am happy to send you the accompanying complete report of my recent two voluntary appearances before the Un-American Activities Committee . . . As you will see, the hearings were thorough and impersonal, and resulted in the kind of vindication I sought when I offered to appear before the Committee and face under oath any evidence which they could produce from any quarter . . . I hope the findings of Congress will be given as much recognition as the unfounded opinions which for a time at least were held by some, and which the hearings have now proved as groundless as they always were.

Not one of the studio executives responded. Robinson was forced to send a similar letter and the transcripts to Hedda Hopper, using mutual friends to plead on his behalf. Hopper would not follow Louella Parsons's example and clear him.

Nor would the crusading Red hunters in the country. The reactionary publication *Alert* had two pages on Robinson's testimony in its January 25, 1951, edition. The first line was clear: "The House Un-American Activities Committee has not cleared actor Edward G. Robinson, as Robinson would have the public believe, and as some of the trade and daily press have reported." Robinson was accused of having tried to "whitewash" his associations, and *Alert* again published the list of the so-called front organizations.

Alert was not impressed by the list of donations from 1939 to 1949 that Robinson had entered into the record at HUAC. The newsletter thought this was just part of the "formula" that Hollywood Reds would be using. *Alert* was not impressed that Robinson had "professed his wholehearted support of the United States." "The fact remains that the subcommittee and the Committee staff did not question him fully about many of his front affiliations," the newsletter noted. "The subcommittee did not recommend, and the Committee as a whole did not pass, any motion stating that Robinson had purged himself of his affinity for joining Communist causes and fronts." *Alert* insisted that Robinson could have "listed those who got him into Communist fronts"—named names. That information, according to the newsletter, "is important to our security." Therefore, as far as the right wing was concerned, Robinson was still suspect. The attitude influenced Hollywood, and no one would give him work.

Nor was the FBI satisfied. The Bureau told all its divisions to reinterview its sources and investigate Robinson anew. The New York Division reported that Robinson frequented two business establishments when in New York—A. Sulka and Company on Fifth Avenue and C. T. Loo and Company on East 57th Street. These stores were to be investigated along with Robinson "for any information of a possible espionage significance not previously reported." In Hollywood terms, this was a page from the classic factual film *The House on 92nd Street*, where the proprietor of a woman's clothing store was a head Nazi agent. But, unlike the movie, there were no espionage agents at A. Sulka and Company.

Oddly enough, Robinson's support came from unexpected sources, such as *The Hollywood Reporter*, where Billy Wilkerson wrote that Robinson "appealed for a hearing, was heard and received absolution." Robinson again made a public statement on February 9, repeating that he had gone before the Committee voluntarily, had laid himself bare, and—he thought—had cleared himself. But, he added, "I have no hesitancy in placing myself at the disposal of the Committee until they are completely satisfied on every score."

But the next day, HUAC reorganized for the 82nd Congress. The Committee said new hearings would take place in both Washington and Los Angeles and that Robinson might be recalled. Several members asserted that Robinson had been permitted to come and make self-serving statements to the subcommittee and investigators. No witnesses were heard who claimed to have proof of his Communist affiliations.

Robinson realized he had not cleared himself but had instead triggered an even bigger witch hunt. The day of purging one's past and friendships was about to begin. Already Ronald Reagan was lining up people on the blacklist and graylist who were willing to tell all before the Committee. He would not see Robinson, but on February 2, Reagan and his aides spoke to Edward Dmytryk, the director and member of the Hollywood Ten who had recently been paroled. Dmytryk told the SAG president he was ready to come clean, and Reagan began using channels to try to get him a hearing. Sterling Hayden would also come clean, and Reagan offered him his help as well. For Robinson there was nothing.

There was no word from the Committee, no word from Reagan, no work. Robinson sat at home with Gladys, who was healthier than she had been in years and sharing the burden of the times with her husband. His hair was thinning, his time was spent painting. Gladys organized a few small dinner parties with close friends, hoping they would cheer Eddie up. At these events, the cigar would bob from hand to mouth, the Yiddish-dialect jokes would be told. But his mind was always on HUAC, always on getting back to work, always on ridding himself of the Red taint.

On March 4, he received a letter from the Red-hunting newsletter *Counter-Action*, offering to help him. Managing editor Hal Denman indicated, "We are writing this letter because we are fairly well convinced that you are innocent." But the letter also sent chills up Robinson's spine. Denman offered to go through Robinson's speeches from 1942 to 1947 and mark passages that would indicate Robinson's "innocence." That, alone, was not chilling, but the fact that Denman had in his possession copies of the speeches was. The text of Robinson's speeches on politics, human rights, civil rights, war bonds, Israel—all were available and circulating, possibly thanks to the FBI file. Robinson refused to become involved with Denman.

It was March, and that meant the annual ritual of the Academy Awards in Hollywood. This year three of the nominees were performers who were on the graylists: Jose Ferrer for *Cyrano de Bergerac*, Judy Holliday for *Born Yesterday*, and Robinson's close friend Sam Jaffe for *The Asphalt Jungle*. Perhaps their nominations were the Hollywood liberals' safe way of making a statement. Whatever the reason, the right wing was up in arms, and the situation in town was inflamed.

Ward Bond, the treasurer of the Motion Picture Alliance for the Preservation of American Ideals, was elected by the right wing to take the offensive on what they perceived to be an affront to the purge. This was long before the television series *Wagon Train*, and Bond—although a pal of John Wayne's—was hardly a household name. He was a journeyman character actor who had appeared with Robinson in such films as *Confessions of a Nazi Spy* and *Manpower*. They had had no scenes together in the former, but Bond along with Alan Hale had broken up the fistfight between Robinson and George Raft during the filming of *Manpower*. Still, Robinson hardly knew him.

In an exclusive interview in *Daily Variety* on March 14, Bond went after Jose Ferrer, Robinson, and other suspected Reds. He boasted that the

MPA had been instrumental in having an award for Ferrer from the California Teachers Association canceled. Bond said, "the teachers will be blasted from coast to coast" if the award were given. Bond was outraged about the Academy Award nominations but didn't stop at just attacking Ferrer. He insisted that if Ferrer and Edward G. Robinson claimed they were not sympathetic to Communists, it was "outright perjury." For the benefit of the reporter, he mouthed off a list of Robinson's "front" organizations, the same groups whose names appeared in *Red Channels*. Bond asserted that Robinson and Ferrer had offered "bland statements merely saying 'I am not guilty.'" He made it clear the right wing wanted much more. He further insisted that if the Academy gave Oscars to Ferrer, Holliday, or Jaffe it would mean very bad press.

Robinson was furious, but there was little he could do. His press agent, William Herbert, sent a letter to the premier Hollywood defense lawyer, Jerry Geisler, who considered launching a libel suit on behalf of Robinson. Nothing ever came of it.

In the same issue of *Daily Variety* as the Bond interview was a statement by Joyce O'Hara, acting president of the Motion Picture Association of America, insisting that the Red-probe hearings upcoming in Washington were doing no good. O'Hara remarked that the fanatical Communist hunters in Hollywood were a greater menace than the suspected Reds. According to the article, he "attributed part of this fanaticism to lack of success in their profession and jealousy of other players and workers who have reached greater eminence than themselves."

O'Hara's message went unheard. HUAC questioned Larry Parks, the actor who had scored a hit in *The Jolson Story*; on March 21, breaking his spirit and ruining his career, Parks was forced to name names. Among those he was specifically asked about was Edward G. Robinson. Parks testified that he had never seen Robinson at a Communist Party meeting. This corroborated Robinson's statements of innocence, but the mere mention of his name signified that HUAC was still investigating. It served their purpose to keep Robinson's name on the list of those yet to be cleared. It did not matter that HUAC investigator Louis Russell had said that there was no evidence of Robinson having been in a Communist Party cell. The militant activist liberals would still be suspect.

Robinson and Gladys attended the Academy Award presentations at the Pantages Theater on March 29, as a gesture on behalf of Jaffe. He lost in the supporting actors' category to George Sanders for *All about Eve*, but Ferrer and Holliday were named best actor and best actress respectively. Bond's attack had not succeeded.

But on April 2, Billy Wilkerson was back on his platform. In his Trade Views, he charged, "There are plenty of hot Commies among us, probably no more than in any other big business, but enough to put a Red stamp on the picture business. These men and women are known and these men and women can be chased out of pictures, an act that will bring back a lot of ticket buyers. This can be accomplished by our big companies *immediately* giving support to the House Un-American Activities Committee."

Sterling Hayden had his day before HUAC on April 10. He named names, and in the course of the questioning was, like Parks, asked if he knew of Robinson's participation. Hayden responded that he knew Robinson only through fund-raising for Israel. He knew of no Communist involvement by the actor. The next day the banner headline in *The Hollywood Reporter* told one side of the story: "Sterling Hayden Tells All." Hayden was cleared. Robinson was not.

The hearings and the paranoia continued. Warner Bros. released a movie entitled *I Was a Communist for the FBI*, no *Confessions of a Nazi Spy*, but enough to get favorable publicity from *The Hollywood Reporter* and the nation. John Garfield testified on April 23 but was not cleared even after three hours of grueling testimony because HUAC decided he had not added any new information to their files.

Two days later, Edward Dmytryk, now confessing and recanting, dealt Robinson yet another blow. Fully naming names, Dmytryk told of the first meeting of the Hollywood 19. "The meeting was held at Edward G. Robinson's house," Dmytryk recalled. "He was not there. The only reason it was held there is that Senator [Claude] Pepper was visiting in Hollywood at the time, and whether he was a house guest with the Robinsons—I know he was quite friendly." Dmytryk later told HUAC, "To the best of my knowledge, he [Robinson] was never a Communist. It is true that he gave some money to Communist-front organizations, but how many people did this without knowing what they were doing? I don't think, however, that he ever gave any money to the Hollywood Ten."

Again, Robinson sat helpless as his name was mentioned. And the revelation of the meeting of the Hollywood 19 at his house started the rumors once again. If Robinson's house had been used that time, could it have been used another time?

Ferrer had his chance on May 22, and he, too, mentioned—as a member of the so-called front—the American Committee for the Protection of the Foreign Born.

The attacks on Reds were now stronger than they had ever been. IATSE strongman Roy Brewer charged that the Communists were still trying to control the screen. Ronald Reagan set himself up as the first step through which actors could clear themselves. This became common knowledge. When the director-producer Mervyn LeRoy was told by actress Nancy Davis that she had been receiving left-wing mail and feared she had been confused with another Nancy Davis, who was on the wrong lists, LeRoy sent her to Reagan. Reagan cleared the matter up and as a bonus for both of them, he and Davis were married in 1952. Reagan also tried to start an industry tribunal to which a person who suspected he or she was being blacklisted or graylisted could go to discuss the situation. The Screen Writers Guild was able to veto this move by pointing out that any person who went before such a council would be admitting guilt before any charges had been leveled.

For Robinson, the picture got darker and gloomier. There was no subpoena from HUAC, no chance to appear again. Although he had reserve funds, money was becoming tighter, and Gladys was told to stop throwing dinner parties. Manny had returned to California with the model, Frances Chisholm, who would later become his wife. The Robinsons were aghast at his behavior with this "older woman" and sent him to a psychiatrist. It meant more pain, more expense, more taxing of Robinson's already aggravated nerves.

One acting job did come through, thanks to old friend and fellow liberal Ben Hecht, who cast Robinson in one of two of the segments of his *Actors and Sin* anthology. Hecht was producer, director, and writer. Robinson portrayed a brilliant actor named Maurice Tillayou who is devoted to his daughter, also an actress. When Marcia Tillayou poisons herself, her father makes the suicide seem like murder to cover up the fact that his daughter's career had been the cause of the action. As part of the ruse, he eventually stabs himself, one last taste of melodrama. The work lasted about one week.

Hecht knew he had taken a big gamble by using Robinson, but it was part of his spirit to buck the Establishment when he thought it was wrong. It took some doing, but he convinced United Artists to distribute his film, knowing it would be a limited second feature. It was set to be in the theaters at the end of May 1952.

That was several months away, and Robinson still knew that pictures were closed to him. But he hoped that the new medium of television might not be. He instructed his agents to try to get him work on the home screen. They did their best, offering Robinson as the star of a television production of *Counselor-at-Law*, by Elmer Rice. Because of *Red Channels*, Robinson was rejected—no advertiser would sponsor such a program. John Garfield and Jose Ferrer were also turned down.

Robinson tried to get something going on his own. He spent $5,000 of his own money for a film script but could get no further financing. His friend Sol Lesser tried in vain to help him, but even the master of independent producers had no luck. An offer came from an independent filmmaker named Sid Kuller to do a project entitled *Duet*, but again financing fell through. None of the major distributors would touch a Robinson project without a name like Ben Hecht attached.

As Robinson sat in his studio painting or took visitors on a tour of his art collection, the Hollywood community was going through its own anxiety. The witch hunt had brought fear, but the studios were now more concerned about the twelve million homes with television—productions for which came mostly from New York. The Hollywood Bowl had run out of funds and was barely saved by philanthropists. The community was going through greater change than it had encountered previously, and there could be no sympathy for Robinson's plight. Even the moderates began to feel that if the Communists and fellow travelers were cleared away the problems would be over. Robinson and others became sacrificial lambs not just for the liberals, but also for a frightened industry.

There was no place for Robinson to turn for work except the stage. He had resisted working on Broadway because he feared the critics would not look favorably on a movie star invading that terrain. Two years previously he had been offered the leading role of Rubashov in *Darkness at Noon*, a vehemently anti-Communist play by Sidney Kingsley and Arthur Koestler. Robinson had turned the part down, not only because it meant Broadway, but also because his character would be on stage the entire two hours, and as a man in his late fifties, he thought the work too arduous. Claude Rains had played the role.

But the road company was forming, and Kingsley, who was also co-producer, offered him the role again. The money was far from what he was used to, averaging $1,500 plus 10 percent of the gross per week. More important, it was a chance for him to make a statement against Communism. A chance to do his penance. Gladys agreed it was a good idea. With her support, he accepted the play and went east for rehearsals.

From the start the experience was not pleasant. Rains was a fine actor, but he was an Anglo-Saxon. Robinson viewed the Rubashov role as an Eastern European would. The play is the story of a Soviet Communist boss who is being purged because his dogma has softened and his view of the purpose of revolution has weakened. Rubashov has openly stated that the revolution has stumbled and he must pay the price—confession, imprisonment, death.

Rehearsals in New York were a trial in themselves. Robinson had just been through the same ordeals his character was experiencing, and he tried to translate that horror to the play. He saw Rubashov as a broken old man. Robinson could understand the agony of a man whose world has turned against him. Kingsley wanted a carbon copy of the spirited Rains performance of a man whose ideals have changed. There were moments when Robinson almost walked off, but he knew there was nothing awaiting him in Hollywood.

In fact, just three days before Robinson was scheduled to open in *Darkness*, HUAC closed its hearings for the season. There could be no absolution, no atonement in the near future.

On September 28, the road company of *Darkness at Noon* opened at the McCarter Theater in Princeton, New Jersey. Robinson was already exhausted from rehearsals and lack of rest. He was nervous, so shaky that his voice was almost inaudible when the curtain went up. The first ten minutes were a disaster, until finally the star took a deep breath and asked the stage manager to begin again. Robinson absorbed this self-inflicted humiliation as he had absorbed the humiliations of the past three years. He completed the play and received decent notices.

The play takes place in a prison and is less dramatic than it is preachy. Rubashov's line says it all: "History has always been an inhumane and unscrupulous builder, mixing its mortar of lies and blood and filth." And the play's point of view in Cold War–torn America is no less subtle, as a Rubashov speech expresses:

> So functional in taking the land, in one year we let five million farmers and their families die of starvation! Deliberately. So functional in freeing the people from industrial exploitation we sent ten million of them to forced labor under worse conditions than galley slaves. So functional, to settle a difference of opinion, the omnipotent Leader knows only one argument—Death!—whether it's a matter of submarines, manure or the party line in Indo-China. Death! Our standard of living is lower than the most backward country in Europe. Labor conditions are harder; discipline's more inhuman. Our country is run by the police.

With dialogue such as this, Robinson set out to tour the country. It was heavy going, and it did not always go well. In Chicago in a scene with Jack

Palance, who portrayed the villainous party-liner Gletkin, Robinson forgot his lines completely and had to walk offstage and look at the script before continuing.

Meanwhile, his lawyers were not having any luck in getting HUAC to reopen its hearings for Robinson. Gladys had had another attack of her mental problems and had left Beverly Hills for Paris. Robinson longed to join her but was still barred from obtaining a passport. Christmas 1951 was spent alone, depressed. Manny was no help either. In February 1952 he married his model girlfriend just one month before his twentieth birthday.

Each performance of the final scene, the death scene, would become harder to complete. But the audience loved him. There were few catcalls, few crank letters backstage. It was as if the country knew nothing of HUAC, and each night the death scene brought down the house.

As his depression turned to anger over his situation, Robinson almost compulsively thought about nothing else but clearing himself. He would look over his notes and records in the evenings after a performance. He would make almost incoherent calls to his lawyers asking if there had been any breakthrough. His friends and agents began to fear for his health.

And he wanted to wash his hands of the so-called transgressions of the past. On February 15, during a brief stay back in Beverly Hills, he wrote and mailed a brief and terse letter to his former friend, Dalton Trumbo, reminding him of the $2,500 loan made in 1948. Trumbo had received a settlement from the studios, and Robinson thought it was high time he was repaid. "I trust that the very pressing financial difficulties that beset you and the family at that time have been met sufficiently so that at least a part payment on the loan can be made by you," he wrote, ending with a formal, "Sincerely yours."

His agent, Bert Allenberg, was working overtime to try to find some sort of project that would allow Robinson to work in Hollywood again. Frightened by his client's mental state, Allenberg sent a telegram to Seattle, Washington, on March 3, where Robinson was appearing in *Darkness at Noon*. "Please, Eddie get hold of yourself," Allenberg wired. "I know you are human and entitled to moments of weakness and depression and God knows you have been strong and courageous beyond belief during this terrible period and you do have good friends who are loyal and working for you myriads of them and you will be on top again higher than ever before so have faith and confidence for yourself just as I have for you. Let me hear from you. All my love, Bert."

Yet, despite the despondency, Allenberg's words were coming true. Doors were starting to open a little, and scripts were starting to appeal for Robinson, even if they were mostly from independent productions. On April 9, Allenberg wrote to Robinson in Minneapolis, telling him there was interest in a television series based on the Nero Wolfe books with Robinson in the title role. There were also two film scripts they were mulling over. And again, Allenberg pleaded with his client to take care: "I sure as hell hope you have gotten over that fit of despondency you were in down in Los Angeles and have gotten hold of yourself again . . . now is not the time to start to go to pieces, when the worst is over and I am sure we are on the threshold of light."

The apparent easing up on his graylisting prompted Robinson's attorneys to try to get him before HUAC. Since Sam Yorty—who had headed California's version of HUAC in 1939 to 1940—had been helpful before, Michael Halperin called the congressman again. Yorty recalled the conversation. "His attorney called me and told me something of the situation. I said I'd be glad to talk to Eddie. He put him on the phone. I thought some guy was kidding, but it really was him. We didn't say much, but it was decided we'd meet in D.C."

Robinson had gone from Minneapolis to Tennessee with *Darkness*, but he flew to Washington, meeting with Yorty at the Statler Hotel. "He said he'd been trying to get a passport, but couldn't," Yorty recalled. "'My wife's in France,' Eddie said. 'I promised to join her.' He told me that there were some Communists who were his friends, but he didn't know they were Communists. This was not Little Caesar. This was a man who was telling me that his career was in shambles. He said, 'I'm doing this play, but I can't get back into pictures because of this.' I said I knew Walter [Francis E. Walter, HUAC chairman]. I promised Eddie I'd talk to Walter, and I did. He said if Eddie wanted to come clean and tell the truth, the Committee would see him. His lawyer got on it and they set something up."

It was agreed that Robinson would again appear before HUAC on April 30, but first he had to finish *Darkness at Noon*. He did his last performance on April 26 and headed immediately for Washington.

Robinson was prepared for HUAC when the public hearing began at 2:00 P.M. on the 30th—in the same room 226 of the Old House Office Building. He knew what questions to expect, and he knew what Walter meant when he said Robinson would have to "come clean." The trick for Robinson would be getting himself off without naming names, especially since he really had no individuals to accuse. Robinson had never been to a Communist Party meeting.

In the first few minutes of the hearing, Robinson wanted the Committee to be very aware of his stage work in *Darkness at Noon*. He apologized for the hoarseness in his voice because he had just finished his season in the anti-Communist play. Then he was allowed to read a statement. As he read the statement, which he had rehearsed with his attorneys, Robinson's voice was clear and direct. He didn't hesitate, he didn't flinch. He had waited too long for this:

> I desire to repeat under oath a denial that I am or ever have been a Communist or knowingly a fellow traveler . . . I have always been a liberal Democrat. The revelations that persons whom I thought were sincere liberals were, in fact, Communists, has shocked me more than I can tell you. That they persuaded me by lies and concealment of their real purposes to allow them to use my name for what I believed to be a worthy cause is now obvious. I was sincere. They were not.
>
> My conscience is clear . . . My loyalty to this Nation I know to be absolute. No one has ever been willing to confront me under oath free from immunity and unequivocally charge me with membership in the Communist Party or any other subversive organization. No one can honestly do so.
>
> I now realize that some organizations that I permitted to use my name were, in fact, Communist fronts. But their ostensible purposes were good, and it was for such purposes that I allowed use of my name and even made numerous financial contributions.

Later in the prepared text he was blunter. He told HUAC, "I was duped and used. I was lied to. But, I repeat, I acted from good motives, and I have never knowingly aided Communists or any Communist cause." And again Robinson wanted the Committee to realize just what kind of play *Darkness at Noon* was: "While you have been exposing Communists, I have been fighting them and their ideology in my own way. I just finished appearing in close to 250 performances of *Darkness at Noon* all over the country. It is, perhaps, the strongest indictment of Communism ever presented. I am sure it had a profound and lasting effect on all who saw it."

When it came time for questioning, the first order of business was the meeting Edward Dmytryk claimed had taken place at Robinson's Rexford Drive home. Dmytryk's testimony was read for Robinson, and he acknowledged its accuracy, noting that "I had never been consulted." Attempting to be honest, Robinson said that even if he had known the meeting was to take place, he would have allowed it since it was prior to the investigations and Senator Pepper was a close friend. Robinson then told HUAC that it was Gladys who had arranged it all, the same Mrs. Robinson whose Americanism was impeccable. She had worked across the country with the USO, begun the Desert Battalion, and had worked so hard for the cause in World War II that she "broke down as a result of it," Robinson told the congressmen. When asked about further meetings at his house that might have been Communist Party meetings, Robinson acknowledged that many who were now revealed as Communists had "been in my home at various times. There were tremendous activities that went on in my house during the war."

Robinson was asked whether he had any information about Communists that would be of interest to the Committee. He responded, "I wish to God I had." When the congressmen told him this seemed to be the same position he took in 1951—when he didn't say enough—Robinson realized the heat was on. "When I found out that certain of the executive secretaries of the Arts, Sciences, and Professions were Communists, as well as some of the other organizations that I had been in, I realized the dirty, filthy work that they had been doing," Robinson said, hoping it would be enough. It wasn't. Chairman Walter took over:

Mr. Walter: Mr. Robinson, you stated you were duped and used—by whom?

Mr. Robinson: By the sinister forces who were members and probably in important positions in these organizations.

Mr. Walter: Well, tell us what individuals you have reference to.

Robinson paused, took a breath and spoke.

Mr. Robinson: Well, you had Albert Maltz, and you have Dalton Trumbo, and you have—what is the other fellow, the top fellow who they say is the commissar out there?

Mr. Walter: John Howard Lawson?

Mr. Robinson: Yes, John Howard Lawson. I knew Frank Tuttle. I didn't know Dmytryk at all. There are the Buchmans, that I know, Sidney Buchman and all that sort of thing. It never entered my mind that any of these people were Communists.

He was asked to give more details.

Mr. Robinson: I came in for a cause that appealed to me. Now, if you take the important organizations that I belonged to—the Arts, Sciences and Professions, principally—they represented to me that they were champions on the Rooseveltian policies, both internal and external. Consequently, I was very much interested in it. I was a great admirer of Mr. Roosevelt.

I have found out now in retrospect, and since these revelations have been made, how many of the important people in that organization were Communists at the time I was a member of it. My interest really waned with the death of Mr. Roosevelt.

As for his participation in the Yugoslav Relief, Robinson said that despite what it said in *Red Channels*, he had never been a member but had been "solicited" by Abe Burrows to make a speech. Robinson hastened to add about Burrows, "I don't know that he is a Communist." Robinson further told HUAC that it was his old friend Donald Ogden Stewart who had solicited him to join the American Committee for the Protection of the Foreign Born. "He was a very personable and likable fellow," Robinson remarked. "I find now that he is a Communist."

After all, Robinson reasoned to the Committee, at a Foreign Born dinner "William Allen White made the principal address; Dorothy Thompson spoke; Grace Moore sang 'The Star Bangled Banner.' There were other people of that kind present." Robinson's contribution was "a funny little talk about not having been born in America."

> Mr. Tavenner: Well, you made a fairly substantial contribution, did you not, to the American Committee for the Protection of the Foreign Born?
>
> Mr. Robinson: It was negligible . . . You will find that amongst the list of the organizations to which I gave between $350,000 and $400,000 in ten years, that so-called subversive organizations got hardly anything. I think it was $10 or something, and $10 again that they have gotten. They still send me literature, although I have asked them not to send it to me, but still it kind of filters in. They follow absolutely, for my purposes, that is, according to my ideas, the Communist line.
>
> Mr. Walter: Practically the entire activities of that organization today are involved in trying to prevent the deportation of known Communists.
>
> Mr. Robinson: That is right. That is exactly it.

The hearing continued with Robinson insisting he was no longer a member of HICCASP. He read into the record once more the statement from 1951 about his contributions to various causes during World War II. Then he was asked about his contribution and loan to Dalton Trumbo. Robinson insisted that the money he lent Trumbo was not to be used in his defense, but in support of his family.

Robinson purged his past. He told the Committee, "I am not a member of any organization except clubs now, my country club and my actors' club—two actors' clubs. Try and get me. I can tell you that actors' clubs are very good, conservative organizations. As you know, the Screen Actors Guild, Actors Equity at that time, is a good conservative organization."

Mr. Walter: You are a little gun shy now?

Mr. Robinson: Oh yes. There ain't room for both of us in this town—one of us had got to go, and it was me.

Robinson reiterated that he had never been to a Communist Party meeting, that he had no sympathy for Communists. Then Congressman Donald Jackson asked him if he thought Communists should be employed in the motion picture industry. Robinson tried to skirt the question, insisting "I am not an employer," but Jackson pressed the issue, saying he wanted Robinson's opinion.

Mr. Robinson: Well, I have no use for people of that kind. I think that whenever you find anyone who works under wraps, and who does things in a clandestine fashion, and, as I said before, masquerades as something he is not, and then you find out that he has been engaged in sinister purposes, which I believe the Communist Party and the Communists represent, drastic measures should be taken.

Jackson responded a few moments later by stating that HUAC had no evidence that Robinson was a Communist Party member but that "some of your activities have lent aid and comfort to the Communist Party, perhaps inadvertently on your part."

Robinson then pressed the Committee for a clean bill of health but was told, "this committee is not in a position to exonerate or to vindicate any person who has been wrongfully accused of being a Communist or who had been smeared as a result of such false accusations." But the congressmen praised and thanked him for coming before the Committee, and Walter summed it up by stating, "Well, actually, this Committee has never had any evidence presented to indicate that you were anything more than a very choice sucker. I think you are No. 1 on every sucker list in the country." Walter admitted that some of the front organizations had his *own* name as a contributor.

Robinson was labeled a "well-meaning individual" and dismissed at 3:20 P.M.

In the House chamber that same day, Sam Yorty had come through. He entered into the *Congressional Record* Robinson's statement and an appeal that Robinson be admired as an artist and that the innuendos against him cease. Yorty also wrote a lengthy letter to the Passport Office on Robinson's behalf, noting that in his opinion the actor "was not and is not a Communist" and that he had just finished 250 performances of the anti-Communist play, *Darkness at Noon.*

Ruth Shipley, the director of the Passport Office, was well aware of Robinson's record. The Office had been keeping a file of its own, with clippings of Robinson's *Darkness* reviews and of numerous newspaper articles suggesting he was a Communist. After meeting with HUAC, Robinson went to see Shipley and Ashley J. Nicholas, an aide, and was required to write a "confession" and "oath" on State Department stationery. "In connection with any application for a passport, I voluntarily swear that I am not now or have ever been a member of the Communist Party," he wrote in his own hand. "I abhor and condemn the tyranny it stands for."

Nicholas wrote a memo dated May 13 stating that Robinson had been given a passport valid for one year only because, "as far as we are concerned he is still on probation." As for the confession—or affidavit, as it was politely called—Nicholas noted, "If during the next ten years evidence should be received which would disprove this statement the matter should be referred to the Department of Justice for prosecution."

In Hollywood, the trade papers heralded that Robinson's "candid testimony wins probe approbation." Congressman Walter noted that he hoped "other people had learned a lesson" by Robinson's experience.

HUAC was through with Little Caesar. The spirit of the militant activist liberal had been broken, he had been brought to his knees, and a pardon had been granted. In a few years it would become evident to writers and historians trying to piece together a rationale for the period that Robinson had never done anything subversive at all. He was what he professed to be—a liberal Democrat, a party member of the people of FDR. His work against Hitler so early on, and his joining of anti-Nazi organizations before others realized the danger of Germany, would earn Robinson the extra tag "premature antifascist." Even Raphael Nixon, one of the investigators for the Committee, would admit when asked that "We never had any evidence that Edward G. Robinson, Jose Ferrer, or John Garfield were Communists." Yet, two careers had been damaged, and Garfield had been sent to an early grave. Nixon never verbalized what can also be seen in the record—that Robinson and Garfield were Jews and Ferrer a Puerto Rican, all minorities that couldn't make it into most country clubs. The list of *Red Channels* victims unable to clear themselves and graylisted artists were overwhelmingly from minority groups.

Robinson took off for Paris to join Gladys, knowing he would have to live with his conscience for the rest of his life. He had said he was duped by Maltz, Trumbo, Lawson, and others. Did he name names? In his autobiography and in interviews over the next twenty years, Robinson always insisted that he did not. Indeed, historians of the period do not include his testimony as one of significance, except that it paved the way for additional witch hunting. Robinson's name never appears on the list of those who exposed others. Still, Albert Maltz, whose name Robinson invoked, remains bitter about the testimony. "He lied about me," Maltz asserted. "I never spoke to him about politics in the brief contact that we had. He was playing the Committee's game. He was a strong-minded man. No one was able to influence him. Even if he thought his back was against the wall—that's no reason to lie. I never asked him to sign as much as a petition. I wrote his film, I wrote two speeches for him. I never tried to influence him."

Robinson had also included the name of director Frank Tuttle in his testimony. By April 1952, Tuttle had already appeared before the Committee and named a host of names himself. Robinson would later explain in interviews why he suspected Tuttle of being a Communist. At a party at Tuttle's house, in about 1940, several men were standing around the piano singing tunes with lyrics lampooning political figures of the day. Roosevelt, Mussolini, Chamberlain, and Hitler had all gone through the biting, ribbing lyrics. When Robinson suggested Stalin as a figure to be dealt with, there was silence from the other men, Tuttle among them. Robinson realized, he would explain, that he was among Communist Party members.

The FBI seems to have been willing to let Robinson go. His file ends as abruptly as it began around the time of the HUAC clearance. There are no further investigations. Hoover called off the dogs. And HUAC had made its point. It would be years before Robinson took an active interest in politics, or at least allowed his name to be used for political purposes. Except on behalf of Zionism, he would not appear publicly for a political cause until the 1960s, when the civil rights movement made it possible for liberals to take a stand again. The Passport Office had forbidden any activities that might smack of being left wing (in the 1950s, that meant liberal).

The liberal had been silenced. The Democrat retreated only to the voting booth. The activism that had been so much a part of Robinson's life since he first stood on a soapbox for Hearst in 1909 was tabled and shelved temporarily. In 1909, Morris and Sarah Goldenberg had become naturalized citizens, and Robinson as a minor automatically became one as well. In 1952 he was allowed to be a citizen once more—but he had been taught a new set of rules.

9

B-MOVIES AND
THE ROAD BACK

I was a fighter when I was a kid. I've never stopped fighting. I wouldn't know how.

—Victor Scott (Edward G. Robinson) in *Illegal*

Eddie and Gladys meandered around Paris for several weeks, enjoying the hospitality of the Plaza Athenée, wandering through the art galleries. Gladys, herself, had paintings on sale in the city. It was a good rest, and Gladys, in love with Europe, suggested that they consider making it their permanent base. There were many films being made throughout the Continent.

Robinson thought about it. He needed work badly, since it had cost $100,000 to clear himself. But to work in Europe would mean admitting that he had done something wrong politically, that he was on the growing list of expatriates, Americans forced to seek work elsewhere. If he were exonerated, Robinson wanted Hollywood to be the place in which he worked. Besides, the art collection was there, Manny was there trying to get his own acting career started. Robinson refused to give in, and they returned to Beverly Hills.

When he did return to Hollywood during the summer, he found that the clearance by HUAC was not enough. Although his agents were working hard, the offers had not been coming in. Instead, it became evident that the film community had its own standards of clearance. In order to work again, Robinson would need a ticket of clean health from Ronald Reagan and Roy Brewer, particularly Brewer.

He met with Brewer, the head of IATSE and one of the leaders of the Motion Picture Alliance, who reviewed his record, putting Robinson through an even bigger ordeal than HUAC had done. Brewer's terms were clear. If Robinson would purge himself further for the benefit of conservative groups in the country, he could work again in Hollywood. Just as Bogart had cleared himself in print, so must Robinson.

It was arranged for Robinson to write an article for the *American Legion Magazine*. The text would be scrutinized by the organization that had once given Robinson its highest award—and by Brewer and others in the MPA. Again, Robinson's relationship with Sam Yorty paid off. Yorty had arranged a lunch with two witch-hunting writers—Victor Reisel and George Sokolsky—for Robinson just before the HUAC hearings. The writers had given Robinson their okay. Now he turned to them for help in writing this final confession. They agreed to be ghostwriters and help him with the text.

Because magazines have long lead times, the articles did not appear until the October issue, with Robinson pacing the rooms of Rexford Drive awaiting its release. The article was entitled "How the Reds Made a Sucker Out of Me" and featured one photograph—that of a disgusted Robinson from the film *Tales of Manhattan*, in which he played an impoverished lawyer helped by his former classmates when his predicament is revealed. Perhaps the Legion saw a parallel.

The article carried the preface from the editors, "Mr. Robinson, whose name, prestige, and money were used by communist causes in the past, here fits action to his words with a statement of how it happened to him."

The text contained the predictable denials and a recap of how Robinson had come to America as an immigrant from oppression. There was a new twist to the suckering, not mentioned before. Robinson now claimed that his name had been lent to front organizations because of Victor Shapiro, a man he had hired to do his public relations during the war. Shapiro had told Robinson he was a member of the Los Angeles Democratic Committee and a past commander of an American Legion Post. Robinson had been skeptical. Shapiro lent his name to many of the Communist fronts, Robinson now insisted. And in 1951, Martin Berkeley, screenwriter, had named Shapiro as a Communist before HUAC (Berkeley was the most prolific of those who named names).

Because of Shapiro, Robinson wrote, "I have changed from a trusting man to a suspicious one. And I blame the Communists for that change. They have poisoned the relations between people in this community for many years . . . they have damaged the fabric of our country." Robinson added that if a man is accused of Communism falsely he should make a statement of his true position. "If he will not do so, I for one would take the charges made against him most seriously."

Again he mentioned *Darkness at Noon* as an anti-Communist statement, then added melodramatically, "As I have said under oath, in the future as in the past I insist before God I have one allegiance and one allegiance only; I am not a Communist, I have never been, I never will be—I am an American. THE END."

The article did the trick. Agent Bert Allenberg could now offer Robinson's services in Hollywood and expect a response. By the end of October, Allenberg came through, thanks in part to Sol Lesser, Robinson's friend from the Hillcrest. The partnership of producers Jules Levy and Arthur Gardner and director Arnold Laven was going to make a film based on the novel *Harness Bull* by Leslie T. White. It was Allenberg's chance to put Robinson back to work. Arthur Gardner recalled:

In 1952 we had made *Without Warning* and had made a small name for ourselves . . . Sol Lesser had bought an interest in the film and after it was successful, he asked us to find something for another project. He gave us *Harness Bull.* We assigned Lawrence Roman to write the screenplay, and he did a good job. Our agent was the William Morris Agency. Bert Allenberg saw the script and called and asked us if we wanted Edward G. Robinson for the part of Captain Barnaby. We laughed. We didn't think we could get him since our entire budget was only $260,000. They said they wanted Eddie to work and we could have him for $50,000. I knew that was less than he had been getting for films in the forties, but who was I to argue? We met with Eddie maybe half a dozen times at his house. He was absolutely the quintessential pro. He was marvelous. I remember that whenever we came to the house with someone he had never met before he would stop everything and show the man the paintings. That always gave him the most joy.

By the time production started, *Harness Bull* had been retitled *Vice Squad* and would be released by United Artists. The film is in the gritty police genre, with Robinson portraying a captain investigating the murder of a police officer by two thugs. Paulette Goddard, whose career was waning, costarred, being paid $5,000 a day for three days. Like Robinson, working on a B picture, however good the script, was a comedown, but she did it. *Vice Squad* was filmed at the old Pathé studios in Culver City for twenty-one days in November–December, coming in only $2,000 over budget.

"Robinson treated us marvelously and gave his all," Gardner added. "There was a clause in his contract that he didn't have to work beyond 6:00 P.M. Occasionally, we would have to work past that time. We'd approach him about it, and he'd look at us with a twinkle in his eye and say, 'For 50 Upmans I'll work.' Upmans were his favorite cigars then. We'd agree, he'd work, and we'd buy him cigars." Gardner remembered that the topic of HUAC or the graylisting was never mentioned. "He never brought it up, we never brought it up. We were in awe of him. We were young. It wouldn't have been right for us to ask about it."

With *Vice Squad* in the can, Robinson and family enjoyed Christmas immensely. He was back in the game. The ice had been broken, and Allenberg wasted no time. He began to appeal to the studio bosses for work for his now available client. Louis B. Mayer thought Robinson right for a low-budget ($425,000) feature entitled *Big Leaguer*, in which Robinson was to play Hans Lobert, an aging baseball player who turns instructor to whip the prospects of the New York Giants into shape.

Robinson now wrote to Joseph C. Keeley, editor of the *American Legion Magazine*, saying,

> It may be of interest to you and your associates to know that since my article appeared in the October issue of *American Legion Magazine* I resumed activity in films after a long lapse. I think the fact that I am returning to the screen is in no small measure due to the presentation of the article ... More than ever, therefore, I am grateful to the Editors of the *American Legion Magazine* that, having ascertained the facts, they encouraged me to present them as a demonstration of the merciless, lying propaganda of the Reds, and the vicious techniques of making a perfectly loyal American appear like a sympathizer and fellow traveler to first use him and then destroy him.

He had learned that respect must still be paid. Robinson was fully aware that the blacklisting and graylisting was still continuing, but the spotlight had turned away from Hollywood and was now on New York, where television was employing a continuing flow of new and old talent. His friend Sam Jaffe was having problems thanks to *Red Channels* as was Zero Mostel. Robinson felt very lucky to be working.

This, despite the fact that his part in *Big Leaguer* was hardly custom made and the pay was $40,000, below what he had earned even for *Vice Squad. Leaguer* was to film in Florida, where the baseball teams trained. Robinson was ready, but apprehensive about the director and producer of the film, both of whom were working on their first feature. The director, Robert Aldrich, who went on to huge successes (among them *The Dirty Dozen, The Killing of Sister George,* and *Whatever Happened to Baby Jane?*), recalled the two-month period:

> Mayer had formed a unit laughingly called "Sons of the Pioneers." Matthew Rapf's father had been one of the first executives around town and Mayer made him the producer. It is my opinion that Bert Allenberg— who was head of William Morris at the time—prevailed upon Mayer and

Dore Schary to give Robinson a chance at a film career again. It coincided with "Sons of the Pioneers" and Mayer must have figured it all fit nicely. Robinson's character—Hans Lobert—was responsible for the baseball farm system. Herbert Baker, the screenwriter, had seen an article in *The New Yorker* and had brought the project to the attention of the studio. It was a pretty good script.

Aldrich's credits prior to the film had been as a director in television and as an assistant director in Hollywood films. Robinson was unaware—and Aldrich did not bring it up—that the young director had once been fired from MGM because a director had heard a rumor, however untrue, that Aldrich was a Communist. Aldrich had been friendly with Dalton Trumbo and believed that he escaped the graylist himself only because of the insignificance of an assistant director in the Hollywood hierarchy, and his young age. Aldrich continued: "Robinson knew this was a charity job . . . He knew he had to prove himself again. But at the same time, he never articulated his anger. Never said, 'I've been worked over by society.' We never, ever, talked politics. I have no idea if he knew of my background. He didn't know that I had spent time with John Garfield trying to get a film going when Garfield was blacklisted. I knew what he had been through."

Leaguer had been given a tight twenty-one-day schedule, most of it at the Giants' training camp in Florida. The crew had to be cleared out before the baseball players returned en masse for spring training. By the second week in February, the crew had begun to arrive. Robinson followed about the middle of the month. Aldrich recalled: "Although he was familiar with baseball and had read all he could, he wasn't quite sure if in the script the character was a coach or a father figure. Before we left I had reported to Robinson's house to answer his questions and I had told him this film was a big opportunity for me. He gave me a tour of the paintings, and when we left a few days later I figured we were getting along."

But Aldrich's pleasure turned toward sour after the first few days at work. As he saw it later: "Robinson had been off for a long time. He wanted to be sure not to make any mistakes in his perception. He had become a great star playing varieties of Edward G. Robinson. I had trouble from the start communicating with him that the nuances he was famous for were not necessarily right for playing a first-generation baseball manager. I tried to get him to be less explosive, but my persuasive powers weren't all that persuasive."

Robinson was not a well-coordinated man. By his own admission he had always been a spectator in sports and had probably not done any serious exercising since boyhood. Aldrich saw that he was clumsy and remembered thinking, "How could I tell him how bad he was?"

There was a catch for the young director, though. In his old contracts, Robinson had always had the right to see the rushes, the first prints of the scenes. He was insecure about his part in *Big Leaguer* and wanted to see the rushes for it. Aldrich was afraid if Robinson saw it wasn't really working out, he'd quit, demand costly retakes, or worse. Robinson pushed to see the rushes, but Aldrich refused. "That started a real, widening argument," the director said. "He thought I was arrogant. Then stupid. Then I was trying to keep something from him. Our relationship was not good. I had gone to medium shots and close-ups to hide his clumsiness. He knew it—it had become a bone of contention. He was determined to get the rushes."

Aldrich had one advantage. The film had to be flown back to MGM in Culver City for processing, and it took two days or more before the film could be returned to Florida. Time was on his side. By the time Robinson's protests got to Dore Schary, head of production, there were only two or three more days left to film. Schary ordered Aldrich to show Robinson the rushes, but the young director threatened to quit. Since the studio executives liked what they were seeing, they let the argument ride, and no rushes were shown.

As a result, when the cameras stopped rolling, Robinson retreated to his hotel suite. Aldrich recalled that he was joined by "a Baltimore socialite" for a few days, "but she had her own room. I don't know if anything happened between them. I do know there was no family spirit on location."

By March 3 the film had wrapped up, five days ahead of schedule. Aldrich was a hero at the studio for bringing the film in under budget.

Robinson got the obligatory pat on the back and returned to Rexford Drive.

Any depression he might have had about his work evaporated almost immediately. A few weeks after he returned, Robinson and Gladys became grandparents when Manny and his wife, Frances, presented them with a granddaughter, named Francesca. Robinson would later say that he immediately put the hopes and dreams he had for Manny into the baby girl. For the next few months, Robinson would feel very much like a family man for the first time in years. Gladys was healthy and at home, busily working on projects and spending money. Manny was scrounging for acting jobs, and Robinson would have to pay for the diaper service, but at least he was trying. Other offers were trickling into Bert Allenberg's office. It appeared as if things might shape up after all.

And he felt like a star again on May 19, when the French consulate in San Francisco presented him with the prestigious Légion d'Honneur, making him the first American film actor to receive the award. Robinson would, in the remaining twenty years of his life, wear the ribbon with pride, intermittently, depending upon the current status of French–Israeli relations.

If the family seemed well and accolades were coming in, Robinson knew that his career was still not on an even keel. In June, Allenberg came through with another offer, sending Robinson back to Universal for *The Glass Web*, in which a young leading man named John Forsythe was cast as a television scriptwriter accused of murdering the star of his show, *Crime of the Week*. But the police cannot prove their case. The research director of the show, portrayed by Robinson, uses the evidence for a script for the series and inadvertently gives himself away as the real murderer while trying to prove the writer's guilt. Robinson tries to shoot Forsythe, but the police kill the murderer before he can do away with the writer.

Robinson was given top billing, and his fee had edged up to $60,000. There was little else to be happy about. Even Forsythe recalled that the script was not the best. "The picture wasn't very good," he admitted. "I was coerced into doing it. They said it would be both a 3-D and a one-dimensional release. I remember Eddie saying, 'Yeah, it's a 3-D picture with a one-dimensional script and two-dimensional acting' . . . It was thrilling for me to work with an actor of Robinson's stature. I remember that I had an image of him as a physically energetic man because of the roles he had played, but at that point he seemed rather low. I assumed—as did the rest of the cast and crew—that it was because of the blacklisting."

But the Robinson humor was still there, and Forsythe fondly remembered Robinson joking on the set and inviting him over to see the art collection. Somehow, they managed to get through the picture, and by July 20 it was completed. Forsythe went off to New York, his contract with Universal completed. Robinson returned home.

Two events occurred about the same time. A few days before *Web* finished, *Big Leaguer* had been released—before *Vice Squad*, which would not premiere until August. *Leaguer* was an instant flop. Aldrich noted, "It was a picture about the Giants and they opened it in Brooklyn—Dodger territory. Of course it wasn't a big success."

And although Robinson read reviews that said he "helps bolster the presentation," many of the publications around the country didn't bother to give the film more than a news item. The film hadn't mattered. He summoned Aldrich for lunch at the Hillcrest. Aldrich remembered:

We had lunch with his cronies. There was Milton Berle, Jack Benny. I remember that I felt out of place and in awe. After lunch Robinson took me into a room at the Hillcrest and said that he wasn't unpleased with his performance. He thought the film was pretty good. Then he said, "Kid, why didn't you show me the rushes?" It was still bothering him. I didn't want to tell him the truth. I told him I was afraid he wouldn't like what he saw and they might replace me. I told him it was my first picture and I wanted to make a good impression. I don't know if he ever found out the truth. I never saw him after that lunch at the Hillcrest. I never even bumped into him around town.

While working on the last scenes of *Glass Web*, Robinson had received a letter from Louis J. Russell, the HUAC investigator he had faced in

Washington. The letter would cause problems, but Robinson didn't realize it. Dated July 11, the correspondence was a plea for a loan. "I regret very much to impose upon you, but of late my financial situation has been beyond my control," Russell wrote, having learned enough about Robinson during his investigation to know the actor was an easy touch. "I urgently need $600 to get myself straightened out," Russell continued. "I have an accumulation of medical and other bills which I must pay."

Russell promised to send $50 or $75 each month if Robinson would give him the loan. The investigator wrote, "Knowing of your desire to assist persons in emergency cases I have come to you for assistance." Robinson sent Russell a check for $300 and forgot the matter. He was afraid not to send the money. He knew there were still those in town who would not hire him, and Robinson felt he just could not go through the graylisting again.

The matter aside, he thought, Robinson decided to take a rest at home and read the scripts that Allenberg was sending over. *Vice Squad* was released in August, and Robinson and the film received mixed reviews. Still, it appeared as if the film would do well at the box office—which it did—and Robinson sat at home with a minor hit on his hands.

Despite all that had happened, he was in good spirits. So was Gladys. Although they had separate bedrooms and much of the union had left their marriage, they seemed to be getting along. Gladys was a spendthrift, but she also had a passion for buying wholesale. Because of who she was—or who Robinson was—Gladys had for years been invited to the private showrooms on Seventh Avenue in New York to look over the seasonal fashions and choose what she wanted. She had managed to become friendly with many of the fashion industry executives, and when they came to California, the Rexford Drive home became a favored stop.

One night during August, Jane Bodenheimer Adler, a divorcée who worked for the Nettie Rosenstein Group as a director, came by to see Gladys. Robinson stayed in his study, not interested in Gladys's guests or the talk that would inevitably center on fashions and designers. While the guests were sipping cocktails, Gladys pulled Eddie out of the study, imploring him to give the tour of the art collection. He always agreed to do that.

Within minutes Robinson and Mrs. Adler had developed a rapport. She was taller than he, but he found her witty and charming, and she passed the important test—she knew something about art. The conversation became enjoyable to him, and Robinson decided to join Gladys, Jane, and her escort for dinner at Romanoffs. By the end of the evening, both Jane and Eddie knew they wanted to see each other again. Robinson told her he hoped she would return.

In the course of his marriage, Robinson had developed relationships with a few other women besides Gladys, but always with complete discretion. Women found him delightful; some even dubbed him a "ladies' man" for his ability to make conversation. Just when Jane Adler became more than an acquaintance remains uncertain, because of the privacy that Robinson guarded. It is certain that Eddie and Jane saw each other again and again, but it would not be until 1956 that their relationship became public knowledge. For he was married, and his Old World ethics told him to stay married: That's the way it was done among Goldenbergs. Although Gladys had sued for divorce several times when mentally unstable, Robinson had never pursued it. He never would.

What Robinson wanted at this point was not a secret affair, but work. But after *Vice Squad* was released, it all dried up again. HUAC had discovered that he had lent $300 to Russell. The investigator had been forced to resign, but the Committee did not take the matter lightly. Robinson was again suspect, this time of crimes much worse than just being a Communist. The reports circulated that it was a bribe, a payoff, a stunt that a Little Caesar might have pulled. Because of a mere $300 his troubles were back.

This time there would be no procrastination on HUAC's part. They wanted to see him. Christmas passed with Robinson again on tenterhooks awaiting news. The lawyers were again contacted, the depression again evident.

HUAC ordered him to appear in executive session on January 25, 1954, but Robinson waived the subpoena, which would have covered his expenses, because he wanted the Committee to know he was fully cooperative. At 2:00 P.M. on the 25th he was back at the Old House Office

Building, back reliving his worst moments. Some of the faces had changed—Harold Velde was now chairman—but the spirit had not.

Robinson took the oath and told HUAC of the events leading to the loan. He read the letter sent by Russell into the record. He read his response of July 13, telling Russell that he was sending the money "Because I am in the habit of never turning down any request from any decent person who is in need." The full amount—$600—had not been sent because, Robinson testified, he could not afford it.

Robinson insisted that Russell had done him no favors, that he had never asked any Committee member for a favor. "I said that I didn't expect a bit of mercy from the Committee," he told them. "And I haven't departed from the truth in my testimony. All I ask is that you give me a clean bill of health."

For Robinson it was the reprise of a nightmare. His mouth opened and the all-too-familiar words came out!

> There was never any real connection between me and the Communists, or any of that sort of thing. I think the finest thing about me is my Americanism. I think I had a very fine reputation as a decent human being, and this means an awful lot to me. I have extended upon the answer you called for. I hope, if you feel justified, that you will make a statement to the press that there wasn't a thing dishonorable about this transaction. I am sorry if it in any way contributed to Mr. Russell's dismissal. I thought I had done a decent and honorable thing, for a decent man who was in want.

Russell had not paid back a penny in the six months he had had the loan, and the Committee was surprised to learn that Robinson did not feel bothered by it. He told them, "When I make a loan I just put it in the red. If I get any of it back it is just found money. I never expect a loan to be repaid."

The Committee gave him absolution when the hour-long session was over. But it had extracted yet another ounce of blood from a body that was already weak. Robinson walked out of room 225 without a smile on his face. He confided in his lawyer that he didn't think he'd ever work again.

To save his career Robinson thought he'd have to humble himself before Roy Brewer and the Hollywood conservatives once more. In the spring of 1954, Brewer was running for reelection as president of IATSE. Robinson contributed money to his campaign parties, spoke on his behalf, and made appearances at his rallies. Brewer sent him a letter on May 7 thanking Robinson for his support.

A few days later General Omar Bradley wrote asking him to lend his name for the United Defense Fund. Robinson agreed immediately. He was back on the establishment's lists.

The added atonement had done the trick, but the first work Robinson got was in television, which he might have declined had he not needed the work and not needed to reestablish himself. There would be appearances on Martha Raye's variety show and on Milton Berle's program. Robinson made a pilot for a proposed series entitled *For the Defense*, but it was never shown. He also did a few *Lux Radio Theatres*.

In June, Manny and Frances—who had been having marriage troubles since before the birth of Francesca—were suffering again. Manny was trying to make it as an actor, but he had a reputation in town as a troublemaker and was a heavy drinker. Each time he was seen in a bar after a few drinks too many, the word would spread through town. The tension had inevitably affected the marriage, and the young couple could be seen battling in public, with columnists Walter Winchell and Dorothy Kilgallen both eager to print the juicier bits. The couple could not manage their money, so Robinson—who was supporting them—assigned them a business manager. It increased the squabbles between Manny and Frances and only widened the gap between father and son.

With his son's problems as a backdrop, Robinson went back to work during the summer in another United Artists' vehicle, *Black Tuesday*. It meant returning to his criminal guise as a killer and mobster whose gang kidnaps the warden's daughter so that Robinson's character—Vincent Canelli—can escape the death house. Canelli's gang ends up at a warehouse with five hostages including a priest. When the police surround the hideout, Canelli threatens to kill the hostages one by one. But when he raises his gun at the priest (Milburn Stone), who is a hostage, Peter Manning (Peter Graves) shoots Canelli.

It was a few weeks' work and not particularly satisfying at that (and he received only $40,000). Robinson felt he had gone full circle, back to the films he did at Warner Bros. in the 1930s, and he complained to his friends that after twenty-five years he didn't find his collection of films artistically sound. His theater work, he thought, had been better. But he was not ready to give up the cameras, nor would he ever be.

His real-life family saga was becoming more dramatic than the films in which he played. In September Frances and Manny had gone to court, and while the judge had kept them from divorcing, he had awarded Frances separate maintenance. Robinson now had to pay for two apartments, as Manny moved into the guesthouse next door to where Frances and his daughter would be.

That was only the start of the troubles. A few weeks later two cab drivers identified Manny as the armed robber who had held them up, and the police took Manny in. The lawyers were able to get Manny out on bail, but in October, at age twenty-one, he was standing trial. Manny was innocent, there can be no doubt. But the jury came back with an 11 to 1 verdict for acquittal, and with a hung jury, Manny would have had to be tried again if the district attorney's office had not dropped the charges.

By this time Gladys had washed her hands of her son. They were barely on speaking terms. Ever taxed financially, Robinson took an offer at Columbia for third billing after Barbara Stanwyck and Glenn Ford in *The Violent Men*, in which Robinson played a crippled, mean, baronial rancher trying to force farmers out of his valley. Little Caesar in buckskin.

It was part of a two-picture deal, and Robinson also accepted the script for *Tight Spot*, in which he would take second billing to Ginger Rogers. The story was weak—about a model released from prison to serve as a material witness for a U.S. attorney. But more important for Robinson, it meant his Red taint was washed away. Rogers's mother Lela had testified about Communists in Hollywood before HUAC. She was a witch hunter. If Rogers accepted Robinson as her costar, she must have felt he was all right.

In December Robinson appeared on the CBS anthology series *Climax*. His was entitled "Epitaph for a Spy," and he portrayed an unsuspecting Iron Curtain refugee used by a pair of French espionage villains. The notices were good, and Allenberg told his client he had a future in television. It was one prophecy from an agent that would turn out to be true.

Christmas turned out to have some joy, as Francesca was now a little girl, not just a baby. Walking and talking a little, she ensured a constant smile on her grandfather's face. When the family was together—or all in the same room, to put it another way—the sight of Francesca would at least reduce the conflicts. Robinson could not be angry at Manny in front of the child. The truce was marred only by a fight between Manny and the business manager a few days before the holiday, when the business manager criticized Manny for buying two bottles of eggnog—extravagance. The business manager insisted that from that point on all bills—even the milk bill—would be monitored by his office. It was more than Manny could bear. His temper exploded, and Robinson gave in. That business manager was relieved of his duties. At other times, other business managers would have to attempt to fulfill the same task.

Manny and Robinson were getting along for another reason. After his well-publicized bout with the law, Manny was sure any chance he ever had of a show business career had gone down the drain. But his godfather, Harry Warner, stepped forward with an offer to help him find work. Manny's spirits were high, his drinking subsided. He even exchanged gifts with Gladys.

The holiday over, Robinson waited anxiously for his 1954 films to be released. *Black Tuesday* was the first—just before New Year's Day—and Robinson had his first strong reviews since *Key Largo*. "It's a pleasure to see Mr. Robinson shedding his good citizenship in such a colorful, lively show," the *New York Times* said. *Variety* noted that he "has lost none of his menacing qualities."

Though the reviews were good, they could bring him no happiness. Robinson felt back at square one, as if *Dr. Ehrlich's Magic Bullet* had never been made. He was making films with no substance, if not quite B or low-budget films. He complained to friends at the Hillcrest that he was doing "crap." The Roundtable gang, all of whom had done their share of junk, was highly sympathetic. Besides, they reminded him that the low-budget films were bringing in some profit.

The Violent Men premiered a few weeks later, and Robinson's notices were better than that of his costars, but he wanted to cry when he read them. Most made mention of Little Caesar, making him seem like a gangster in a different uniform. He asked Bert Allenberg if he was "old hat." Allenberg reassured him and booked him on a *Ford Theater* on NBC. A quick $4,000.

The work was coming, and Allenberg was now in a position to negotiate "points" for his client—the show business expression meaning Robinson would share in the net profits. Robinson would get 16 percent of the net on his next United Artists' film, *A Bullet for Joey*. He'd have top billing and play the cunning Canadian inspector who rounds up a gang of criminals. The script excited him. It was not an A, but it seemed good.

That is, until the name of his costar was announced. George Raft. They had barely spoken to each other—and then only reluctantly—since the fist fight in front of Stage 11 while filming *Manpower*. It had been more than a decade. If Robinson had wanted to find a gimmick to get his name back on the lips of the in-crowd at Ciro's or Romanoffs, he couldn't have dreamed of anything better. There's little the gossips in Hollywood like more than a good feud.

But things were different now. The two men were no longer competing superstars vying for top-dog status at the same studio. Raft had passed his prime, and his involvement with gangsters and his gambling and womanizing had extracted their price. His career was on the skids, and he was almost broke. Robinson had been through the witch-hunting horror, he had lost his status, and at age sixty-one—two years older than Raft—the juicy character parts were not coming his way.

It was Robinson who took the first step by sending flowers to Raft's dressing room before they had met again face to face. When Raft saw him, he gave Robinson a suspicious look as they walked toward each other across the stage. When their eyes met, Raft broke into a laugh. There were hugs all around, much to the shock—and perhaps disappointment—of the community.

Little good can be said about the film, though. *A Bullet for Joey*, in which Raft was the gangster, did not make money. One critic said of the stars, "Age cannot wither, nor custom stale the infinite uniformity of Edward G. Robinson and George Raft."

Robinson did not even notice the outcome. By the time the film was released, the truce with Gladys had broken down. She told the press in March that she was filing for divorce. On April 15, she told them the rift had healed. Robinson was in a daze. He only knew he liked it better when Gladys was away. There was no question but that their marriage was finished. What they had to decide now was whether to continue it on paper.

With Gladys and Robinson living separate lives, there were no fancy parties at Rexford Drive. Robinson's life outside of work revolved almost completely around the Hillcrest and time spent with his granddaughter. The bills were mounting: Manny and family; Gladys and her doctors and clothing bills; Robinson himself and his art collection. There would be little else in this period of Robinson's life but work.

He went back to Warner Bros. for *Illegal*, about a defense attorney who goes crooked then straight again. Weeks later, he was still at the Burbank Studios, taking second billing to Alan Ladd in *Hell on Frisco Bay*. It was directed by Frank Tuttle who, like Robinson, had suffered at the hands of HUAC—Robinson had even mentioned Tuttle's name as one of those who "suckered" him. But Tuttle had named thirty-six names of his own in his 1951 testimony, so the two men dared not discuss what happened in the past. Instead, Tuttle teased Robinson ever so gently about finally being taller than a fellow actor. Ladd was 5' 4," and even in his sixties Robinson did better than that.

In *Frisco*, Robinson is a gang leader and Ladd the former cop whom he framed and who has returned to town after serving a term for manslaughter. As in his films of the thirties, Robinson plays a brutal boss, and as in *Key Largo* the climax takes place on a boat. In years to come, Robinson would dismiss *Hell on Frisco Bay* as superficial, but it remains one of the few films of his B period that stands up after nearly half a century.

His next film is best forgotten. Later in 1955, Robinson went to work for producers William Thomas and Howard Pine on *Nightmare*, which would give him top billing but become one of the biggest box office disasters of his career. A mystery, the film had Kevin McCarthy as a jazz musician who has a nightmare that he has killed a man. Robinson played his brother-in-law, Rene, a detective. It turns out that the musician's neighbor had hypnotized him into thinking he had committed the crime. The audience understandably found it contrived.

Robinson worked more in 1955 than he had worked in years—not since his early contract days at Warners had he been so busy. Still, the big roles in the choice movies eluded him—and his agent. Robinson suspected it was because of the graylisting, that there was still too much fear left for the studios to trust him with a major investment. The executive suites at the studio had begun to be filled with college-educated men, many with business degrees. The moguls Robinson had known, pioneering men with vision but often little or no education, had been eased out or lost much of their power. Within two years the biggest of them all— Louis B. Mayer—would be dead.

One by one the studios would become more like corporations than families run by a sometimes benevolent, sometimes tyrannical dictator. The studios were also, by 1955, starting to dabble in television. One of the most popular films of the year—*Marty*—had originally been a television drama, giving the new medium credibility. Two other films—*East of Eden* and *Rebel without a Cause*—starred James Dean, who, like Marlon Brando, was a star cut from a mold created for a national mood alien to the glitter and glamour of the 1930s.

Robinson feared he was a dinosaur, a relic because of his age, and an outcast because of his political past. His friends at the Hillcrest could sympathize. They had seen vaudeville die but had found their way into radio. With radio breathing its last, they were finding their way into television. But television was a demanding medium, one of quick-paced productions. Robinson was not used to that. If only for his pride and ego, his self-respect, he wanted one more big-screen spectacular.

Cecil B. DeMille gave Robinson that chance. DeMille had always been known for screen spectaculars, and with the rise of television, all-star casts and special effects were one way of getting patrons back into the cinemas. The pioneer producer was casting for his biggest screen epic, *The Ten Commandments*, a Paramount picture that would tell, in four hours, the story of Exodus. Robinson's name was suggested for the part of Dathan, the agnostic Israelite who becomes a slave overlord, leaves Egypt with his people, then invokes the wrath of Moses and Jehovah by persuading the Israelites to build the Golden Calf. It was the one role in the film that was not sympathetic.

The producer's associates vetoed Robinson on first glance, citing his political past. DeMille disagreed. Robinson was right for the role, and the producer figured he had paid whatever debt was necessary for his political transgressions. Robinson was not only cast, he received $100,000 and fourth billing after Charlton Heston, Yul Brynner, and Anne Baxter. He was to be treated with the respect he deserved, ordered DeMille.

Robinson steals his scenes in *The Ten Commandments*, in a powerful performance. There was no doubt that he was a gang boss, but this time in costume. The old energy was back. A fierce snarl, this time in the face of the ultimate power. As one of only a few Jews, Robinson felt a certain honor in being in the cast. He mixed well with his costars, the crew showed him full respect. It felt like old times.

He would tell friends, "Cecil B. DeMille restored my self-respect," and he meant it. Hollywood would see the film and marvel at how the sixty-three-year-old body seemed much younger thanks to the power of Robinson's voice.

10

DIVORCE AND
A RETURN TO
BROADWAY

*Now, I want an end to this business. Is that clear? I'm very an-
noyed by this.*

—The Manufacturer, portrayed by Edward G. Robinson in
Middle of the Night

With a solid film under his belt, Robinson had one more ego-related
subject to take care of. He didn't want his atonement, *Darkness at
Noon,* to be his last play. He wanted one more Broadway success, just for
himself. Plus, with his relationship with Gladys over and with Jane in New
York, it seemed like a good idea to get out of town for a while.

During the filming of *The Ten Commandments,* Josh Logan had sent
him the script for *Middle of the Night,* by Paddy Chayefsky, the hottest
writer in television. The story was strong—a twenty-four-year-old woman
about to get a divorce pursues a love affair with a fifty-three-year-old
clothing manufacturer, a widower, despite the objections of their families.
It meant being on stage most of the time. The scenes were tender and
emotional, but not as wrenching as *Darkness at Noon* had been. At sixty-
four, Robinson figured it would be his last chance for a stage success.
With a financial offer of $6,375 per week plus 5 percent of the profits to

start, it was also a job he could afford to take. He wired Logan and accepted the offer, heading for New York right after Christmas.

Rehearsals in New York were a trial. Paddy Chayefsky was perhaps the most brilliant writer of his generation, but his view was often a humorless one. When the play previewed in Philadelphia in the middle of January at the Locust Street Theater, the playwright was furious. His serious work was getting laughs. Logan argued that it was a comedy since the couple marries, but Chayefsky saw it as serious drama. Robinson also wanted a few laughs—not gags, but human comedy. Chayefsky complained to Logan that he was cuing the audience to laugh.

"Eddie was just a marvelous actor," Logan still remembered. "I never had any real problems with him. But if you asked me about Chayefsky I could write a book. There were some very funny lines in the original script, but Paddy didn't think they should be in. Maybe Eddie was handling them too well. I had to tell him to take five or six of the lines out. He reluctantly cut them, discussing it all along. But I never saw him lose his temper."

For Gena Rowlands, who would go on to become a leading actress on screen and television, *Middle of the Night* was her first big break. Eva Marie Saint had played the part when the play had appeared on television, but she had left for Hollywood, and Rowlands, an unknown with but a few little parts behind her, had been hired. She had been forced to read for the role nine or ten times, as the producers still hoped Saint could return to New York.

"I didn't see Eddie until I had got the part," she remembered. "I don't even recall where our first meeting was. I do remember that I was terrified. At rehearsals there were big talents and big temperaments. I only wanted to do well . . . From the outset Eddie and I got along. He was surprisingly gentle for a man who had played so many gangsters. He was one of the most gentle men I have ever known. But he was tough, too. Eddie was no pussycat. But when he touched you on stage, he was very gentle. It made rehearsals and breaking the ice so much easier."

Robinson made sure the newcomer was kept out of the creative arguments that were going on between himself, Logan, and Chayefsky.

He was always considerate of her, and Rowlands never forgot it. She recalled:

> He was going through a lot personally, and he hadn't done Broadway in a long time. But he displayed a very good sense of humor, he laughed easily. He didn't display any big ego or star trip . . . I remember he smoked cigars all the time, but he still managed to always smell sweet. He was a sweet-smelling man, very clean. I get deathly ill around people who smoke cigars, especially when I'm nervous and queasy. But what could I do? I couldn't tell him not to smoke. I remember after the first rehearsal we got into a limousine. He had just started smoking a cigar when the car arrived, but he put it out when I got into the limo. He would always do that. It was the same way with elevators—even if he had just lit it. I never saw him light a cigar without saying, "Do you mind if I smoke?" Some stars would not be that way.

Logan and the producers had seen to it that Robinson was treated with all the respect due to him. He was given an East Side apartment, the limousine, splendid furniture, and a living allowance. A few days before *Middle of the Night* opened, his old rival Paul Muni, who was appearing in *Inherit the Wind* on Broadway at the time, came to call. The two men patched up their differences, but Muni was amazed at Robinson's perks. He immediately went back to his producers and demanded the same.

Middle of the Night opened at the ANTA Theater in New York on February 8. Robinson immediately fell into the pattern he would adopt for the run of the play—going off by himself on the set ten minutes prior to curtain and remaining alone and unseen when he was not on stage. His concentration was amazing to cast and crew. The first-night audience was not overwhelmed by the play. The story touched some hearts, and Robinson earned a standing ovation, but there was no rush at the box office. Gena Rowlands remembered the circumstances: "The reviews were mixed, although they were glowing for Eddie. Mostly Paddy was heavily attacked by the critics. This was the first television show that was enlarged into a play and there was some out-and-out snobbery. We had bad business for the first few weeks, but then we went on the *Ed Sullivan Show* and from that night on there was never an empty seat in the house."

But events back in Hollywood would knock the wind out of Robinson's sails. On February 25, Gladys, perhaps jealous over his good press, filed for divorce and announced it to the press. This time there would be no reconciliation. On the same day, Frances Chisholm Robinson filed for divorce against Manny. The newspaper articles on these events ran side by side in Los Angeles, and the columnists had a field day. Robinson could not get away, but he was most concerned over the fate of Francesca. He wired immediately that all bills for Frances and the baby would be paid.

There also seemed no reason to pretend about his relationship with Jane any longer. After performances, Robinson would go to unwind at Sardi's, the Stork Club, the Copa, 21, or the Empire Room. Jane was always at his side, always at the penthouse with him. There was no doubt he had found his next companion. This fact was not lost on Gladys either. She contended in court that Robinson had given Jane $25,000 in gifts from money that was community property, and she demanded to be compensated. She also lost her temper when Robinson lent some of the paintings for a showing in San Francisco. She claimed he had no right to do that without her permission.

Gladys's revenge was to demand that the paintings be split between them. On June 12, she hosted a party at the Rexford Drive home to display the paintings one more time. "Now we'll divide it 50–50," she told the press. "A van Gogh for Eddie and one for me . . . A Rouault for him, a Rouault for me . . . some of the choices will be almost impossible to make." Around her that afternoon were Elizabeth Taylor, Michael Wilding, Susan Hayward, Rosemary Clooney, Jose Ferrer, John Huston, and Greer Garson.

The next day the story made national headlines. Robinson did not say a word to the press or to his coworkers, but Rowlands remembered that he was not himself that day: "When it came out in the papers that he was losing his art collection it was the first time he forgot a line. He looked at me, got up and left the stage. He came back out and said to the audience,

'I was so upset, I didn't know what to say.' The audience was well aware of his personal problems, and they roared with applause. I thought at the time, 'That's what they mean by a great actor.' I'm sure he got a standing ovation that night, too."

Gladys's idea of punishment did not stop at the good-bye party for the paintings. On June 30, the newspapers carried further reports that Gladys was naming Jane as the other woman, insisting that she was living with Robinson in his New York City apartment.

The divorce settlement was being hammered out. As it stood, Gladys was entitled to 50 percent of the value of their art collection and home—in cash if she so desired—plus $3,500 per month for eleven months and 25 percent of his gross income for life. Gladys now wanted the paintings sold so she could have the money. Robinson went into a panic. He would do almost anything to save the collection. Her lawyers agreed to give him one year to raise the money to buy her half of the collection.

Throughout all the personal problems, he never brought them into his relationships backstage. Rowlands remembered, "He was very quiet about everything. We became extremely close friends. Jane was always at the theater and they were open about their relationship. Eddie, Jane, John [her husband John Cassavetes], and I would go out to dinner. He wouldn't mention a thing. He was a very proud man. We were only aware of what was going on because it was in the newspapers. Naturally, we wouldn't bring it up."

As *Middle of the Night* picked up in business, so did Robinson's star rise on Broadway. He became the toast of the town. What had been missing for the last few years—during the B-picture phase—were interviews in the press. Now, they couldn't get enough of Edward G. Robinson.

And Robinson couldn't get enough of New York. After two shows on Saturday, Robinson could be seen leaving the theater in a tuxedo ready for a night on the town, while Rowlands, Martin Balsam, and the other young members of the cast would be exhausted. Robinson would look at Rowlands and joke, "Go home, old lady. Go to bed," then take Jane out on the town. In an odd way he was courting her the same way he had wined and dined Gladys in the 1920s. The situations were parallel. He was again a Broadway star.

Back in Beverly Hills, Manny was despondent. In April he had tried to commit suicide with sleeping pills but was found in time. In July, a few weeks after Gladys's pronouncements, he was driving his automobile when he skidded and crashed into a parked car just a few blocks from the UCLA campus. Manny was fine, but the passenger, a friend, would lose one eye. Because of his past record, there was a police investigation. Manny was charged with reckless driving under the influence of alcohol. It could mean five years in prison if counted as a felony.

The first trial in October resulted in a hung jury. After it was over, the courts allowed him to fly twice to New York. His second trip, in March, coincided with his birthday. Robinson arranged a big birthday party for his son—and Gladys was also in New York on her way to Europe. She would attend the party until 11:00 P.M., then quietly leave when the curtain went down on *Middle of the Night* and she knew Eddie and Jane would be arriving. For Manny, it was like old times. For a few minutes he took his mind off the trial in Santa Monica.

But only for a few minutes. In April he was back in court, this time found guilty of drunk driving—a misdemeanor. He'd spend sixty days in jail.

Middle of the Night had closed after 488 performances, and while Robinson planned to tour with it, he returned to Hollywood to take care of business. He made sure he was there for his son during the trying time. He also had to do something that tore his heart out—sell the paintings. Robinson and Gladys had not been able to come to terms. He would have to pay her off. The Rexford Drive house would be sold, as well.

Robinson made a deal with Greek tycoon Stavros Niarchos to purchase fifty-eight of the seventy-two paintings in the world-famous collection. As part of the gentleman's agreement, Robinson would claim that he had the right to purchase the works back from Niarchos at a later date. That would not come to pass.

As the house was being cleared, Robinson could see his loves gone from their places on the walls. Gone were Gauguin's *After the Ball,* worth $200,000, Renoir's *Dinner Table* ($75,000), Corot's *Italian Woman* ($200,000), as well as Seurat's *Le Crotoy*, van Gogh's *Portrait of Père Tanguy*, and his prize, Cézanne's *Black Clock*. The sale brought him $3.25 million, certainly enough to keep Gladys comfortable. An unhappy Robinson was pictured in *Life* magazine with three of the remaining paintings.

At least Hollywood treated Robinson like a star again. Because he had been on Broadway, Robinson had barely noticed that *The Ten Commandments* had turned into a box office smash, grossing the then rare sum of $43 million. His reviews had been good, and while he had been on stage, there had been a movement in Hollywood to get him an Academy Award nomination for his work. There had been no nomination, but the fact that the community was still congratulating him on his performance was enough. In that town, you are only as good as your last picture, and Robinson was labeled good for the present.

Before he had left the East, Robinson had fulfilled an obligation that touched his heart and in a way closed an era in his life. Eleanor Roosevelt had asked him if he would say a few words at the Memorial Day ceremonies in honor of FDR at Hyde Park, New York. He could not refuse, and said: "I was flattered that this great lady had singled me out for the occasion, but it was a far deeper emotion that I felt—an emotion, I think, that mingled deep love and gratitude and something else—that it is very difficult for me to define. And it is difficult to define, probably, because there is no single word that says it. But it is an emotion that I have always felt—and will always feel—toward Franklin Delano Roosevelt."

He credited Roosevelt—accurately—with his own political reawakening in the 1930s. "Mr. Roosevelt changed politics from the small, limited thing it was so that it embraced the whole world. He made it no longer merely a politician's job, he made it the concern of every human being, he gave it scope equal to the scope of any art, and in doing so he left the artist with no excuse to remain aloof from it." Roosevelt, he concluded, "blew away from many minds the smug, complacent hypocrisy that was there. And this breath still breathes. It will never die. Never!"

Reagan, Brewer, and HUAC be damned. Robinson had had his final say. On this day he had closed his books on the graylisting. With *Ten Commandments* and *Middle of the Night* under his belt, he could go back to working where and when he wanted. Only a decade had passed.

Robinson wasn't through with *Middle of the Night*, though. He agreed to tour with the play, beginning in New Haven, Connecticut, on October 9, 1957. Jane would have a job on the production staff so she could tour with him. This time there were no repeats of the mishaps of the Broadway run, no loss of memory on stage. In December he celebrated his sixty-fourth birthday, but his energy and vitality had returned. He no longer worried about his hair turning gray, he had accepted his age.

In January 7 the play was set for three weeks of performances in Washington, D.C. As of New Year's Eve Robinson had become a bachelor once again, but not for long. He married the thirty-eight-year-old Jane on January 16 in a civil ceremony in Arlington, Virginia. His mother would have been happy—he had found a Jewish wife. Robinson would later say that he had also—and more importantly—found the deep love he thought a marriage was meant to have. Jane would be his support for the rest of his life.

As for Gladys, she took an apartment at the Century Towers, Los Angeles, as her base but would spend most of the rest of her life traveling, painting, sponsoring new artists in the United States and Europe. Outside of affairs involving their granddaughter or Manny, she would see Eddie only about one more time—when she asked Sam Jaffe to bring him to her apartment. On that occasion, they would chat about her artwork, about Francesca, perhaps about old times. They would never be friends.

Nor would all of Gladys and Eddie's friends stay the same. As in any divorce, people have a tendency to choose one partner or the other. Sam Jaffe managed to remain friendly with Gladys, but never socially. Robinson's niece Beulah would see little of the aunt who she says had such a great influence on her life. But it would not be because of a rift, rather because the relationship had run its course. Gladys's name would remain in the news columns from time to time, always about her setting off on another trip, seeming bubbly and happy. In truth, her last decade was sometimes lonely, estranged from her son and without a male partner.

But on the road with Jane and *Middle of the Night*, Robinson was glad to be rid of Gladys. He was the toast of the town as he passed through Cincinnati, Boston, Montreal, Indianapolis, St. Louis, Kansas City, Los Angeles in February 1958, and finally closing in *Middle of the Night* on March 29 at the Curran Theater in San Francisco, eight hundred performances after the premiere.

The tour was a triumph, but there were disappointments as well. Although the role was tailor-made for Robinson, and he thought it needed a Jew to give it its full life, Frederic March was the actor chosen by Hollywood when *Middle of the Night* was made into a film. Robinson would comment for years on how March was unable to capture the inherent Jewishness of the garment manufacturer. Although it was and still is common practice not to cast the Broadway star of a play in the film version, losing the *Night* part would remain a bitterness to Robinson.

There was another role he lost at this time that was an even harder disappointment. Robinson had been considered for the role of the elderly and humanistic doctor in *The Last Angry Man*, and he had even had a clause inserted in his *Middle of the Night* contract allowing him to leave the production if he was awarded the film part. When the final casting decision was made, the choice lead part was given to another actor who had just appeared in a triumph on Broadway—Paul Muni. It would be Muni's last film; the irony of losing yet another film to him was not lost on Robinson. Friends dared not ever mention Muni's name around him.

Robinson had sold the Rexford Drive home to pay Gladys's settlement, but he was able to buy it back when he and Jane returned to Beverly Hills to settle down. His art collection was, for the most part, still in the hands of Niarchos, and Robinson set out to buy new pieces though he'd never be satisfied with what he had again.

Jane was well trained in design, but she viewed the Rexford Drive home as a museum, and so she set out to "turn it into a home," as Robinson would say. A Renoir was hung in the foyer to greet guests. The sunken living room still had the eighteenth-century Chippendale fireplace, but the deep darkness was lessened by softening the effect of the beams. The porch was filled with African wood carvings, which Robinson joked was "my room of ancestors." A Modigliani was hung in the den.

Jane hired a staff of five to run the house—a maid, laundress, houseman, gardener, and butler—and she and Robinson frequently entertained. They acquired four miniature Dobermans, and Robinson would spend free afternoons playing canasta, for which he developed a passion, or stopping by the Hillcrest to kibitz.

Through the William Morris Agency, which had taken Manny on as a client to please his father, Robinson's son also found some work in 1958, appearing in small roles in *Some Like It Hot* and *Gunsmoke*, while taking the lead and star billing in a very low-budget feature, *Piranha*, which was produced in a mere two weeks. Manny was working, he was off booze, he was coping with his own life.

In 1958, too, Manny had his revenge and cleared the air at the same time. He published his autobiography, *My Father, My Son*, written with William Duffy, a bitter memoir of a mother and father who battled, who ignored him, and the misunderstandings that had got him into trouble. One of the most striking passages of the book has Manny explaining that show business stars are like royalty: "To be born into such a family is to be raised like a prince, the way I was raised. To be born into such a family gives you all the rights, privileges, duties, and obligations that your family has, except the gimmick which keeps royalty in business—the right of succession."

The resultant publicity horrified Gladys, and she criticized her son publicly, and privately swore never to speak to him again. Robinson took it more in his stride, telling Sam Jaffe that if the book in some way acted as a sort of catharsis for Manny, then it had served its purpose.

Much of the summer of 1958 was spent at home, enjoying an extended honeymoon with Jane. He had been working during most of their courtship and marriage, and they needed time to get acquainted, to allow Jane to become part of the Hollywood community. Her warmth gave her easy entrée into Robinson's world.

Robinson also tried television again in October, with a *Playhouse 90* performance in "Shadows Tremble," about a retired toy manufacturer who moves to Vermont but is seen as an interloper by the residents of the village. There were also a good number of scripts for both television and film coming his way, and the next one he chose was *A Hole in the Head*. This was to be a coproduction by two old friends, Frank Capra and Frank Sinatra, and starred the latter as the proprietor of a run-down Miami Beach hotel who is still searching for the big, get-rich-quick deal. In the play by Arnold Schulman, on which the film would be based, the lead characters were Jews. For Sinatra's sake, they were now Italians, with Robinson cast as the staid, successful older brother and Thelma Ritter as his wife.

Filmed partly on location and partly at the Goldwyn Studios, *Hole in the Head* didn't start as an enjoyable experience at all. In the early days of filming, director Capra realized that Sinatra was at his best when there was little or no rehearsal. More than one or two rehearsals and he turned stale before the rolling cameras. Robinson, on the other hand, was an obsessive rehearser, which is one of the reasons he was known to do his scenes in one or two takes. He was always prepared. Capra was in a quandary when it was time to film the scenes between Robinson and Sinatra. Robinson needed and wanted the rehearsals. So, he took a chance and had the stand-in read Sinatra's lines to the older star, hoping that would suffice. It did not.

Robinson flew into a rage. "I was a star at Warners for twenty years and no one ever refused to rehearse with me," he shouted at Capra, insisting that Capra was not ordering Sinatra to the set because he was intimidated by the star. Capra tried to calm him, but to no avail. He stormed off the set while morning rehearsals were going on, demanding that Sinatra report to rehearsals or he would quit. Capra shouted at Robinson as he walked away that if he didn't report back for the 1:00 P.M. call, he'd sue. Robinson, in *Little Caesar* fashion, would not be moved.

Within minutes he had called his agents at William Morris. They telephoned Capra, who tried to explain the situation, reiterating that he'd sue

Robinson for damages if he quit and the part had to be recast. Within an hour, agent Phil Kellogg was at the Goldwyn Studios, in Robinson's dressing room. Capra and crew kept an eye on the door, not knowing what was going on. Would they have a star? Sinatra, for his part, was unaware of the events until he arrived and went to his own dressing room.

Like all stars, Robinson had displayed his share of temperament, but he had never been known as being difficult. Even during the filming of *Manpower*, the finger had been pointed at George Raft. That was the first thing Kellogg reminded him. Kellogg explained to Robinson Capra's reasons for not rehearsing with Sinatra, which Robinson had heard and hadn't found too convincing.

Then Kellogg laid it on the line. At this stage of Robinson's career, he ought to relish and enjoy the work he had. There were other character actors his age who could play the roles he was getting, but at a far lower fee. Besides a nice salary, Robinson had been given a 10 percent profit share in *Hole in the Head*. He had a lot to lose financially, and even more to lose in terms of career and ultimate prestige. "Eddie," Kellogg finally said. "Do you want to go years without work again?"

Robinson knew what he meant. In show business there could be a continuous sort of blacklist that had nothing to do with one's political leanings. A star who did not guarantee box office by his name alone could not afford to be difficult. It was a lesson to be learned. This was not Warner Bros. 1938. This was Sinatra's picture.

Kellogg summoned Capra to Robinson's dressing room. Before the director could say a word, Robinson with tears in his eyes and emotion in his voice, gave Capra a bear hug, sobbing, "How could I do this to you, Frank. My old dear friend. Me! Who's been in the theater since before I could blow my own nose. How could I do this to you?"

Capra didn't want apologies; he wanted Robinson on the set. Robinson followed him back to face the crew, and Capra called for quiet, announcing, "Our first set-up is a big head close-up of the best damned actor in the world, Mr. Edward G. Robinson." The assembled company applauded, including Sinatra, who had just walked onto the set. Sighting him, Robinson ran up to Sinatra and repeated the hug he had given Capra, the sentiment again flowing. All was forgotten, and the filming continued.

As work progressed, Sinatra and Robinson became better and better friends. When they learned that they shared a birthday—December 12—Robinson and Sinatra decided to have a joint birthday party on the set. It was such a success that they did it again, wherever they were, for many years to come.

When *A Hole in the Head* was completed, Robinson found himself a member of the Hollywood elite again. Invitations to the big community events poured in, and he'd attend with Jane on his arm. The house at 910 Rexford Drive was again the scene of parties. When it came to work, age was now the only obstacle, but not in Robinson's mind—only in the minds of producers. Robinson hounded his agents and let the word out in interviews and by any means possible that he wanted more roles. He was willing to accept small parts, however unfulfilling, because he wanted to keep busy, to earn the money necessary to rebuild his art collection. At sixty-five, producers would have to pay higher insurance if he participated, but they'd also get a professional, a name recognized by the audience.

He also found chances to help Manny. The two appeared as father and son in a CBS *Zane Grey Theater* story entitled "Loyalty," telecast on April 2, 1959, and it gave Robinson satisfaction to know that his relationship with his son was stronger than it had been in years. He still subsidized Manny's income, but there were no more drinking and brawling incidents.

A Hole in the Head was released in July 1959, and Robinson's reviews were excellent. The *New York Times* said he was "Superb, funny while being most officious, and withering while saying the drollest things." Hollywood took notice as the film made money, and Robinson's name was second to Sinatra's in the credits, and in the same size type. Robinson was back on top, back in the minds of the community as a reigning character actor. He could walk with his head held high.

And his price for a picture was now firmly back at a respectable level. Late in 1959 he was cast in *Seven Thieves* at Fox, playing a gangster trying to make one last score by robbing a Monte Carlo casino. Rod Steiger had first billing as one of Robinson's cohorts and, as later revealed, his son. Robinson's character suffers a fatal heart attack, and Steiger goes straight. It was only mediocre fare, but Robinson didn't worry about it any longer. It was not his name and reputation that were at risk. He was no longer a headliner.

But this wasn't true on television, where his presence alone could carry weight. Early in 1960 he went to New York to do *The Devil and Daniel Webster* as a one-hour NBC special. The third act was prerecorded for the February 17 airing, but the rest had to be done live. Robinson was enthused by the work, but shocked by the fee—$10,000. He found he had to do as much work as he would have for a film.

Next, he was cast as himself in *Pepe*, a Columbia production for producer-director George Sidney. The film, which starred Cantinflas, had Robinson as a film producer who buys the beloved white stallion belonging to the title character in order to fund a film being produced by Dan Dailey. He earned $90,000 for his work and also lent five paintings to the production for an additional $10,000, although he had to pay the insurance himself. Film buffs can see on the wall Hazeltine's *Head of a Fox Hunter*, Bonnard's *Winter Landscape*, Pissarro's *Avenue de l'Opéra*, Derain's *Portrait of a Young Man*, and Monet's *A Landscape*.

Some of the individuals involved in the production would prove to be important in Robinson's later life. Producer-director Sidney would become a close friend of both Robinson and Jane, and a shoulder for Jane to lean on when illness struck her husband. They would later marry. Leonard Spigelgass, who is credited with writing the story along with Sonya Levien, would become a close friend and cowriter of Robinson's autobiography. Robinson would enjoy working on the film, although it would not be a financial success. He survived the bad reviews.

Early in 1961 he was back on the small screen on the CBS *General Electric Theater* for a drama that received much notice from the audience, although Robinson mused that the attention was probably generated by teen star Billy Gray from *Father Knows Best*. The program, called "The Drop-Out," dealt with a confused young man whose father puts him to work in his business when the boy leaves school. By the end of the hour, the young man decides that dropping out of school was a hasty decision. The theme touched too close to home for Robinson, and he didn't enjoy the job.

Luckily, there were more offers for films. Soon after, he was cast with Shirley MacLaine and Yves Montand in *My Geisha*, a Paramount film in which Robinson played the producer of MacLaine's films. MacLaine's character is masquerading as a Japanese geisha, so her director-husband (Montand) can think he is, for once, directing a film without the performance of his wife. When the film was released in the summer of 1962, a critic noted, "Robinson gives his customary relaxed and beautifully-timed performance."

It became evident to Robinson that if he wanted to keep active, it would mean traveling. He and Jane didn't mind. When *Pepe* opened in Japan, he was there. In June of 1961, he went to Paris, where Niarchos allowed him to visit the art collection Robinson had lost in the divorce settlement. The Greek shipping tycoon was not present, and the experience was emotionally draining. For Robinson the paintings were more than art, they had been friends. Although the original agreement with Niarchos had been that Robinson would be allowed to buy back most of the paintings, the tycoon knew this was a verbal agreement, not a legal one, and he reneged. Robinson would only be able to repossess a few of the more than fifty paintings sold. He would never get over it.

But in August, he went on to Rome to begin filming *Two Weeks in Another Town*, produced by John Houseman and directed by Vincente Minnelli. Robinson would have second billing to Kirk Douglas, and he never liked the script by Charles Schnee. Like *Pepe* and *My Geisha*, it was a backstage movieland story. Former star Jack Andrus (Douglas) has been in a sanatorium for three years and on his release manages to get a small role in Maurice Kruger's (Robinson) latest film. Kruger suffers a heart attack, and Andrus takes over the reins as film director, thus embarking on a new career.

There was a lot of spare time in Rome, time to sit and sip espresso or wine and chat with the stars of the picture. Robinson had resigned himself to the weak script, feeling at this point that *Two Weeks* meant little more than a free trip to Europe and some necessary activity. His spirits were good, and his sense of humor on the set was in rare form. He especially enjoyed working with Claire Trevor again, only this time she was actually his wife—not his ignored girlfriend as in *The Big Town* or his battered broad in *Key Largo*. They enjoyed talking over old times.

The epic film *Cleopatra* was shooting in Rome at the same time, and the casts and crews visited socially during off hours. Robinson enjoyed the company of Eddie Fisher, whose wife, Elizabeth Taylor, was busy with *Cleopatra*, and—as it would later be discovered—Richard Burton. Robinson insisted that Fisher was one of his favorite singers, chiefly because Fisher would often either sing in Yiddish or do English translations of Yiddish songs. The young performer obliged the star, and Robinson and Fisher spent much time together in Rome. The language and culture of Yiddish became a passion for Robinson.

After filming was completed on *Two Weeks*, Robinson and Jane returned to Beverly Hills, where Robinson's press agents had an interesting clipping awaiting him. The *Milwaukee Sentinel* had listed an advertisement in its television section for one of Robinson's 1930 films, noting "WITI-TV presents the late Edward G. Robinson in *The Last Gangster!*"

It was a different world now, both in Hollywood and the rest of the country. People visited the cinemas less and stayed at home and watched television more. Increasingly, films were being made for the teen and young adult audience, often sleazy horror or weak beach movies. The studios had all but plunged into television by now, and the base of the new industry had moved from New York. Among the permanent immigrants was Sam Jaffe, who had been cast as Dr. Zorba in *Ben Casey*, and his wife, Bettye Ackerman, also on the show. Television stars now turned more heads than film stars. If Robinson didn't want to be forgotten—or thought dead—he'd have to appear at least occasionally on the small screen. As he told friends, it was "a different game. A lot of hard work for a lot less money. I should really leave it to the young guys." But the reality of the business told him he could not turn his back on television.

After more than forty years of acting, Robinson had also developed a finely tuned and fully cultivated voice, and the William Morris Agency was able to convince him that there was respectable money to be made doing narrations or voice-overs. He obliged them by narrating a television documentary called *Project Twenty—Cops and Robbers* for NBC.

He enjoyed all the work, but he wanted to work in films whenever possible. In the spring of 1962, another chance came, when producer Hal Mason and director Alexander MacKendrick cast him—with top billing—in their film *A Boy Ten Feet Tall*, also known by the name of the book on which it is based, *Sammy Going South*. It focuses on a young boy, portrayed by Fergus McClelland, whose parents have died in an air raid on Port Said during the Suez crisis in 1956. The ten-year-old sets off alone for Durban, South Africa, to find his only living relative, an aunt. Along the way he meets Cocky Wainwright, a bearded diamond smuggler (Robinson), who teaches him about manhood. It meant filming in Kenya.

Traveling with Jane, Robinson was filming his scenes, when on June 18, in the middle of the bush country far from the capital city of Nairobi, he suffered a heart attack. Jane, beside herself with worry and fear, attempted to find suitable medical treatment, but the only doctor in their vicinity was a German, who refused to allow Jane to telephone any of their acquaintances in Nairobi, all of whom happened to be Jewish. There was one call she was able to make—to a British doctor in the capital, luckily not Jewish. A medical team was sent in via airplane the next day and transported Robinson in an unpressurized cabin back to Nairobi. Each moment was critical, and there were times when they didn't think Robinson would survive.

Robinson spent several days in Nairobi convalescing, but the thin air of the high-altitude country made it difficult for him. Meanwhile, the producers scrambled to save their investment. Representatives of the insurance company holding the policy on *Sammy* were in the hospital within days, threatening to close the picture. The suspicion was that Robinson would never act again. Jane knew if they canceled the project or replaced her husband it would kill him. She begged the producers, the doctors, the insurance people—anyone—to help the situation. A heart specialist was flown in from London. He examined Robinson and said that he would survive and could make the film, but he would have to recuperate in England—and all filming would have to be done there. Jane and the producers had no choice but to agree. On the 4th of July weekend, Robinson was taken by plane to London. His plane arrived at 5:00 P.M., and as he was being whisked to the hospital by ambulance, Robinson, looking haggard and with a full white beard, glanced out the window to see a lone photographer snapping his picture. The actor flashed the *V* for *Victory* sign with his fingers, and the photograph was reproduced around the world. Hollywood knew Robinson was ailing, but that he would survive.

But he needed rest and medical supervision. Frank Sinatra called, and he was one of the few people Robinson would speak to. The London art galleries—whose dealers Robinson had cultivated as friends and with whom he had done much business—sent over Impressionist paintings to decorate Robinson's hospital room for the duration of his stay. After a few days, the doctor told Robinson he would be all right after rest and offered to light his cigar. It was decided that the almost seventy-year-old actor should be allowed to smoke—the doctor reasoning that taking the privilege away would only make Robinson nervous and fidgety.

Another famous cigar smoker was also in the hospital at the time, and Robinson gladly did a cigar swap. It was an unusual introduction to Winston Churchill, who had always been starstruck and had once dreamed of working and writing in Hollywood.

After several weeks, Robinson was released from the hospital and finished the film. Although he often insisted to friends that he had had acute indigestion, not a heart attack, he was more candid with an interviewer, whom he told, "The best thing you can do is forget it ever happened. It takes you to the side of the road and then you go on."

He returned to Rexford Drive for further recuperation, bowing out of any more work for a while. By Christmas he was eager to get back, and he busied himself by doing fund-raising work for Israel, traveling a bit, and making speeches. Jane held a few parties, and they attended many more. There were very frequent visits to the Jaffes, and Robinson took delight in knowing that thanks to television, Sam had more recognition with the younger set than he had. There had never been a competitive spirit between the friends.

In late March, a friend from the Hillcrest Country Club, the famous producer Pandro Berman, had contracted Paul Newman for his latest film, *The Prize*, and offered Robinson the second-billed part, guaranteeing him $75,000 and a commitment for another film at $100,000. Robinson eagerly accepted.

It was a challenging assignment. Stratman and Craig (Robinson and Newman) are two Americans on their way to Stockholm to receive Nobel Prizes. Through the deceit of Stratman's niece (Diane Baker), the eminent physicist is kidnapped by an Iron Curtain power that puts his "twin" in his place. Craig is suspected of knowing about the plot and is pursued by the kidnappers, eventually rescuing Stratman and rushing him to Stockholm in time to accept his prize.

Robinson was pleased with his work. He felt good about himself, and his spirits were high. He especially liked the look of his beard, which Tommy Furlong, barber at the Hillcrest, had designed for him based on that of Commander Whitehead, international symbol of Schweppes tonics.

In May of 1963, Maxwell House Coffee, through its advertising agency, contacted Robinson asking if he'd be interested in doing a television commercial for the product. Stars and celebrity endorsements had been common for years—Robinson himself had had pipe tobacco carrying his name on the market since the 1930s. But up to this point most celebrity endorsements on television and radio had merely been by the hosts or stars of the particular program the sponsor was supporting. The era of celebrities doing actual commercials had not yet begun. Robinson hesitated. Maxwell House came back with an offer guaranteeing him $75,000 for what would only be a few days' work. He didn't know what to do.

Robinson called his friend Jack Benny, who had been identified with Jello for years and had done many endorsements. He told Robinson not to be ashamed, but Robinson was still not sure, and the discussion filtered to the Roundtable at the Hillcrest Country Club. George Burns remembered what happened: "Eddie was saying that they had offered him $75,000 to do the commercial, but he didn't think he wanted to do it. I asked him what his objections were, and he told me, 'George, I'm a big actor.' I said to him, 'Eddie, you're only 5'5"! You're a little actor. Do the commercial.'"

Robinson was convinced. The spots, which eventually ran for two years and were reshot several times, pictured Robinson enjoying the coffee and telling the potential buyers to purchase Maxwell House, with Robinson's text ending with a Little Caesar "Now do it my way, see . . .," with a tongue-in-cheek smile, and a "You'll like it." Robinson had made his peace with the characterization of the gangster role that made him famous.

"Eddie always insisted that he didn't know how to do that Little Caesar dialogue," Burns continued. "When he did Jack Benny's show, they had to get some comedian who impersonated Eddie to come backstage and show him how to do it. Even at all the great parties Eddie had, you never heard him doing the voice. And he did have a good sense of humor. We all loved going to parties at the Robinsons'. The real entertainment always began when we'd take our shoes off and run barefoot through Sam Jaffe's head of hair," Burns kidded.

At least the audience identification was back. And Robinson had opened the doors for other big stars to do television spots. Soon Bette Davis would be singing the praises of orange juice and Eddie Albert would be using a detergent prewash.

His name was mostly out of the news until December, when several events occurred in rapid succession. On the first of the month, he joined Betty Hutton, Cornel Wilde, and Barbara Stanwyck in hosting a ninety-minute NBC salute to Cecil B. DeMille, the man Robinson always credited with restoring his respectability in Hollywood, and his self-respect as an actor. The program was called *The World's Greatest Showman*.

On December 8, just days before his seventieth birthday, Robinson received the Eleanor Roosevelt Humanitas Award for his work selling Israeli bonds. He had long since stopped wearing his French Légion d'Honneur pin since he had developed a distaste for Charles de Gaulle, and the Roosevelt prize became his prime personal achievement, earning a place among the art treasures in his home.

A few days later, on the 15th, Manny, aged thirty, married an actress named Ruth Elaine Menold Conte in Arlington, Virginia—where Robinson had wed Jane Adler. About this time, Jack Haley Jr. became reacquainted with Manny, whom he hadn't really seen since childhood. "He'd been rather notorious as a kid. Now he was notorious as an adult," Haley remembered. "He was trying to kick the drinking. I invited him up to the house. I had people over every other Friday. He came. He was quiet. He had fun."

"I'd see him on and off," Haley continued. "At least once a month. I'd invite him over. He was trying to substitute grass for liquor. I remember I cast him in a picture and Hal Wallis was nervous. He said, 'How can you control him?' But I think it was because of Big Eddie's prominence that Little Eddie took a bigger attack from the town. I would occasionally run into his father and he'd always thank me."

After several years of renewed friendship, Haley and Manny drifted apart again. Haley reported that "the last time I saw him, which I guess was 1973, he had gone off the wagon. He was kind of a gypsy, moving around a lot."

Robinson gave nodding approval to Manny's marriage—hoping it would settle his son down—and went to work in a solid and fun supporting role in Jack Lemmon's film for Columbia entitled *Good Neighbor Sam*, in which he was cast out of type as a hyperpure and conservative milk magnate named Simon Nurdlinger. His work took only a few weeks, and he enjoyed every minute of it.

At the end of January, *The Prize* was released to dismal reviews, except for Robinson, whose dual performance was called the best work in the picture. In the lingo of the industry, "he swam."

Frank Sinatra then convinced Robinson to play an unbilled part as the top hoodlum in *Robin and the Seven Hoods*. Robinson's character, Big Jim, is feted at the commencement of the film on his birthday, then is gunned down. But his smiling—almost laughing—pictures and paintings are seen throughout the film, haunting the killers, including Sinatra, Dean Martin, Sammy Davis Jr., and Allen Jenkins, Robinson's old comrade from several 1930s gangster films.

Robinson found himself tremendously in demand in 1964, so busy he didn't have to resort to television for work. He was back with Paul Newman for *The Outrage*, fulfilling the commitment of his *The Prize* contract, playing a character aptly called merely Con Man, who meets a preacher and a prospector at a railroad station and listens to their tale of the trial of Juan Carrasco, played by Newman. Robinson was heartened by the casting of Howard da Silva as the prospector; da Silva suffered through the blacklisting period with a complete loss of film income. The two men did not discuss their past, but there was a bond between them.

In his next film, which went into production soon after *The Outrage* was completed, Robinson was cast in the role of Carl Schurz—an actual character from the pages of history—in *Cheyenne Autumn*, a semihistorical epic of Indian wars and Indian truces. Spencer Tracy had originally been offered the role. Robinson was back at Warner Bros. for the film, and back with director John Ford, whom he had demanded for his Columbia film *The Whole Town's Talking* thirty years before. Robinson received fifth billing but was calm about it. Jimmy Stewart had got only fourth billing after Richard Widmark, Carroll Baker, and Karl Malden.

There were good tidings in 1964, but heartbreak as well. Robinson wrote to Niarchos in May noting that he had just come back from New York and Chicago, where he had done fund-raising work for Israel. Robinson indicated to Niarchos that sellers in New York and Chicago—whom he described as "mutual friends"—had told Robinson that Niarchos was doing a lot of buying. Robinson hoped that Niarchos was "rearranging and changing the character" of his collection and might be trying to rid himself of some of the paintings that did not fit the new mood. "You may be having second thoughts about some of your earlier acquisitions, particularly those I know so well," he wrote. "In which case, I would like to feel you would give me the opportunity of considering their purchase before making other arrangements concerning them. I would deeply appreciate such consideration and courtesy."

Niarchos had no interest in selling to Robinson. Something so sought after is something worth keeping.

If there was no response from Niarchos, there were more offers to act. In November, Robinson signed for ten weeks at $10,000 per week for what he would consider to be his last film of importance, *The Cincinnati Kid*. Steve McQueen was cast as a gambler—the Kid—who is a top-notch poker player in New Orleans, thinking of moving his gambling career on to Miami, until the Man, Lancey Howard (Robinson), makes an appearance on the scene and forces the Kid into one more big game.

The Cincinnati Kid had been written by Ring Lardner, Jr., one of the Hollywood 10, and Terry Sothern—and Robinson was pleased that Lardner could now get full credit on the screen. He also was satisfied working with Joan Blondell, hired by producer Martin Ransohoff and director Norman Jewison for a supporting part. Robinson and Blondell had worked together in *Bullets or Ballots*, and now she too was active in character roles.

Mostly, though, Robinson liked the role, which he would later say in interviews was more like himself than any part he had done. Lancey Howard, like Robinson, was a man in his seventies who had been on top and was now being challenged. The only difference was that Lancey was still top dog, and Robinson knew that McQueen was the star. In one scene Lancey returns to his hotel room, totally fatigued, where the proud, strong man crumbles on his bed, his face filled with the agony of the competition, the fear of defeat, and the strain of age. For Robinson, it was not a difficult scene to do. And though Lancey eventually beats the Kid with a straight flush to a full house, for Robinson the film was a climax to his career, a public reckoning of his own age and mortality.

Emotionally drained when the filming was completed, Robinson did not want to work for the first time in years. He had had four releases in

1964, his largest output ever—even more films in the theaters in one year than in his heyday at Warner Bros.

But there was one commitment he needed to take care of. On January 9 he made the first of several appearances on ABC's *The Hollywood Palace*, this time reading a patriotic essay entitled "This Is It" for a $7,500 fee.

When he returned to the Rexford Drive home with no work immediately ahead and a chance to relax and do some painting, Robinson felt professionally secure for the first time in years. *The Cincinnati Kid* had been a lesson to him. He was back in mainstream Hollywood, and he no longer had to look over his shoulder for conservatives attempting to make his life miserable. The film had taught him that he still had the knack as an actor, but more important, that he need not feel he should be a top star anymore. Although he had convinced himself intellectually that he was a character actor years before, now he realized that he could thrive as a supporting character actor. What was important now was to keep busy, to keep the creative juices flowing. He had an art collection of note (although not what it had been), and he had a wife he adored more than ever.

Jane was keeping busy, also, starting a company called Adler Enterprises, which made gadgets such as the "handy band," a four-way rubber band that stretched out to hold objects and containers, and the "guarder," a sleeve garter with a zipper in which a woman could hide money and lipstick when she didn't want to carry a purse.

Friend George Sidney was working on his first television project in February, and he asked Robinson to join the cast. For the drama *Who Has Seen the Wind*, Robinson was the captain of a tramp steamer whose passengers include stateless victims of World War II. The reviews made it clear that Robinson had made George Sidney's directorial debut on television a success.

And in April he participated in an event that was most important to Robinson's self-esteem. On April 17, he went to Steve Allen's home to participate in the reading of *Letter from Birmingham Jail* for KABC Radio. Robinson was participating actively in liberal politics again, this time not against the Nazis, but against racists, and for civil rights. It would be the first of numerous appearances he would make for that cause, and because it was a popular one there would be no studio consequences. He had moved into the realm of elder statesman in Hollywood, and he could do as he saw fit.

In May he gave an interview in *Daily Variety*, having made his peace with the trade papers that had shamed him during the witch hunts. It was the old Robinson speaking, the man of political commitment in the 1930s and 1940s. "We are beholding marvels in the realm of speculative thought," he said, noting the giant steps that had been taken in science. Then, he spoke of the activity taking place on college campuses—the Vietnam protests were beginning—and he called the actions at the University of California campus at Berkeley "a bursting of the bounds fettering the limits of free speech and academic freedom although they are doing it the wrong way. I don't believe in upsetting the morale and curriculum of a great university. Let them do their search for new ideas off the campus."

But he had nothing but praise for the other actors he said "were thrusting themselves into the great debates of the day." Robinson asserted, "Voltaire and the Enlightenment carried us forward. I believe we are living in a New Enlightenment. Man is racing to new frontiers of the mind and spirit as adventurous as landing on the moon or probing the secrets of Mars." The article ended with the reporter's "Little Caesar has come a long way!" It was a misstatement: Little Caesar had returned.

GOLDEN CHARACTER YEARS

Most people don't live. They worry about the afterlife and they haven't really lived here.

— Edward G. Robinson

Robinson's screen appearances in 1965 centered on a few forays into television, and though he wanted to work more, he was content with what came his way, still always pressing for that solid character part.

His reviews for *The Cincinnati Kid*, which was released in October, were stunning. The film had put McQueen firmly on the road to superstardom, and for Robinson it was increased recognition. So he flew to New York to do one of the popular panel shows of the age, *What's My Line?*, appearing as the mystery guest and charming the regulars with a Mr. Kitzel accent that he had not used publicly since his stage success in the 1920s. America knew he was alive again.

"Robinson was a delight," recalled Stephen Pinkus, who as a fledgling William Morris agent was assigned to "cover" the client, or spend the day with him, whenever Robinson had to make an appearance of any sort in New York. He continued:

I remember during rehearsals there was, as usual, much commotion, and no one was paying much attention to Robinson. He signaled me to come over and whispered something in my ear. I didn't understand a word of it, so I asked him to repeat what he had said. He did, and I realized he was speaking to me in Yiddish. I said to him, "Mr. Robinson, I'm Jewish, but I don't speak that language." He looked at me with a sigh, mumbled some lament about the younger generation of Jews, and then whispered "Where can I go to take a piss?" All he wanted was the bathroom! He was really a great guy. All the young agents enjoyed it when he came to town.

Work started to flow in for Robinson early in 1966. On February 4, he did a makeup test for a movie in development entitled *Planet of the Apes*. Robinson was testing for the part of Dr. Zaius, the leader of the new civilization. It meant wearing a heavy suit and makeup, but he was offered $150,000 to play the role of an ape and he signed. There was, at this point, no starting date.

He also agreed to do *The Angel Levine*, expecting to play an aged and impoverished Jew coping with his lot in life and with a world that has passed immigrant Jews by. The rub is that an angel sent by God is black. In addition, he was offered the role of Hassan Bey, a Turkish warlord, in a film to be entitled *Cervantes*.

All three parts were strong roles, and he was expecting a good year. Fate changed all that. Late in the afternoon of June 10, he was driving home on Rexford Drive, heading north from Santa Monica Boulevard, when he either fell asleep at the wheel of his car or had a seizure. The doctors were never sure.

What is certain is that the car mounted the pavement, bounced off a tree, and plowed across several front lawns until it came to a halt in front of 710 Rexford Drive. Robinson was immediately rushed to Mt. Sinai Hospital and listed in critical condition with hemorrhaging in his ruptured abdomen and spleen, and cuts and lacerations over much of his body.

Jane and Manny rushed to the hospital, and at 4:15 P.M. Robinson was wheeled into surgery, with the doctors not offering much hope. He was in the operating theater until 2:00 A.M. then was sent to intensive care. For days it was touch and go, as the newspapers published preliminary obituaries and Jane found no time for rest. Sinatra was on hand through it all, as were other friends. But Robinson survived and left the hospital on June 25, carrying a skateboard that Sinatra had given him as a joke. There were smiles for the waiting photographers and press.

But back on Rexford Drive, he needed time to convalesce. Even Robinson stubbornly knew it would take time, and he was forced to bow out of *Angel Levine*. The part eventually went to Zero Mostel. *Cervantes* went to Jose Ferrer and was a dismal failure.

He still wanted to do *Planet of the Apes*, but the producers would not wait for him, and they cast Maurice Evans in the Dr. Zaius role that was to be his. Since Robinson had signed a contract, his agents were furious. Many months later he agreed to a $50,000 settlement, but it was never the money he had been after. It was the challenge.

He would not work for the rest of the year, but despite his age, the body healed. Yet, age has a way of creeping up on even the most vital. Robinson found that his eyesight and hearing were starting to fade, although it would be a few more years before it became truly noticeable.

Much of his time now was spent with family, particularly worrying about the future of his granddaughter, Francesca. The girl's mother had had a mental breakdown and had gone to recuperate with her family in Florida. Manny was remarried, but unable to care for the child. Robinson and Jane sought to take Francesca into their home, but Gladys would not allow it. At the same time, Robinson didn't think Gladys capable of caring for a girl barely in her teens.

The outcome of the squabbles was that Francesca went to live with Augustine Cole, who had been Manny's trusted governess and his friend in times of trouble. Robinson and Jane sent support money for Francesca and saw her often. Gladys took her to Europe. She was still part of the family, but circumstances had dictated that she be left in the care of someone who was not blood. It was a bitter pill for Robinson to swallow, but he had no choice.

After the first of the year in 1967 things began to happen for Robinson again, and the next two years would be as active as any in his life. In fact, there were few weeks when he wasn't working, and he couldn't have been happier. Work meant travel, and that pleased Jane, too.

On February 20 he went into rehearsals with Dick Van Dyke for *Never a Dull Moment*, from the Disney studio. Directed by Jerry Paris, who had acted with Van Dyke on *The Dick Van Dyke Show*, *Never a Dull Moment* gave Robinson second billing. Again he was a gangster chief, this time trying to mastermind an art theft with Van Dyke as an out-of-work actor mistaken for a hired killer by the gang.

Before *Never a Dull Moment* was released—in 1968—Robinson would have several other films in the can. With Jane, he went to Paris for *La Blonde de Pékin* (The Blonde from Peking), with Robinson in the small but key role of a CIA agent trying to obtain a Chinese pearl. In Italy, he'd do *The Biggest Bundle of Them All*, with Robert Wagner and Raquel Welch, one of the hottest names in show business at that point. Robinson played a cultured professor hired by a gangster (Vittorio de Sica) to plan a job.

Robinson was hot internationally and in Italy, with *Variety* noting he was in demand as much as Lee Van Cleef, the spaghetti Western star. He had top billing—in *Grand Slam* (Ad Ogni Costo) as an old teacher trying to put together a big heist, and *Uno Sacco Tutto Matto* (Mad Checkmate), the latter never released as a feature but eventually shown on television under the title *It's Your Move*.

In August he was in Rome for *Operation St. Peter's*, as the thief of Michelangelo's *Pietà* from the Vatican. Again, there was an international cast, but for $75,000 and a few weeks' work, Robinson did his job.

Back home, niece Beulah Robinson, now a designer, had temporarily moved to California to try her luck. Manny's marriage had faltered, and the two cousins took an apartment together. She vividly recalled that period in the Robinson family life:

> Manny was not drinking. He was with Alcoholics Anonymous at the time. We'd get together with my uncle and Jane for dinner. I always thought my uncle found me a good influence on him. Manny was doing some acting

and he had started a production company. I don't know what it was or if anything came of it. I don't think so.

My uncle and Manny were getting along at this time, Sam Jaffe always said to me, "Y'know, the greatest thing that Eddie had about Manny was hope." That kept my uncle going. The sad part is Manny really was bright, he was sharp. After his troubles, no one could take him seriously, and it was a shame, because he was bright.

But, my uncle and Gladys were not awful parents. There was one thing about my uncle. He emphasized the intellectual. If you mispronounced a word he quickly corrected you. I remember when I was a kid it used to bother me because he'd come to New York and he'd ask me "How are your grades?" and "What are you learning in school?" You felt like you were on the carpet sometimes. But I realize now what he was trying to do. He really wanted for you to be interested in learning. I don't know if Manny ever realized this. Maybe he just built up resentment. They indulged him too much; they loved him too much. But Manny could never live things down. I remember when he came to New York and he went to some clubs and the columns published "Edward G. Robinson Jr. was seen at such and such a club on his best behavior. He was with a girl cousin." That item always killed me.

Beulah also remembered Robinson's love for his dogs. One time a butler took the collie to have his hair cut, and instead of it just being thinned, the dog came back shorn. The butler was fired.

Things were really good then. It was "Come to breakfast"—my uncle always ate prunes—and there was laughing and joking. It was really family. When I was leaving after living with Manny, they both took me to the airport. Manny had tears in his eyes, and said I had to come back even if it meant he was going to New York to get me.

But always there were crowds when my uncle was in public. When they walked me to the gate, people suddenly gathered and began asking for his autograph. We were used to it. The people were handing pieces of paper to my uncle and he was signing them. As the crowd grew they started handing the papers to Manny to give to his father, and my uncle turned to him and said, "Please Manny, don't drum me up any more business." We all laughed and it was a lovely send-off.

Autograph hounds seeking Robinson's signature had been common for forty years, but around him Hollywood had changed once again. Between the so-called new morality in the country and the pervasive nature of television, the movies had reached their lowest point ever. Fewer were being made, and fewer still were making money. Box office receipts were low. Studios, which for years had been at the mercy of bankers, were now being acquired by larger corporations. The families that once ran them were scattered and no longer in power. For an actor of Robinson's age, it was particularly damaging, but still he continued, telling interviewers that he wanted jobs, not testimonials.

It is a credit to his talent that Robinson was able to retain the screen power he had in the 1930s. Never tall, he had, with age, diminished in height and gained a few inches around the waist. The face grew older and scraggy, even with the beard. The eyes were still penetrating, although there were bags underneath them, and his screen persona was kept intact by his mouth, still able to snarl.

"I don't know anyone who didn't like Eddie," said Phil Weltman, who was with the William Morris Agency for thirty years and, as head of the television department, got Robinson placed on the network shows. "But he developed a cantankerous streak. One day I picked him up at his house to drive him to CBS. He sat in the car bitching and moaning about the fee he was getting. I said, 'Eddie, if you're unhappy, screw it, I'll take you home.' 'Naw,' he said, 'I okayed it.'"

"Eddie was not tight," Weltman continued. "And he could show you lavish parties. He did complain about his salaries. He knew every penny he was supposed to be getting. He was very interested in the money. But it didn't bother you because he was such a doll of a guy. He had a great sense of humor and he'd do anything for you if he liked you. There wasn't a more loyal person in Hollywood."

If 1967 had been one of Robinson's busiest years, 1968 would be a time for some relaxation. He had stopped going to too many movies and even shied away from watching his old ones on television. When he was fitted for a hearing aid, though, he said he found his old movies comforting, claiming they were one of the few things he could watch with the hearing aid turned off.

His major work in 1968 consisted of *MacKenna's Gold* for Carl Foreman, Dmitri Tiomkin, and Columbia, a tale of greed for gold with Gregory Peck and Omar Sharif in key roles. Robinson was cast as an old, blind prospector, the only living white man who has seen the El Dorado gold-filled canyon. It meant one week of work, at $45,000. At his side in *MacKenna's Gold* is John Garfield Jr., son of the late actor, who was trying his own hand at acting. Garfield played the blind prospector's companion. For Robinson, it was a bittersweet presence, since young Garfield's father had died as a result of the anguish of HUAC. It also brought to Robinson's mind the status of his own son, Manny, who like young Garfield was trying to act in the shadow of a famous father.

In April, Robinson was back on a public political platform, as he appeared at the Martin Luther King Friendship Rally at the Hollywood Bowl on the 24th. His remarks were carried on local KLAC Radio.

In all he had six films released in 1968, topping his previous highs. It didn't matter to him whether they made money—and with the state of films being what it was, most of them did *not* in their domestic runs.

What had begun to interest Robinson again was the state of the world. After so many years, he once again sought political involvement. In the November election, Robinson favored Hubert Humphrey, although he would quip that the candidate needed "a good director." With the Democratic Party fragmented and Humphrey held responsible for the sins of Lyndon Johnson, many friends who were normally on the same side as Robinson switched their allegiance to Richard Nixon, whom Robinson disliked. Among the names in Nixon's column was Frank Sinatra, and that saddened Robinson. It also cooled their friendship slightly. Sinatra was still part of the Robinson inner circle, but the tight camaraderie was never the same again.

One thing Robinson always admired Sinatra for, though, was the latter's work for Israel, which had remained Robinson's passion for twenty years. Sinatra's work for the country and for Jewish charities was unique among those not of the faith. Robinson's work was preeminent. Israel honored him with its Distinguished Artist's Award in 1968, and at a special seventy-fifth birthday celebration held in his honor at a Chanukah festival in Madison Square Garden, he received the Tree of Life Award for his Israeli bond work.

Robinson also received a letter in December that had such an ironic twist to it, he showed it to friends, amid laughter. The letterhead read, "Office of the President-Elect Richard M. Nixon." The text was simple, in which Nixon says: "I have pledged to bring into this Administration men and women who by their qualities of youthfulness, judgment, intelligence and creativity can make significant contributions to our country . . . You as a leader are in a position to know and recommend exceptional individuals. The persons you select should complete the enclosed form and return it to you. I ask that you then attach your comments . . . I will appreciate greatly, Mr. Robinson, your taking time from your busy schedule to participate in this all-important program."

That a Republican leader was soliciting aid from a leading Democrat seemed like crazy politics to Robinson. That it was from Richard Nixon, one of the members of HUAC in its early days, a man who had labeled Helen Gahagan Douglas "the pink lady," and who had been responsible for the blacklist in both the entertainment industry and the country at large made it less than palatable. For this one time, Robinson shunned his patriotic duty. Nixon was one president he didn't hanker to meet.

Early in 1969 Robinson was cast in *UMC*, a two-hour television movie for CBS that would become the pilot for the long-running series *Medical Center*. Richard Bradford portrayed Dr. Joe Gannon in the pilot, although he was later replaced for the series by Chad Everett. Robinson played an old doctor given a heart transplant by his young protégé. As part of his deal, Robinson got the producers to give Manny a small part as a reporter for $2,000, many times above scale. The movie ran on April 17 to fine reviews and, more important, excellent ratings.

Bill Haber, who later became one of the most powerful agents in Hollywood thanks to his partnership in Creative Artists' Agency, was with William Morris's television department when Robinson filmed *UMC*. He made many of Robinson's deals after that and became close friends with the actor. "The first time I met him was when he did the pilot," Haber recalled. Like a good agent, he also remembers Robinson received a $50,000 fee. "I found Robinson to be extraordinary," he continued. "He had an overview and joy of life more than most people I remember. You'd sit with him and he'd do five things at once. I've known few people who were as interested in life."

Haber had the job of finding work for Robinson, and he relished the assignment, although he indicated, "He used to think it was the 1930s–40s features. He didn't really get to like the quick pace of television." He continued:

> But Eddie was in demand. He was still a major movie star. I remember he had a $1 million offer to host all of a documentary series, but he was getting older and wasn't all that well. He made a decision not to do it. He said it was better to die and be remembered as Edward G. Robinson than die and be remembered as the host of a syndicated series. Anthony Quayle did it, but I'm sure he didn't get the same fee.
>
> It was a really tough decision for him, because Robinson loved money. He was always broke, he said. I guess he spent his money on art. And what art! I remember being at his house for a party and watching some guy crush out his cigar in one of the ash trays. I suddenly realized the ashtray was a Picasso ceramic.

Haber found that he sought out reasons to be with Robinson:

> He liked to play the sage. Robinson was comfortable in that role. He'd push you as far as you could be pushed. But he'd honor you when you told him it was no good. He also looked to other people by their Jewishness. It was important to him that someone was a strong Jew.
>
> When you'd sit at his house he'd like to reminisce. He was also very political. I've never known anyone so interested in everything. He was as politically

involved as Jane Fonda in his own way. And he loved to travel. He loved to give dinner parties. I remember that George Burns was always there and he'd bring twenty-year-olds. Eddie always got a kick out of that. Eddie was someone you could care about very quickly.

That ability to make people care carried over to the set. Haber remembers being amazed at how well Robinson was treated on the set of *UMC*. When Robinson arrived, the producer had left a box of cigars in his dressing room. Even the crew knew that Robinson would treat them with utmost respect. "What makes stars irreplaceable is when no one else can play them," Haber asserted. "Robinson was one of those stars. The secret of Edward G. Robinson the man was that he lived life to the fullest and was interested in everyone and everything. I consider it a gift to have known him."

Thanks to Robinson, Manny was also with the William Morris Agency, and Haber had some dealings with the son. He recalls Manny's frustrations in not making it big as an actor. "Manny once went in the William Morris Agency with a gun threatening them," Haber said. "He tried it on the Fox lot. You learned not to discuss Manny around Eddie unless Eddie mentioned him."

Robinson was now in the twilight of his life, and he knew it. He needed a hearing aid, which he often turned off because it annoyed him; his eyesight was failing, and sometimes even the strongest glasses did not help. Hurting his pride even more was that he could no longer drive his own car. A chauffeur was needed, even when he went to the Hillcrest.

The biggest shock came in 1970, when after a routine physical examination it was discovered he had cancer of the bladder. He was given the maximum allotment of cobalt treatments, and for a while, it appeared as if he had recovered from the disease. It was enough of a recovery to send him back to work in short spurts. He made a brief appearance as a piano dealer in *Song of Norway* with Florence Henderson. He picked up a quick $10,000 for giving a two-minute pep talk in Little Caesar tones at an Anheuser-Busch sales convention. He earned $15,000 to do a Michelob industrial film and pocketed another $25,000 for a commercial for General Foods' Toastems.

For the extra income, he allowed a reproduction of one of his own still life paintings, "Still Life of Fruit," to be given as an inducement to subscribe to the *National Observer*. The money he received was used to increase his own collection.

Two other performances that year proved to be even dearer to him. A family friend, Stanley Rubin, was producing *Bracken's World* as an NBC television series, and Jane came up with a story idea that could utilize Robinson. The series was a backstage drama set at a movie studio. In the episode entitled "The Mary Tree," which ran in December 1970, Robinson played a famous author about whom a documentary is being made. The rub is that the author is estranged from his daughter (Diana Hyland), who appears to destroy the image the author had taken great pains to construct through the years. Robinson and Jane arranged for Manny to have a small role, and he later made recurring appearances in the series as a sound mixer.

On the same night that *Bracken's World* was screened—October 23—Robinson could be seen on ABC's *This Is Tom Jones*, doing dramatic readings of the Rudyard Kipling poem "The Betrothed."

An ABC movie-of-the-week that was also shown that month was very special for Robinson, as it united him with Sam Jaffe for the first time since they acted with Jacob Ben-Ami on stage in the early 1920s. Called *The Old Man Who Cried Wolf*, it concerned an elderly man (Robinson) who witnesses the murder of his friend (Jaffe), but who cannot convince the authorities of what he has seen. Martin Balsam, who played Robinson's son-in-law in *Middle of the Night*, was his son; Diane Baker, who was his niece in *The Prize*, was his daughter-in-law. Edward G. Robinson Jr. is billed as the assistant to executive producer Aaron Spelling. Walter Grauman—known in Hollywood as Wally—produced and directed and had fond memories of the experience:

> Gosh, I loved that old guy. He knew his position in the industry, and he played it. He wouldn't really rehearse thoroughly. He'd walk through and

indicate what he'd want to do. Then, as the cameras were rolling he was really full blown. His use of voice was better than the words on the page.

Television shoots quickly, and you have to push hard. We did the film in about ten days. He'd call me "kid" or "a goddamn fucking machine" if I wanted to work too hard or too quickly.

I remember we were shooting in San Pedro. I had hoped to finish at 1:00 A.M.—it was night shooting so his schedule had been adjusted accordingly. Eddie had fallen asleep in his motor home. I got the alley lit for the shot I needed and I told them to call Robinson. It was late, and they had to wake him up. All of a sudden I look up the alley and there he comes like Little Caesar down the alley, a big cigar in his mouth, a felt hat, an overcoat. He marches over and says, "Go ahead, shoot, you fucking computer." We did the shot, and there was some tension. But the next day he came on the set and said, "Kid, you're all right. I just got a little hot." How can you not love a man like that?

But Robinson held his ground. On another day, it was a minute before 6:00 P.M., Robinson's contractual quitting time, and Grauman wanted one more shot. Robinson asked his director, "Kid, how long does it take?" Grauman told him two and a half minutes, and Robinson smiled and responded, "I'm having cocktails at the Hillcrest. See you tomorrow." That was it. Grauman added:

Of course, his hearing was going. At one point I was trying to give him instructions and I just wasn't getting through. Eddie Jr. leaned over to him and told him to put in his hearing aid.

And I'll always remember that no one could steal a scene better than Robinson. He'd make a move or something and Marty Balsam would say to me, "Watch him, watch him." Marty would say that scene stealing was taught in the Yiddish theater—but Robinson didn't act in the Yiddish theater. He just knew the cameras. No matter where the camera was, he'd find some way to make the shot his. I don't think he even realized it.

Grauman remembered Manny performing his duties, but thought he was an unhappy man. "I think he couldn't cope with the image of his father," Grauman related. "The word was that he drank, but luckily he was sober on our set."

And like others with whom Robinson worked and liked, Grauman was invited to Rexford Drive to see the art collection. While they were touring, Grauman remembered Robinson saying to him, "Always buy more than you can afford because it will keep your nose to the grindstone." The lessons of Morris Goldenberg had never died.

Robinson still sought work, but he was becoming aware of his limitations, even if he didn't want to admit them. While on sets, he would turn to actors and say quietly, "What's the director saying?" when the instructions were yelled from a distance.

At age seventy-seven, Robinson did interviews insisting he'd never retire, and there was no reason to expect he would. He had become a legend. He was not going to stop. In May he delivered the prologue and the epilogue for the PBS production of John Dos Passos's *USA*, and the Wilkinson Sword Blade company paid him $25,000 to do a commercial for their product. Again, there was the Little Caesar lilt, as Robinson explained he had tried the new Wilkinson Bonded Shaving System and it worked well, adding, "I told them they had passed my test and they had better sell me some or else! Soon after, they started selling them everywhere. Huh, they still remember who's boss. Try 'em. If you know what's good for you. See."

Now it was done with a smile.

There was tragedy on June 6 when Gladys collapsed at Francesca's high school graduation ceremonies at Marymount High School (she had been raised a Roman Catholic). Gladys died soon after, aged seventy-five, at Culver City Hospital, of a stroke and a heart attack. Robinson attended the June 8 memorial service, and Sam Jaffe remembered he cried openly. Gladys was survived by Manny, Jeanne, three granddaughters, and one great-granddaughter.

Even in death, she managed to bring headlines to the Robinsons. When her will was read, it revealed that Gladys had left Manny "one baby chair, one baby picture and one tea set," because of his "unbearable conduct towards me." Manny sued the estate—worth $750,000—for leaving him penniless.

That same month there was a rumor published in the trade papers that Robinson would do *The Steps of My Forefathers*, a Rumanian film. Niece Beulah Robinson recalled that her uncle still spoke Rumanian in his later years and did visit his birthplace, but no film was ever made.

Robinson also made up for losing *The Angel Levine* role in 1971 by playing in an episode of *Night Gallery* on NBC. He was cast in an episode entitled "The Messiah on Mott Street," about an impoverished old Jew who refused to die until the coming of the Messiah. Robinson did not realize at the time that it would be his last dramatic performance on television.

Now age and illness were beginning to slow him down, even more than he wanted to admit. The public appearances were fewer. The spirit was still there, but the energy would run out earlier and earlier each day.

In early 1972 he agreed to be a presenter for the Golden Globe Awards, given by the Hollywood Foreign Press Association and syndicated on television. Paul Hunter, a prominent Hollywood writer-producer, was producing the event and had the privilege of working with Robinson this one time. "He was a charming, dignified man," Hunter recalled. "When I went to his house to give him his script, he asked me to read it to him. I understood. His eyesight was poor. We ended up the meeting by swapping Yiddish stories. And at the ceremonies, I made sure to have cue cards three times normal size for him."

Paul's son, Neil Steinberg, was then a high school student invited by his father to visit the set. He, too, never forgot his contact with Edward G. Robinson. "I was at rehearsal and there he was, Little Caesar. During lunch break I was eating by myself and he came over. We had deli sandwiches. I put mustard on mine and he looked and said, 'That stuff will kill ya.' Then he proceeded to smear it all over his sandwich, and I mean smear it. I remember saying to my father later, 'Dad, he sounds just like Edward G. Robinson.'"

Perhaps Robinson sensed that his time was running out, as he passed through the days of 1972. But he had no intention of stopping his activities. He made one more visit to Israel, this time to do a cameo in a film entitled *Neither by Day or by Night*, in which he was cast as a New York furrier who flies to the Holy Land to see his son, who has been injured while picking oranges on a kibbutz during the Six-Day War. The film was never released in the United States, but it played in British theaters in 1975, after his death.

After Labor Day he went to work on what would be his last major film, *Soylent Green*, announced as *Thorn: 2022*. Robinson was paid $62,500 to appear as Sol Roth in this futuristic film starring Charlton Heston. The theme was pessimistic; life in the year 2022 is filled with overcrowded cities, little food, police-state tactics, and the final horror, a new food source, Soylent Green, made from human flesh.

With beret, beard, and a pale and thin appearance, Robinson portrayed an old man who remembers the old days and does research and provides wisdom for Heston, a policeman. Because the character chooses euthanasia over living in the world, many film reviewers would try to make comparisons between Roth and Robinson. Robinson did not see it that way. In one of his last interviews, he insisted, "My character in *Soylent Green* is a weak liberal who hasn't done enough to stop the rot in society." Robinson had always done his part. It had almost ruined his life and his career.

Since most sensed *Soylent Green* was to be Robinson's last picture, producers Walter Seltzer and Russell Sathacher threw a party in his honor at MGM Stage 20 on October 10, with the theme being Robinson's "second hundred films." Robinson was in his glory, saying in his remarks, "I suppose I've been a perennial to most of you." He tossed a posy to "my old warden, Jack Warner," and needled the former mogul on his dyed brown hair by quipping, "I knew him when he had grey hair."

But Robinson was not ready for testimonials. He continued work on his autobiography, which would be written by Leonard Spigelgass, although Robinson managed to dictate only up until the early 1950s. And he continued work on yet another project. Producer Ron Lyon, through his Filmsense Productions, had conceived an idea for a PBS documentary series about people over the age of seventy who were great artists, still active and in love with life. Robinson planned to narrate it, but the project would never be made.

"I went to Robinson and he fell in love with the idea," Lyon recalled. "Eddie would write the letters to the artists—Pablo Casals, Arthur Rubinstein, Jacques Lipschitz, Helen Hayes, Duke Ellington—that is, he'd dictate and I'd type. Eddie was a perfectionist . . . We'd have monthly dinners at restaurants and lunches at the Roundtable at the Hillcrest. He was like a grandfather figure. When we went out to eat, my wife, Linda Hall, would have to sit next to him. Eddie liked that. He was very sly and charming with her, but never lascivious." Lyon added that Robinson would have a tendency to go without his hearing aid, or when asked, just say, "It's on, but the damn thing doesn't have any batteries."

He also remembered that Jane went to most of the dinners, and George Sidney would attend as well. It was obvious to Lyon that Jane and Sidney had already become close friends. "Jane was so good to Eddie," he said. "She really took care of him. I don't know what her relationship was with George Sidney then, but I think Eddie knew how close they were. It didn't seem to bother him."

In this, the last year of his life, Robinson also would make almost daily visits to the Beverly Hills home of Sam and Bettye Jaffe. Bettye remembered him telling her many times, "There's a lot of love in this house, Bettye." The friendship had not waned for fifty or more years.

But by Christmas, the cancer had returned and had spread throughout much of Robinson's body. The doctors knew the end was near, as did Robinson. He went back into the hospital. Although attempts were made to suppress any publicity, the community always knows when one of its own is nearing the final curtain. The Academy of Motion Picture Arts and Sciences had planned to bestow an honorary Oscar on Robinson at their March ceremonies, and fearing the end was near, the organization jumped into action. It announced early that Robinson would have the tribute and sent an unmarked Oscar to his bedside.

With Spigelgass, Robinson wrote a statement for the press. "It couldn't have come at a better time in a man's life. Had it come earlier, it would have aroused deep feelings in me. Still, not so deep as now. I am very grateful to my rich warm creative talented intimate colleagues who have been my life's associates. How much richer can you be?"

The end was coming. Ironically, Spigelgass had reached the point of the HUAC hearings in his writing, but Robinson could dictate no further. There were frequent guests. George Burns stopped by to tell Robinson funny stories, some new, some old, to perk up his spirits. Spigelgass was a daily visitor. And, of course, the family was there—Jane, Manny, and brother Willie and his wife, Rhea, from New York, as well as the Jaffes.

The prospect of being able to accept his Oscar in person kept his spirits alive. It was reported that Laurence Olivier would present the award, and Robinson talked of being there even if he had to do it in a wheelchair.

But it was all for naught. In the afternoon of January 26, 1973, the doctors came to the waiting room where Manny, Jane, Spigelgass, the Jaffes, Willie and Rhea, and other friends had been holding vigil. It was all over. Robinson was dead.

Two days later, on January 28, mourners flocked to Temple Israel on Hollywood Boulevard, entering the chapel to melodies by George Gershwin, one of Robinson's friends in his New York days. As such melodies as "For You, For Me, For Evermore," "I Got Plenty o' Nuttin,'" and "Love is Here to Stay" filled the synagogue, friends and those he had worked with filed in: Henry Fonda, Zero Mostel, Karl Malden, Raymond Massey, Gregory Peck, Danny Thomas, and Milton Krims (writer of *Confessions of a Nazi Spy* and several film projects that Robinson had wanted to make). And of course, his friends from the Hillcrest: Jack Benny, Groucho Marx. Sam Jaffe was an honorary pallbearer, along with George Burns and men who had been there from the very beginning: Jack Warner, Hal Wallis, and Mervyn LeRoy. Rabbi Max Nussbaum conducted the services.

Charlton Heston, who had been the last actor to work with Robinson in a film and worked with him twice, delivered the eulogy, borrowing from notes Spigelgass had made for the autobiography.

Calling Robinson a "Renaissance man," Heston noted that his first stage performance was the Antony soliloquy in *Julius Caesar*, and in tribute, Heston chose a passage from the speech:

"His life was gentle, and the elements so mixed in him that Nature might stand up and say to all the world, 'This was a man.'"

EPILOGUE

Sixty years before his death, Emanuel Goldenberg had used the Antony soliloquy from *Julius Caesar* for his audition before the Sargent School. It had been his entrance into show business, and now it was his farewell. Robinson's body would not rest in Hollywood. Instead, it was flown to New York, where Robinson would take his place in the Goldenberg mausoleum at the Beth El Cemetery in Brooklyn.

On March 27, 1973, Jane was at the Dorothy Chandler Pavilion to receive Robinson's posthumous Oscar, engraved "To Edward G. Robinson, who achieved greatness as a player, a patron of the arts, and a dedicated citizen . . . in sum, a Renaissance man, from his friends in the industry he loves."

By her late husband's request, Jane did not wear black; instead, she walked out on stage in a light, sleeveless dress. Softly, she read the words that Robinson had wanted said that night: "It couldn't have come at a better time in a man's life. Had it come earlier, it would have aroused deep feelings in me. Still not so deep as now. I am so grateful to my rich, warm, creative, talented, intimate colleagues who have been my life's associates. How much richer can you be?"

There was a standing ovation, but a limited amount of tearful emotion from Jane. She knew the way Eddie would have wanted it done.

Jane returned to the Rexford Drive home, and remained there, soon married to George Sidney.

Sam Jaffe's grief would not allow him to enter the Rexford Drive home or the Hillcrest Country Club again. To the day he died in 1984, he would gaze daily at the portrait Robinson painted of him and a Robinson self-portrait hanging in the Jaffe living room in a more modest section of Beverly Hills, along with artwork by George Gershwin, Zero Mostel, and John Huston. Jaffe remained close to Ira and Lee Gershwin, and Lee's sister, Emily Paley, all from the New York crowd that Robinson had helped him become a part of in the 1920s.

Manny had been told by his father, "All us Goldenbergs live to our eighties. Enjoy yourself, but make it work for you." It was not a prophecy that would come true. On February 26, 1974, shortly after midnight, Manny's third wife found him retching uncontrollably in their bathroom. He was rushed to the hospital, but died en route. His death was listed by the coroner as a "possible heart attack," but that was later changed to "natural causes." Services were held at the Hollywood Memorial Cemetery (now Hollywood Forever) for the son who one month before his forty-first birthday had literally burned himself out.

Amidst all the tragedy, it was probably Francesca who suffered the most. Her grandmother died at her high school graduation, her grandfather two years later. Then, coupled with her father's passing was the slow, painful death by cancer of Augustine, the governess who had become her guardian. Francesca lived for a while with Jane, then headed out on her own, building a life as an artist and marrying Ricardo Sanchez. She lives today in Malibu, still close to her Aunt Jeanne, Gladys's daughter. Until Sam Jaffe's death, he and his wife Bettye traditionally spent Christmas with the Sanchez family, and cousin Beulah Robinson stays at her house when she is in California. Francesca has remained a Robinson and kept the love of art her grandparents cherished.

In his will, Robinson had left Jane the house and split the bulk of the rest of his estate, giving her half and giving quarter shares each to Manny and Francesca. Sam Jaffe received the portrait Robinson had done of him.

His Steinway piano, autographed inside by the great musicians of the age, was willed to UCLA after Jane's death, and his papers were to go to the University of Southern California.

The estate was valued at anywhere from $2.5 million to $3 million, the bulk of it in the art collection. Five per cent of the money was set aside to be split equally between six charities—the Actors' Fund of America, the Motion Picture Relief Fund, City College of New York, the American Academy of Dramatic Arts, the Jewish Community Fund of the Jewish Federation-Council of Los Angeles, and the NAACP Legal Defense and Education Fund.

Robinson had known that Jane would have to sell the collection, including the three prized works, Pissarro's *The Dead Tree,* Vuillard's *Madame Vuillard au Déjeuner,* and Morisot's *Avant le Théâtre.* There were eighty-eight paintings in all, and Robinson had hoped they could be held together in a collection, not sold separately. He had suggested Sotheby's in London or a New York auction house for the job.

The sale was swift. Armand Hammer of Occidental Petroleum bid $5,124,000 through his M. Knoedler and Co. Galleries, of which he was the principal stockholder. In April, the deal was accepted, and Hammer quipped, "We were prepared to go much higher. It's kind of a letdown." Robinson's wish to have the collection stay intact had proved impossible. It went to the gallery to be sold piece by piece.

Later in 1973, *Soylent Green* was released, and though the film did only moderate box office business, the critics could not help praising Robinson one more time. The film, *The Hollywood Reporter* wrote, "provides Edward G. Robinson with as moving a screen farewell as any actor has ever had." The image of a thin, bearded, pale Robinson on a stool, one of the publicity photos from *Soylent Green,* remains his farewell.

Praise continued to pour in from all quarters. Richard Burton told columnist Joyce Haber in November that Robinson and Spencer Tracy were tops on his list of best actors. In all press and documentary recaps of the events of 1973, Robinson's last days took a prominent place. There were attempts to launch his life as a stage musical, all unsuccessful.

An advertisement in the *Los Angeles Times* on July 28, 1977, heralded the public auction of Edward G. Robinson's effects at the Fine Art Gallery of Scottsdale in Newport Beach, California, on July 29 and 30. Offered were jewelry, period furniture, crystal and art glasses, oriental art, silver, oriental and Persian rugs. "A wonderful opportunity to acquire the world's great art treasures by competitive bidding at an investment level," the copy stated.

Jane was divesting herself of the past. For this and what he considered other slights to the memory of his friend, Sam Jaffe's relationship with Jane became at best strained, and she was not close to Francesca. Jane not only declined virtually all interviews and opportunities to talk about Robinson, she admonished those who did, frequently with pressuring phone calls. Her reasons died with her in July 1991, when she succumbed to cancer. George Sidney married again before the year's end.

The legacy of Edward G. Robinson nevertheless continues. It sometimes surfaces in small ways, such as a recruiting advertisement for the American Academy of Dramatic Arts, which used a 1913 photo of Robinson in a display of its famous graduates.

When media mogul Ted Turner purchased the MGM film library in 1986, it contained the pre-1948 Warner Bros. films, the period in which Robinson made the bulk of his movies. Turner then launched the cable television channel Turner Classic Movies (TCM) to exploit the MGM-UA and Warner Bros. libraries, and through that service nary a month goes by without some Robinson film available to cable subscribers. Naturally, his films appear elsewhere as well, and his "tough guy" image remains the symbol of the 1930s screen gangster.

That image did not deter the U.S. Postal Service from honoring Robinson with his likeness on a postage stamp as part of its Legends of Hollywood series. A ceremony on October 24, 2000, in front of a mostly packed house at the Egyptian Theatre in Hollywood featured Robert Osborne, the film critic–historian, and Turner Classic Movies as host and such Robinson costars as Karl Malden, Charlton Heston, Florence Henderson, Nanette Fabray, and Norman Lloyd speaking in praise of their friend. Francesca was in attendance, keeping the bond, and extending it—

with her was Adam Edward Sanchez, Robinson's great-grandson. *The Cincinnati Kid* was screened for those gathered.

Of his generation of Lower East Side immigrants, Robinson's name would always remain preeminent. No other Jew from that background would rise to equal stardom on the big screen. Manny Goldenberg had never forgotten his roots, and not just as a Jew. The Manny who had stood on a soapbox and campaigned for Hearst was, in his last days, preaching for civil rights; the Manny who had spent his afternoons poring over books at the Astor Place Library was in his last days still learning, still reading and acquiring knowledge. The son of Morris Goldenberg, who had been told to pursue the full life as an incentive for doing his best, had probably fulfilled his father's every wish.

While art collecting became the vogue among the Hollywood elite in the 1980s, no one would ever boast a collection that could equal Robinson's or open their homes to hundreds each year as if it were a museum. No one in Hollywood could claim their home as a mecca for the international creative community. In fact, the elite of the art and music world would be rare visitors to the screen capital.

The debate as to whether Hollywood actors should become active in politics continues, but for all the vocalizing by a Barbara Streisand for liberal causes, or a Charlton Heston for the conservatives, there would never again be the mobilization for an objective such as the antifascist movement Robinson had helped lead in the late 1930s and early 1940s. The blacklisting had destroyed any chance of that. True, many star names would work for political candidates and causes, both liberal and conservative, but while controversy might follow, punishment was not as easy to ascertain as the blacklisting surely was. For example, Jane Fonda would face the lions of the Right and the outrage of many in the nation in the 1970s for her stance against the Vietnam War but win two Academy Awards nevertheless.

The negative results of political activism were usually less devastating, but some suffered nevertheless. Ed Asner, who had appeared with Robinson in a small role in *The Old Man Who Cried Wolf*, and who achieved fame as Lou Grant, would rise to the presidency of the Screen Actors

Guild and become outspoken for liberal politics in the 1980s. His condemnation of U.S. foreign policy in El Salvador coincided with the surprise cancellation of his television series in 1982, and Asner, a multiple Emmy Award winner, claimed finding work difficult after that. Did advertisers not want to be associated with an anti-Reagan political activist? A whisper of *blacklist* followed, but except for a few articles in *The Hollywood Reporter*, the press did not wish to utter the word, and there seemed little interest even among more-outspoken liberals of taking up Asner's cause.

At the same time, Ronald Reagan, who had done Robinson's career so much damage because of their political differences, would become president of the United States, still claiming that not only had he never participated in hurting anyone's career, there had never even been a *blacklisting*. Rather, Reagan insisted, it was *his* career in Hollywood that was damaged because he was a conservative.

History speaks otherwise, but that aside, Robinson would have been saddened to see Reagan in the office once held by Franklin Delano Roosevelt. The political exchanges between Asner and spokespersons for Reagan that played in the press would have brought chills to Robinson's spine. Asner placed his career on the line, as Robinson had done years before, and like Robinson, suffered the consequences.

Actors who mix liberal or left-of-center politics with celebrity continue to tempt a backlash. In 2003, the Baseball Hall of Fame canceled a charity event honoring the film *Bull Durham* because two of its stars, Susan Sarandon and Timothy Robbins, were at the same time activists against U.S. involvement in the war with Iraq. The right wing countered by noting that actor Tom Selleck, said to be conservative politically, was ambushed on air by talk show host Rosie O'Donnell a few years earlier for allegedly being an opponent of gun control. While studios seem to let the audience decide if off-camera politics is bad business, the fear that activism will lead to career damage remains from the era of the blacklisting.

If Robinson suffered because of his politics, his career was ultimately hardly destroyed. It is indicative of his ability and talent that he lasted on stage, screen, radio, and television for sixty years. To this day he is impersonated by comedians and performers, with the Little Caesar role he grew to spurn still shadowing him. Mention his name in Hollywood to someone still around "from the old days," and a smile appears on that person's face, followed by many stories. But few people will mention the graylisting. Robinson made that period of his life his personal agony. He was determined to best his attackers, and he did. Others who went through the same hell wallowed in their sorrow or guilt for the rest of their lives. Robinson overcame it.

"Most people don't live. They worry about the afterlife and they haven't really lived here."

APPENDIX

STAGE APPEARANCES

1911

Appeared in various plays and recitals while a student at City College of New York, billed as Emanuel Goldenberg.

1912

Bells of Conscience: Performed in "circuit" (rotating performances) at Loew's Theatres during the summer while a student at the American Academy of Dramatic Arts. He considered this the first time his name appeared on a professional program, the first time as Edward G. Robinson, and the first time his name appeared above the title. First performed at the Loew's Plaza Theatre on Lexington Avenue in Manhattan.

1913

Number 37: Appeared as "fill-in" for three performances beginning March 10 in the role of the D.A. at the West End Theatre in New York City. Billed as Edward Golden, these were his only appearances in a Yiddish theater production. Though he was nineteen at the time, he played a fifty-year-old character opposite Yiddish theater legend Rudolph Schildkraut.

Paid in Full: Opened in April in Binghamton, New York. Edward G. Robinson played the role of Sato.

1915

Under Fire: Opened on August 12 in the Hudson Theater, New York City. Edward G. Robinson played the role of André Lemaire.

1916

Under Sentence: Opened on October 3 in the Harris Theater, New York City. Edward G. Robinson played the role of Fagan.

1917

The Pawn: Opened on September 8 in the Fulton Theater, New York City. Edward G. Robinson played the role of Hushmaru.

1918

The Little Teacher: Opened on February 4 in the Playhouse Theater, New York City. Edward G. Robinson played the role of Batiste.

1919

First Is Last: Opened September 17 in the Maxine Elliott Theater, New York City. Edward G. Robinson played the role of Steve.

Night Lodging: Opened December 22 in the Plymouth Theater, New York City. Edward G. Robinson played the role of Satan.

1920

Poldekin: Opened September 9 in the Park Theater, New York City. Edward G. Robinson played the role of Pinsky. George Arliss starred.

Samson and Delilah: Opened November 17 in the Greenwich Village Theater, New York City. Edward G. Robinson played the role of the Director. Jacob Ben-Ami starred. Sam Jaffe was also in the cast.

1921

The Idle Inn: Opened December 20 in the Plymouth Theater, New York City. Edward G. Robinson played the role of Mendel. Jacob Ben-Ami starred. Sam Jaffe was also in the cast.

1922

The Deluge: Opened January 27 in the Plymouth Theater, New York City. Edward G. Robinson played the role of Nordling.

Banco: Opened September 20 in the Ritz Theater, New York City. Edward G. Robinson played the role of Louis.

1923

Peer Gynt: Opened February 5 in the Garrick Theater, New York City. Edward G. Robinson played the roles of the Button Molder and Von Eberkopf.

The Adding Machine: Opened March 19 in the Garrick Theater, New York City. Edward G. Robinson played the role of Shrdlu.

Launzi: Opened October 10 in the Plymouth Theater, New York City. Edward G. Robinson played the role of Louis.

A Royal Fandango: Opened November 12 in the Plymouth Theater, New York City. Edward G. Robinson played the role of Pascual. Ethel Barrymore starred. Spencer Tracy was also in the cast.

1924

The Firebrand: Opened October 15 in the Morosco Theater, New York City. Edward G. Robinson played the role of Octavius.

1925

Androcles and the Lion: Opened November 23 in the Klaw Theater, New York City. Edward G. Robinson played the role of Caesar.

The Man of Destiny: Opened November 23 in the Klaw Theater, New York City. Edward G. Robinson played the role of Giuseppe.

1926

The Goat Song: Opened January 25 in the Guild Theater, New York City. Edward G. Robinson played the role of Reb Feiwell.

The Chief Thing: Opened March 22 in the Guild Theater, New York City. Edward G. Robinson played the role of the Stage Director.

Henry Behave: Opened August 23 in the Nora Bayes Theater, New York City. Edward G. Robinson played the role of Wescott P. Bennett.

Juarez and Maximilian: Opened October 11 in the Guild Theater, New York City. Edward G. Robinson played the role of Porfirio Diaz.

Ned McCobb's Daughter: Opened November 29 in the John Golden Theater, New York City. Edward G. Robinson played the role of Lawyer Grover.

1927

The Brothers Karamazov: Opened January 3 in the Guild Theater, New York City. Edward G. Robinson played the role of Smerdiakov.

Right You Are If You Think You Are: Opened March 2 in the Guild Theater, New York City. Edward G. Robinson played the role of Ponza.

The Racket: Opened November 22 in the Ambassador Theater, New York City. Edward G. Robinson played the role of Nick Scarsi.

1928

A Man with Red Hair: Opened November 8 in the Ambassador Theater, New York City. Edward G. Robinson played the role of Mr. Crispin.

1929

The Kibitzer: Opened February 18 in the Royale Theater, New York City. Edward G. Robinson played the role of Lazarus. Robinson cowrote with Jo Swerling.

1930

Mr. Samuel: Opened November 10 in the Little Theater, New York City. Edward G. Robinson played the role of Samuel Brisach.

1951

Darkness at Noon: Opened (on tour) September 28 at the McCarter Theater, Princeton, New Jersey. Closed on April 26, 1952, at the Cox Theater, Cincinnati, Ohio. Edward G. Robinson played the role of Rubashov.

1956

Middle of the Night: Opened February 8 at the Anta Theater, New York City. On tour from October 9, 1957, at the Shubert Theater, New Haven, Connecticut, to March 29, 1958, at the Curran Theater, San Francisco, California. Gena Rowlands, Martin Balsam, and Betty Walker were also in the cast.

FILM APPEARANCES

1923

The Bright Shawl (Associated First National): 80 min. Presenter, Charles H. Duell; director, John S. Robertson; based on the novel by Joseph Hergesheimer; adapter, Edmund Goulding. Cast: Richard Barthelmess; Edward G. Robinson; Margaret Seddon; Mary Astor; William Powell.

1929

The Hole in the Wall (Paramount): 73 min. Supervisor, Monta Bell; director, Robert Florey; based on the play by Fred Jackson; adapter–dialogue, Pierre Collings. Cast: Claudette Colbert, Edward G. Robinson, David Newell, Nellie Savage, Donald Meek.

1930

Night Ride (Universal): 5,418 feet. Presenter, Carl Laemmle; director, John S. Robertson; based on the story by Henry La Cossitt; dialogue, Tom Reed, Edward T. Lowe Jr.; adapter, Edward T. Lowe Jr. Cast: Joseph Schildkraut, Barbara Kent, Edward G. Robinson.

A Lady to Love (MGM): 92 min. Director, Victor Seastrom; based on the play *They Knew What They Wanted* by Sidney Howard; screenplay, Sidney Howard. Cast: Vilma Banky, Edward G. Robinson, Robert Ames, Richard Carle.

Outside the Law (Universal): 76 min. Presenter, Carl Laemmle; associate producer, E. M. Asher; director, Tod Browning; screenplay, Tod Browning, Garrett Fort. Cast: Mary Nolan, Edward G. Robinson, Owen Moore, Edwin Sturgis.

East Is West (Universal): 75 min. Presenter, Carl Laemmle; associate producer, E. M. Asher; director, Monta Bell; based on the play by Samuel Shipman, John B. Hymer; adapter, Winifred Eaton; screenplay, additional dialogue, Tom Reed. Cast: Lupe Velez, Lew Ayres, Edward G. Robinson, Mary Forbes.

The Widow from Chicago (First National): 64 min. Director, Edward Cline; story–screenplay, Earl Baldwin. Cast: Alice White, Neil Hamilton, Edward G. Robinson, Frank McHugh, Lee Shumway.

Little Caesar (First National): 80 min. Director, Mervyn LeRoy; based on the novel by William R. Burnett; screenplay, Francis E. Faragoh. Cast: Edward G. Robinson, Douglas Fairbanks Jr., Glenda Farrell, Sidney Blackmer, Thomas Jackson, Ralph Ince, William Collier Jr., Maurice Black, Stanley Fields, George E. Stone.

1931

Smart Money (Warner Bros.): 90 min. Director, Alfred E. Green; story, Lucien Hubbard, Joseph Jackson; screenplay, Kubec Glasmon, John Bright; additional dialogue, Lucien Hubbard, Joseph Jackson. Cast: Edward G. Robinson, James Cagney, Evalyn Knapp, Ralf Harolde, Noel Francis, Margaret Livingston, Boris Karloff, Gladys Lloyd.

Five Star Final (First National): 89 min. Director, Mervyn LeRoy; based on the play by Louis Weitzenkorn; screenplay, Byron Morgan. Cast: Edward G. Robinson, H. B. Warner, Marian Marsh, Anthony Bushell, Frances Starr, Ona Munson, George E. Stone, Aline MacMahon, Boris Karloff, Gladys Lloyd.

1932

The Hatchet Man (First National): 74 min. Director, William A. Wellman; based on the play *The Honorable Mr. Wong* by Achmed Abdullah, David Belasco; screenplay, J. Grubb Alexander. Cast: Edward G. Robinson, Loretta Young, Dudley Digges, Leslie Fenton, Edmund Breese, Tully Marshall, J. Carroll Naish, Ralph Ince, Gladys Lloyd.

Two Seconds (First National): 68 min. Director, Mervyn LeRoy; based on the play by Elliott Lester; screenplay, Harvey Thew. Cast: Edward G. Robinson, Preston Foster, Vivienne Osborne, J. Carroll Naish, Guy Kibbee, Adrienne Dore.

Tiger Shark (First National): 80 min. Director, Howard Hawks; based on the story "Tuna" by Houston Branch; screenplay, Wells Root; assistant director, Richard Rosson. Cast: Edward G. Robinson, Zita Johann, Richard Arlen, Leila Bennett, J. Carroll Naish.

Silver Dollar (First National): 84 min. Director, Alfred E. Green; based on the biography of H. A. W. Tabor by David Karsner; screenplay, Carl Erickson, Harvey Thew. Cast: Edward G. Robinson, Bebe Daniels, Aline MacMahon, Leon Ames, Bonita Granville.

1933

The Little Giant (First National): 74 min. Director, Roy Del Ruth; story, Robert Lord; screenplay, Robert Lord, Wilson Mizner; music conductor, Leo F. Forbstein. Cast: Edward G. Robinson, Helen Vinson, Mary Astor, Kenneth Thomson, Russell Hopton.

I Loved a Woman (First National): 90 min. Director, Alfred E. Green; based on the book by David Karsner; screenplay, Charles Kenyon, Sidney Sutherland. Cast: Kay Francis, Edward G. Robinson, Genevieve Tobin, J. Farrell MacDonald.

1934

Dark Hazard (First National): 72 min. Director, Alfred E. Green; based on the novel by William R. Burnett; screenplay, Ralph Block, Brown Holmes. Cast: Edward G. Robinson, Genevieve Tobin, Glenda Farrell, Robert Barrat, Gordon Westcott, Hobart Cavanaugh, Sidney Toler.

The Man with Two Faces (First National): 72 min. Director, Archie Mayo; based on the play *The Dark Tower* by George S. Kaufman, Alexander Woollcott; screenplay, Tom Reed, Niven Busch. Cast: Edward G. Robinson, Mary Astor, Ricardo Cortez, Mae Clarke, Louis Calhern, John Eldredge, Milton Kibbee.

1935

The Whole Town's Talking (Columbia): 93 min. Producer, Lester Cowan; director, John Ford; based on the novel by William R. Burnett; screenplay, Jo Swerling; dialogue, Robert Riskin. Cast: Edward G. Robinson, Jean Arthur, Arthur Hohl, Wallace Ford, Arthur Byron, Donald Meek, Lucille Ball.

Barbary Coast (United Artists): 91 min. Producer, Samuel Goldwyn; director, Howard Hawks; screenplay, Ben Hecht, Charles MacArthur; music director, Alfred Newman. Cast: Miriam Hopkins, Edward G. Robinson, Joel McCrea, Walter Brennan, Frank Craven, Brian Donlevy, Otto Hoffman, Donald Meek, Harry Carey.

1936

Bullets or Ballots (First National): 81 min. Associate producer, Louis F. Edelman; director, William Keighley; story, Martin Mooney, Seton I. Miller; screenplay, Miller. Cast: Edward G. Robinson, Joan Blondell, Barton MacLane, Humphrey Bogart, Frank McHugh, Joseph King, George E. Stone, Louise Beavers, Frank Faylen, Jerry Madden.

1937

Thunder in the City (Columbia): 76 min. Producer, Alexander Esway; director, Marion Gering; screenplay, Robert Sherwood, Aben Kandell. Cast: Edward G. Robinson, Luli Deste, Nigel Bruce, Constance Collier, Ralph Richardson, Annie Esmond.

Kid Galahad (Warner Bros.): 101 min. Associate producer, Samuel Bischoff; director, Michael Curtiz; based on the novel by Francis Wallace; screenplay, Seton I. Miller; music, Heinz Roemheld, Max Steiner. Cast: Edward G. Robinson, Bette Davis, Humphrey Bogart, Wayne Morris, Jane Bryan, Harry Carey, Veda Ann Borg, Frank Faylen, Harland Tucker, Milton Kibbee.

The Last Gangster (MGM): 81 min. Director, Edward Ludwig; story, William A. Wellman, Robert Carson; screenplay, John Lee Mahin. Cast: Edward G. Robinson, James Stewart, Rose Stradner, Lionel Stander, Douglas Scott, John Carradine, Sidney Blackmer, Edward Brophy, Louise Beavers.

1938

A Slight Case of Murder (Warner Bros.): 85 min. Producer, Hal B. Wallis; associate producer, Sam Bischoff; director, Lloyd Bacon; based on the play by Damon Runyon, Howard Lindsay; screenplay, Earl Baldwin, Joseph Schrank; songs, M. K. Jerome and Jack Scholl. Cast: Edward G. Robinson, Jane Bryan, Willard Parker, Ruth Donnelly, Allen Jenkins, Edward Brophy, Bobby Jordan, Margaret Hamilton, George E. Stone.

The Amazing Dr. Clitterhouse (Warner Bros.): 87 min. Associate producer, Robert Lord; director, Anatole Litvak; based on the play by Barre Lyndon; screenplay, John Wexley, John Huston; music, Max Steiner. Cast: Edward G. Robinson, Claire Trevor, Humphrey Bogart, Gale Page, Donald Crisp, Allen Jenkins, Maxie Rosenbloom, Ward Bond.

I Am the Law (Columbia): 83 min. Producer, Everett Riskin; director, Alexander Hall; based on the magazine articles by Fred Allhoff; screenplay, Jo Swerling; music director, Morris Stoloff.

Cast: Edward G. Robinson, Barbara O'Neil, John Beal, Wendy Barrie, Otto Kruger, Arthur Loft, Marc Lawrence, Ronald Reagan (Announcer's Voice).

1939

Confessions of a Nazi Spy (Warner Bros.): 102 min. Director, Anatole Litvak; based on the book *The Nazi Spy Conspiracy in America* by Leon G. Turrou; screenplay, Milton Krims, John Wexley. Cast: Edward G. Robinson, Francis Lederer, George Sanders, Paul Lukas, Henry O'Neill, Lya Lys, Grace Stafford, James Stephenson, Ward Bond.

Blackmail (MGM): 81 min. Producer, John Considine Jr.; director, H. C. Potter; based on the story by Endre Bohem, Dorothy Yost; screenplay, David Hertz, William Ludwig. Cast: Edward G. Robinson, Ruth Hussey, Gene Lockhart, Bobs Watson, Victor Kilian.

1940

Dr. Ehrlich's Magic Bullet (Warner Bros.): 103 min. Producers, Jack L. Warner, Hal B. Wallis; associate producer, Wolfgang Reinhardt; director, William Dieterle; story, Norman Burnside; screenplay, John Huston, Heinz Herald, Norman Burnside; music, Max Steiner. Cast: Edward G. Robinson, Ruth Gordon, Otto Kruger, Donald Crisp, Sig Rumann, Maria Ouspenskaya, Henry O'Neill, Harry Davenport, Albert Bassermann, Donald Meek, Louis Calhern.

Brother Orchid (Warner Bros.): 91 min. Executive producer, Hal B. Wallis; associate producer, Mark Hellinger; director, Lloyd Bacon; story, Richard Connell; screenplay, Earl Baldwin; music, Heinz Roemheld. Cast: Edward G. Robinson, Ann Sothern, Humphrey Bogart, Ralph Bellamy, Donald Crisp, Allen Jenkins, Charles D. Brown, Cecil Kellaway, William Hopper, Frank Faylen.

A Dispatch from Reuters (Warner Bros.): 89 min. Producer, Hal B. Wallis; associate producer, Henry Blanke; director, William Dieterle; story, Valentine Williams, Wolfgang Wilhelm; screenplay, Milton Krims; music director, Leo F. Forbstein. Cast: Edward G. Robinson, Edna Best, Eddie Albert, Albert Bassermann, Nigel Bruce, Gene Lockhart, Montagu Love, Otto Kruger, James Stephenson, Dickie Moore.

1941

The Sea Wolf (Warner Bros.): 100 min. Producers, Jack L. Warner, Hal B. Wallis; associate producer, Henry Blanke; director, Michael Curtiz; based on the novel by Jack London; screenplay, Robert Rossen; music, Erich Wolfgang Korngold. Cast: Edward G. Robinson, John Garfield, Ida Lupino, Alexander Knox, Gene Lockhart, Barry Fitzgerald, Howard da Silva.

Manpower (Warner Bros.): 105 min. Executive producer, Hal B. Wallis; producer, Mark Hellinger; director, Raoul Walsh; screenplay, Richard Macaulay, Jerry Wald; music, Adolph Deutsch. Cast: Edward G. Robinson, Marlene Dietrich, George Raft, Alan Hale, Frank McHugh, Eve Arden, Barton MacLane, Ward Bond, Barbara Pepper, William Hopper.

Unholy Partners (MGM): 94 min. Producer, Samuel Marx; director, Mervyn LeRoy; screenplay, Earl Baldwin, Bartlett Cormack, Lesser Samuels; music, David Snell. Cast: Edward G. Robinson, Laraine Day, Edward Arnold, Marsha Hunt, Frank Faylen, Milton Kibbee.

1942

Larceny, Inc. (Warner Bros.): 95 min. Producer, Hal B. Wallis; associate producers, Jack Saper, Jerry Wald; director, Lloyd Bacon; based on the play *The Night before Christmas* by Laura and S. J. Perelman; screenplay, Everett Freeman, Edwin Gilbert. Cast: Edward G. Robinson, Jane Wyman,

Broderick Crawford, Jack Carson, Anthony Quinn, Edward Brophy, Harry Davenport, William Hopper, Pat O'Malley.

Tales of Manhattan (20th Century Fox): 118 min. Producers, Boris Morros, S. P. Eagle; director, Julien Duvivier; stories-screenplay, Ben Hecht, Ferenc Molnar, Donald Ogden Stewart, Samuel Hoffenstein, Alan Campbell, Ladislas Fodor, Laslo Fodor, Laslo Vadnay, Laszlo Gorog, Lamar Trotti, Henry Blankford; music, Sol Kaplan. Cast: Sequence D—Edward G. Robinson, George Sanders, James Gleason, Harry Davenport.

1943

Destroyer (Columbia): 99 min. Producer, Louis F. Edelman; director, William A. Seiter; story, Frank Wead; screenplay, Frank Wead, Lewis Melzer, Borden Chase; music, Anthony Collins. Cast: Edward G. Robinson, Glenn Ford, Marguerite Chapman, Edgar Buchanan, Leo Gorcey, Regis Toomey, Ed Brophy, Bobby Jordan, Tristram Coffin, Larry Parks, Lloyd Bridges.

Flesh and Fantasy (Universal): 93 min. Producers, Charles Boyer, Julien Duvivier; director, Julien Duvivier; based on the story "Lord Arthur Saville's Crime" by Oscar Wilde, and stories by Laslo Vadnay, Ellis St. Joseph; screenplay, Ernest Pascal, Samuel Hoffenstein, Ellis St. Joseph; music, Alexandre Tansman. Cast: Edward G. Robinson, Charles Boyer, Barbara Stanwyck, Betty Field, Robert Cummings, Thomas Mitchell, Charles Winninger, Anna Lee, Dame May Whitty, C. Aubrey Smith, Robert Benchley, Peter Lawford, Marjorie Lord.

1944

Tampico (20th Century Fox): 75 min. Producer, Robert Bassler; director, Lothar Mendes; story adapter, Ladislas Fodor; screenplay, Kenneth Garnet, Fred Niblo Jr., Richard Macaulay; choreography, Geneva Sawyer; music, David Raksin. Cast: Edward G. Robinson, Lynn Bari, Victor McLaglen, Robert Bailey, Marc Lawrence.

Mr. Winkle Goes to War (Columbia): 80 min. Producer, Jack Moss; director, Alfred E. Green; based on the novel by Theodore Pratt; screenplay, Waldo Salt, George Corey, Louis Solomon; music, Carmen Dragon. Cast: Edward G. Robinson, Ruth Warrick, Ted Donaldson, Hugh Beaumont.

Double Indemnity (Paramount): 106 min. Associate producer, Joseph Sistrom; director, Billy Wilder; based on the novel by James M. Cain; screenplay, Billy Wilder, Raymond Chandler; music, Miklos Rozsa. Cast: Fred MacMurray, Barbara Stanwyck, Edward G. Robinson, Porter Hall, Jean Heather, Tom Powers, Byron Barr, Richard Gaines.

The Woman in the Window (RKO): 99 min. Producer, Nunnally Johnson; director, Fritz Lang; based on the novel *Once off Guard* by J. H. Wallis; screenplay, Nunnally Johnson. Cast: Edward G. Robinson, Raymond Massey, Joan Bennett, Edmond Breon, Dan Duryea, Spanky McFarland.

1945

Our Vines Have Tender Grapes (MGM): 105 min. Producer, Robert Sisk; director, Roy Rowland; based on the book by George Victor Martin; screenplay, Dalton Trumbo; music, Bronislau Kaper. Cast: Edward G. Robinson, Margaret O'Brien, James Craig, Agnes Moorehead, Jackie "Butch" Jenkins, Morris Carnovsky.

Scarlet Street (Universal): 103 min. Executive producer, Walter Wanger; producer-director, Fritz Lang; based on the novel and play *La Chienne* by Georges de la Fouchardière; screenplay, Dudley Nichols; music, H. J. Salter. Cast: Edward G. Robinson, Joan Bennett, Dan Duryea, Jess Barker, Margaret Lindsay.

1946

Journey Together (English Films): 80 min. Producer, Royal Air Force Film Unit; director, John Boulting; story, Terence Rattigan; screenplay, John Boulting; music, Gordon Jacob. Cast: Sergeant Richard Attenborough, Aircraftsman Jack Watling, Flying Officer David Tomlinson, Edward G. Robinson, Bessie Love.

The Stranger (RKO): 94 min. Producer, S. P. Eagle; director, Orson Welles; based on the story by Victor Trivas, Decia Dunning; screenplay, Anthony Veiller; adapters–dialogue, Anthony Veiller, John Huston, Orson Welles. Cast: Edward G. Robinson, Loretta Young, Orson Welles, Richard Long.

1947

The Red House (United Artists): 100 min. Producer, Sol Lesser; director, Delmer Daves; based on the novel by George Agnew Chamberlain; screenplay, Delmer Daves; music and music director, Miklos Rozsa. Cast: Edward G. Robinson, Lon McCallister, Judith Anderson, Allene Roberts, Julie London, Rory Calhoun, Ona Munson.

1948

All My Sons (Universal): 94 min. Producer, Chester Erskine; director, Irving Reis; based on the play by Arthur Miller; screenplay, Chester Erskine; music, Leith Stevens. Cast: Edward G. Robinson, Burt Lancaster, Mady Christians, Louisa Horton, Howard Duff, Frank Conroy, Arlene Francis, Henry "Harry" Morgan, Herbert Vigran.

Key Largo (Warner Bros.): 101 min. Producer, Jerry Wald; director, John Huston; based on the play by Maxwell Anderson; screenplay, Richard Brooks, John Huston; music, Max Steiner. Cast: Humphrey Bogart, Edward G. Robinson, Lauren Bacall, Lionel Barrymore, Claire Trevor, Thomas Gomes, Harry Lewis, John Rodney, Marc Lawrence, Dan Seymour, Monte Blue, William Haade, Jay Silverheels, Rodric Redwing.

Night Has a Thousand Eyes (Paramount): 80 min. Producer, Endre Bohem; director, John Farrow; based on the novel by Cornell Woolrich; screenplay, Barre Lyndon, Jonathan Latimer; music and music director, Victor Young. Cast: Edward G. Robinson, Gail Russell, John Lund, Virginia Bruce, William Demarest, Richard Webb, Jerome Cowan.

1949

House of Strangers (20th Century Fox): 101 min. Producer, Sol C. Siegel; director, Joseph L. Mankiewicz; based on the novel by Jerome Weidman; screenplay, Philip Yordan; music, Danièle Amfitheatrof. Cast: Edward G. Robinson, Susan Hayward, Richard Conte, Luther Adler, Paul Valentine, Efrem Zimbalist Jr., Debra Paget, Esther Minciotti, Hope Emerson, Diana Douglas.

It's a Great Feeling (Warner Bros.): C-84 min. Producer, Alex Gottlieb; director, David Butler; story, I. A. L. Diamond; screenplay, Jack Rose, Melville Shavelson; music numbers staged by LeRoy Prinz; music director, Ray Heindorf; music, Jule Styne; songs, Julie Styne, Sammy Cahn. Cast: Dennis Morgan, Doris Day, Jack Carson, Bill Goodwin, David Butler, Michael Curtiz, King Vidor, Raoul Walsh, Gary Cooper, Joan Crawford, Errol Flynn, Sydney Greenstreet, Danny Kaye, Patricia Neal, Eleanor Parker, Ronald Reagan, Edward G. Robinson, Jane Wyman, Maureen Regan (all as themselves), Errol Flynn (Jeffrey Bushdinkel).

1950

My Daughter Joy (aka *Operation X,* Columbia): 79 min. Producer, Gregory Ratoff; associate producer, Phil Brandon; director, Gregory Ratoff; based on the novel *David Golder* by Irene Nemirowsky; screenplay, Robert Thoeren, William Rose. Cast: Edward G. Robinson, Nora Swinburne, Peggy Cummins, Richard Greene.

1952

Actors and Sin (United Artists): 85 min. Producer-director-screenplay, Ben Hecht; codirector, Lee Garmes; music, George Antheil. Cast: "Actor's Blood"—Edward G. Robinson, Marsha Hunt, Dan O'Herlihy.

1953

Vice Squad (United Artists): 88 min. Producers, Jules Levy, Arthur Gardner; director, Arnold Laven; based on the novel *Harness Bull* by Leslie T. White; screenplay, Lawrence Roman. Cast: Edward G. Robinson, Paulette Goddard, K. T. Stevens, Porter Hall, Adam Williams, Edward Binns, Lee Van Cleef, Jay Adler.

Big Leaguer (MGM): 73 min. Producer, Matthew Rapf; director, Robert Aldrich; story, John McNulty, Louis Morheim; screenplay, Herbert Baker. Cast: Edward G. Robinson, Vera-Ellen, Jeff Richards, Richard Jaeckel.

The Glass Web (Universal): 81 min. Producer, Albert J. Cohen; director, Jack Arnold; based on the novel by Max S. Ehrlich; screenplay, Robert Blees, Leonard Lee; music director, Joseph Gershenson. Cast: Edward G. Robinson, John Forsythe, Marcia Henderson, Kathleen Hughes, Kathleen Freeman, Beverly Garland, Benny Rubin.

1954

Black Tuesday (United Artists): 80 min. Producer, Robert Goldstein; director, Hugo Fregonese; story-screenplay, Sydney Boehm; assistant director, Sam Wurtzel; music, Paul Dunlap. Cast: Edward G. Robinson, Peter Graves, Jean Parker, Milburn Stone, Warren Stevens, Jack Kelly.

1955

The Violent Men (Columbia): C-96 min. Producer, Lewis J. Rackmil; director, Rudolph Mate; based on the novel by Donald Hamilton; screenplay, Harry Kleiner; music, Max Steiner. Cast: Glenn Ford, Barbara Stanwyck, Edward G. Robinson, Dianne Foster, Brian Keith, Richard Jaeckel, Jack Kelly.

Tight Spot (Columbia): 97 min. Producer, Lewis J. Rackmil; director, Phil Karlson; based on the novel *Dead Pigeon* by Leonard Kantor; screenplay, William Bowers; music director, Morris Stoloff. Cast: Ginger Rogers, Edward G. Robinson, Brian Keith, Lorne Greene, Kathryn Grant.

A Bullet for Joey (United Artists): 85 min. Producers, Samuel Bischoff, David Diamond; director, Lewis Allen; story, James Benson Nablo; screenplay, Geoffrey Homes, A. I. Bezzerides; music, Harry Sukman. Cast: Edward G. Robinson, George Raft, Audrey Totter, George Dolenz, Peter Hanson.

Illegal (Warner Bros.): 88 min. Producer, Frank P. Rosenberg; director, Lewis Allen; based on the play *The Mouthpiece* by Frank J. Collins; screenplay, W. R. Burnett, James R. Webb; music, Max Steiner. Cast: Edward G. Robinson, Nina Foch, Hugh Marlowe, Robert Ellenstein, De Forrest Kelley, Jay Adler, Edward Platt, Albert Dekker, Ellen Corby, Jayne Mansfield.

1956

Hell on Frisco Bay (Warner Bros.): C-98 min. Associate producer, George Bertholon; director, Frank Tuttle; based on a novel by William P. McGivern; screenplay, Sydney Boehm, Martin Rackin; music, Max Steiner. Cast: Alan Ladd, Edward G. Robinson, Joanne Dru, William Demarest, Paul Stewart, Fay Wray, Perry Lopez, Renata Vanni, Nestor Paiva, Stanley Adams, Jayne Mansfield.

Nightmare (United Artists): 89 min. Producers, William Thomas, Howard Pine; director, Maxwell Shane; based on the novel by Cornell Woolrich; screenplay, Maxwell Shane. Cast: Edward G. Robinson, Kevin McCarthy, Connie Russell, Virginia Christine, Rhys Williams.

The Ten Commandments (Paramount): C-221 min. Producer, Cecil B. DeMille; associate producer, Henry Wilcoxon; director, Cecil B. DeMille; based on the novels *Prince of Egypt* by Dorothy Clarke Wilson, *Pillar of Fire* by the Reverend J. H. Ingraham, *On Eagle's Wings* by the Reverend G. E. Southon, in accordance with the Holy Scripture, the ancient texts of Josephus, Eusebius, Philo, the Midrash; screenplay, Aeneas MacKenzie, Jesse L. Lasky Jr., Jack Gariss, Fredric M. Frank; music, Elmer Bernstein. Cast: Charlton Heston, Yul Brynner, Anne Baxter, Edward G. Robinson, Yvonne De Carlo, Debra Paget, John Derek, Sir Cedric Hardwicke, Nina Foch, Martha Scott, Judith Anderson, Vincent Price, John Carradine, Eduard Franz, Frank DeKova, Mike Connors, Gail Kobe, Carl Switzer, Clint Walker, Michael Ansara, Robert Vaughn.

1959

A Hole in the Head (United Artists): C-120 min. Producer, Frank Capra; coproducer Frank Sinatra; director, Capra; based on the play *The Heart Is a Forgotten Hotel* by Arnold Schulman; screenplay, Arnold Schulman; music, Nelson Riddle; songs, Sammy Cahn, James Van Heusen. Cast: Frank Sinatra, Edward G. Robinson, Eddie Hodges, Eleanor Parker, Carolyn Jones, Thelma Ritter, Keenan Wynn, Joi Lansing, Jimmy Komack, Dub Taylor, Connie Sawyer, Benny Rubin.

1960

Seven Thieves (20th Century Fox): 120 min. Producer, Sydney Boehm; director, Henry Hathaway; based on the novel *Lions at the Kill* by Max Catto; screenplay, Sydney Boehm; music, Dominic Frontière. Cast: Edward G. Robinson, Rod Steiger, Joan Collins, Eli Wallach, Alexander Scourby, Sebastian Cabot, John Beradino.

Pepe (Columbia): C-195 min. Producer, George Sidney; associate producer, Jacques Gelman; director, George Sidney; based on a play by Ladislas Bush-Fekete; screen story, Leonard Spigelgass, Sonya Levien; screenplay, Dorothy Kingsley, Claude Binyon; music and music supervisor, Johnny Green; special musical material, Sammy Cahn, Roger Edens; songs, André Previn, Dory Langdon; Hans Wittstatt, Dory Langdon; André Previn; Augustin Lara, Dory Langdon. Cast: Cantinflas, Dan Dailey, Shirley Jones, Carlos Montalban, Joe Hyams, Joey Bishop. Michael Callan, Maurice Chevalier, Charles Coburn, Richard Conte, Bing Crosby, Tony Curtis, Bobby Darin, Sammy Davis Jr., Jimmy Durante, Zsa Zsa Gabor, the voice of Judy Garland, Greer Garson, Hedda Hopper, Ernie Kovacs, Peter Lawford, Janet Leigh, Jack Lemmon, Dean Martin, Jay North, Kim Novak, André Previn, Donna Reed, Debbie Reynolds, Edward G. Robinson, Cesar Romero, Frank Sinatra, Billie Burke, Ann B. Davis, William Demarest, Jack Entratter, Colonel E. E. Fogelson, Jane Robinson, Bunny Waters (as themselves).

1962

My Geisha (Paramount): C-120 min. Producer, Steve Parker; director, Jack Cardiff; screenplay, Norman Krasna; assistant director, Harry Kratz; music, Franz Waxman; song, Waxman, Hal Davis. Cast: Shirley MacLaine, Yves Montand, Edward G. Robinson, Bob Cummings.

Two Weeks in Another Town (MGM): C-107 min. Producer, John Houseman; associate producer, Ethel Winant; director, Vincente Minnelli; based on the novel by Irwin Shaw; screenplay, Charles Schnee; music, David Raksin; assistant director, Erich Von Stroheim, Jr. Cast: Kirk Douglas, Edward G. Robinson, Cyd Charisse, George Hamilton, Dahlia Lavi, Claire Trevor, Stefan Schnabel, Erich Von Stroheim Jr., Leslie Uggams.

1963

The Prize (MGM): C-135 min. Producer, Pandro S. Berman; associate producer, Kathryn Hereford; director, Mark Robson; based on the novel by Irving Wallace; screenplay, Ernest Lehman; music, Jerry Goldsmith. Cast: Paul Newman, Edward G. Robinson, Elke Sommer, Diane Baker, Micheline Presle, Gerard Oury, Sergio Fantoni, Kevin McCarthy, Leo G. Carroll, Virginia Christine.

1964

Good Neighbor Sam (Columbia): C-130 min. Producer, David Swift; associate producer, Marvin Miller; director, David Swift; based on the novel by Jack Finney; screenplay, James Fritzell, Everett Greenbaum, David Swift; music, Frank DeVol. Cast: Jack Lemmon, Romy Schneider, Dorothy Provine, Edward G. Robinson, Michael Connors, Edward Andrews, Louis Nye, Robert Q. Lewis, Anne Seymour, Charles Lane, Joyce Jameson, Neil Hamilton, Riza Royce, David Swift.

Robin and the Seven Hoods (Warner Bros.): C-123 min. Executive producer, Howard W. Koch; producer, Frank Sinatra; associate producer, William H. Daniels; director, Gordon Douglas; screenplay, David R. Schwartz; music conductor, Nelson Riddle; songs, Sammy Cahn, James Van Heusen. Cast: Frank Sinatra, Dean Martin, Sammy Davis Jr., Bing Crosby, Edward G. Robinson, Peter Falk, Barbara Rush, Victor Buono, Allen Jenkins.

The Outrage (MGM): 97 min. Producer, A. Ronald Lubin; associate producer, Michael Kanin; director, Martin Ritt; based on the film *Rashomon*, from stories by Ryunosuke Akutagawa and the play by Fay and Michael Kanin; screenplay, Michael Kanin; music–music conductor, Alex North. Cast: Paul Newman, Laurence Harvey, Claire Bloom, Edward G. Robinson, William Shatner, Howard da Silva, Albert Salmi, Thomas Chalmers, Paul Fix.

Cheyenne Autumn (Warner Bros.): C-156 min. Producer, Bernard Smith; director, John Ford; associate director, Ray Kellogg; based on the novel by Mari Sandoz; screenplay, James R. Webb; music–music conductor, Alex North. Cast: Richard Widmark, Carroll Baker, Karl Malden, James Stewart, Edward G. Robinson, Sal Mineo, Dolores Del Rio, Ricardo Montalban, Gilbert Roland, Arthur Kennedy, Patrick Wayne, Elizabeth Allen, John Carradine, Victor Jory, Mike Mazurki, Ken Curtis, Harry Carey Jr., Ben Johnson, Denver Pyle, Carleton Young.

1965

A Boy Ten Feet Tall (Paramount): C-88 min. Producer, Hal Mason; director, Alexander MacKendrick; based on the novel *Sammy Going South* by W. H. Canaway; screenplay, Denis Cannan. Cast: Edward G. Robinson, Fergus McClelland, Constance Cummings.

The Cincinnati Kid (MGM): C-113 min. Producer, Martin Ransohoff; associate producer, John Calley; director, Norman Jewison; based on the novel by Richard Jessup; screenplay, Ring Lardner, Jr., Terry Southern; music, Lalo Schifrin. Cast: Steve McQueen, Edward G. Robinson, Ann-Margret, Karl Malden, Tuesday Weld, Joan Blondell, Rip Torn, Jack Weston, Cab Calloway, Jeff Corey, Ron Soble, Irene Tedrow, Dub Taylor, Robert Do Qui.

1968

La Blonde de Pékin (aka *The Blonde from Peking,* Paramount): C-80 min. Director, Nicholas Gessner; based on the novel by James Hadley Chase; adapter, Jacques Vilfrid; screenplay, Nicholas Gessner, Mark Behm; music, François de Roubaix. Cast: Mireille Dare, Claudio Brook, Edward G. Robinson.

The Biggest Bundle of Them All (MGM): C-110 min. Producer, Josef Shaftel; associate producer, Sy Stewart; director, Ken Annakin; story, Josef Shaftel; screenplay, Josef Shaftel, Sy Salkowitz, Riccardo Aragno; music, Riz Ortolani, the Counts. Cast: Robert Wagner, Raquel Welch, Vittorio de Sica, Edward G. Robinson, Godfrey Cambridge, Danny Kaye.

Ad Ogni Costo (aka *Grand Slam,* Paramount): C-121 min. Producers, Harry Colombo, George Papi; director, Giuliano Montaldo; screenplay, Mino Roli, Marcello Fondato, Antonio de la Loma, Caminito; music, Ennio Morricone. Cast: Janet Leigh, Robert Hoffman, Edward G. Robinson, Adolfo Celi, Klaus Kinski.

Uno Sacco Tutto Matto (aka *Mad Checkmate,* Kinesis/Miniter/Tecisa): C-89 min. (television title: *It's Your Move*) Producer, Franco Porro; director, Robert Riz; screenplay, Robert Riz, Massimilliano Capriccoli, Ennio De Concini, Jose G. Maesso, Leonardo Martin, Juan Cesarabea; music, Manuel Asins Arbo. Cast: Edward G. Robinson, Terry Thomas, Maria Grazi Buccella.

Operation St. Peter's (Paramount): C-88 min. Producer, Turi Vasile; director, Lucio Fulci; screenplay, Ennio De Concini, Adriano Baracco, Roberto Gianviti, Lucio Fulci. Cast: Lando Buzzanca, Edward G. Robinson, Heinz Ruhmann.

Never a Dull Moment (Buena Vista): C-100 min. Producer, Ron Miller; director, Jerry Paris; based on the novel *Thrill a Minute* by John Godey; screenplay, A. J. Carothers; music, Robert F. Brunner. Cast: Dick Van Dyke, Edward G. Robinson, Dorothy Provine, Henry Silva, Joanna Moore, Tony Bill, Slim Pickens, Jack Elam, Ned Glass, Tyler McVey, Jerry Paris.

1969

MacKenna's Gold (Columbia): C-128 min. Producers, Carl Foreman, Dmitri Tiomkin; director, J. Lee Thompson; based on the novel by Will Henry; screenplay, Carl Foreman; music, Quincy Jones. Cast: Gregory Peck, Omar Sharif, Telly Savalas, Camilla Sparv, Keenan Wynn, Julie Newmar, Ted Cassidy, Lee J. Cobb. Raymond Massey, Burgess Meredith, Anthony Quayle, Edward G. Robinson, John Garfield Jr., Victor Jory.

1970

Song of Norway (Cinerama): C-142 min. Producers, Andrew L. and Virginia Stone; director, Andrew L. Stone; suggested by the stage play by Milton Lazarus (music and lyrics, based on the works of Edvard Grieg, by Robert Wright, George Forrest) from a play by Homer Curran; screenplay, Andrew L. Stone. Cast: Toralv Maurstad, Florence Henderson, Christina Schollin, Frank Poretta, Harry Secombe, Robert Morley, Edward G. Robinson, Oscar Homolka.

1973

Soylent Green (MGM): C-97 min. Producers, Walter Seltzer, Russell Thacher; director, Richard Fleischer; based on the novel *Make Room! Make Room!* by Harry Harrison; screenplay, Stanley R. Greenberg; music, Fred Myrow. Cast: Charlton Heston, Leigh Taylor-Young, Edward G. Robinson, Chuck Connors, Joseph Cotten, Brock Peters, Paula Kelly, Stephen Young, Mike Henry, Lincoln Kilpatrick, Whit Bissell, Celia Lovsky, Dick Van Patten.

Neither by Day or Night (Monarch): 95 min. Producer, Mordechai Slonim; associate producer, Mischa Asherov; director, Steven Hilliard Stern; based on the play by Avraham Raz; screenplay, Steven Hilliard Stern, Gisa W. Slonim; music–music director, Vladimir Cosma; songs, Vladimir Cosma, Steven Hilliard Stern. Cast: Zalman King, Miriam Bernstein, Dalia Friedland, Edward G. Robinson.

APPEARANCES AS SELF IN NEWSREELS, DOCUMENTARIES, AND SHORT FILMS

1931

The Slippery Pearls: Two-reel comedy made for the Masquers Club, in which EGR appears among more than forty other screen stars.
How I Play Golf, by Bobby Jones (#10 in a series from Warner Bros.): Uncredited appearance.

1939

Verdensberomtheder I Kobenhaven: Produced by Dansk Films. EGR made an appearance along with Myrna Loy, Robert Taylor, Charles Lindbergh, and Duke Ellington.
A Day at Santa Anita: Uncredited appearance in one-reel short film about Los Angeles–area racetrack.

1941

Polo with the Stars (Warner Bros. novelty shorts): Seen watching polo match.

1942

Moscow Strikes Back: Narrator of war propaganda film. Short was distributed by Artkino and cowritten by Albert Maltz.
Screen Snapshots (Series 22, #4): Produced as part of a series by Columbia Pictures. EGR provided humorous introductions to a ten-minute performance of Russian music.

1943

The Red Cross at War: War propaganda film with EGR as narrator.
Projection of America: Made for the Office of War Information. EGR spoke extemporaneously about love of country, cowboys, and also Chicago gangsters.
Magic Bullets: Military training film warning against the spread of syphilis. EGR hosts and narrates.

1944

Screen Snapshots (Series 23, #9): Produced by Columbia Pictures. A one-reel record of cinema history as a fiftieth anniversary of filmmaking. EGR appears alongside Fred Astaire, John Barrymore, Carole Lombard, Irene Dunne, Rosalind Russell, Cary Grant, Humphrey Bogart, and others.

1946

Okay for Sound: Produced by Vitaphone. Commemorated twenty years of "talkies." EGR seen in clips from *Little Caesar* and *Dr. Ehrlich's Magic Bullet.*

1948

Where Do You Get Off? Short film made for the United Jewish Appeal with EGR narrating.

1950

Screen Snapshots (Series 29): Produced by Columbia Pictures. EGR appears at an Ice Capades premiere.

1951

Screen Snapshots: Hollywood Memories (Series 30): Produced by Columbia Pictures; director, Ralph Staub. EGR seen in archival footage.

1954

"A Star Is Born" World Premiere: Seen attending event.

1956

When the Talkies Were Young: Produced by Vitaphone. A clip from *Five Star Final* is incorporated into this seventeen-minute short.

1957

The Heart of Show Business: Produced by Columbia Pictures. Forty-minute documentary on the history of Variety Clubs International charity. EGR, Bing Crosby, Bob Hope, James Stewart, Burt Lancaster, and Cecil B. De Mille narrate.

1959

Israel: Produced by Warner Bros. Pictures. EGR narrated twenty-nine-minute tour of Israel; writer, Leon Uris; director, Sam Zebba; music arranged and conducted by Elmer Bernstein.

1971

Mooch Goes to Hollywood: Writer, Jim Backus; director, Richard Erdman. A fifty-five-minute film narrated by Zsa Zsa Gabor with Lynne Lipton as voice of Mooch. Appearances by Vincent Price, James Darren, Jill St. John, Jim Backus. EGR has uncredited appearance.

1973

A Look at the World of "Soylent Green": Promotional short film.

1988

The 1950's Music, Memories, and Milestones (Direct to Video production). Seen in archival footage. Executive producer, David McWhinnie.

2001

Pulp Cinema (Direct to Video production): Seen in archival footage. Produced by David Kalat for All-Day Entertainment. Distributed by Image Entertainment, Inc.

APPEARANCES IN ANIMATED SHORTS

1936

Coconut Grove, a Merrie Melodies cartoon directed by I. Freleng: EGR appears as animated character.

1945

Hollywood Canine Canteen, a Merrie Melodies cartoon directed by Robert McKimson: EGR appears as animated character.

1947

Racket Rabbit, a Looney Tunes cartoon directed by I. Freleng: EGR menaces Bug Bunny as a faux "Little Caesar" gangster.

RADIO APPEARANCES

1933

March 21, *The Jack Benny Program* (NBC): Appeared as himself.
April 21, *The Jack Benny Program* (NBC): Appeared as himself.
November 7, *California Melodies* (CBS).

1935

February 1, *Hollywood Hotel* (CBS).

1936

January 13, *Lux Radio Theatre* (CBS): "The Boss."
May 8, *Hollywood Hotel* (CBS): "Bullets or Ballots."

1937

January 18, *Lux Radio Theatre* (CBS): "Criminal Code."
March 10, *Hollywood Showcase* (CBS).
April 29, *Kate Smith A & P Bandwagon* (CBS): "Thunder in the City."
August 2, *CBS Shakespeare Theater* (CBS): "The Taming of the Shrew," with Frieda Inescourt.
October 19–July 2, *Big Town* (CBS): A weekly series that in its heyday was the second-highest-rated radio program. Robinson packaged the show and starred as Steve Wilson, crusading editor of *The Illustrated Press.* Claire Trevor portrayed Lorelei Kilbourne, the society editor. Ona Munson later took over the role.

1938

December 19, *Lux Radio Theatre* (CBS): "Kid Galahad," with Wayne Morris, Andrea Leeds, Joan Bennett.

1939

April 4, *Lux Radio Theatre* (CBS): "Silver Dollar."
April 17, *Lux Radio Theatre* (CBS): "Bullets or Ballots," with Mary Astor, Humphrey Bogart, Otto Kruger.

1940

February 25, *Gulf Screen Guild Theater* (CBS): "Blind Alley," with Joseph Calleia, Isabel Jewell, Leatrice Joy.

1941

November 2, *Gulf Screen Guild Theater* (CBS): "The Amazing Dr. Clitterhouse," with Humphrey Bogart, Marsha Hunt.

1942

May 15, *Command Performance* (Armed Forces Radio Service): Radio series produced for military; appeared as himself.
March 16, *Lux Radio Theatre* (CBS): "Manpower," with Marlene Dietrich and George Raft.

1942-1943

Various airtimes and networks, *Treasury Star Parade*: Series made by Treasury Department to stimulate sale of war bonds. EGR appears in two fifteen-minute installments, numbers 45 and 58.

1943

January 4, *Lockheed's Ceiling Unlimited* (CBS): EGR substituted for regular narrator, Orson Welles.
February 8, *Lux Radio Theatre* (CBS): "The Maltese Falcon," with Laird Cregar and Gail Patrick.
March 15, *DuPont Cavalcade of America* (NBC): "A Case for the FBI."

March 31, *The Eddie Cantor Show* (NBC): Appeared as himself.

April 18, *Radio Reader's Digest* (NBC Blue).

April 26, *Lockheed's Ceiling Unlimited* (CBS): "The World of Tomorrow."

June 30, *Broadcast Salute to the Motion Picture Committee for Hollywood War Savings* (NBC): EGR was master of ceremonies.

July 4, *U.S. Rubber Hour* (CBS): "Our American Scriptures"; EGR did readings from the U.S. Constitution and from the letters of Thomas Jefferson.

July 15, *Mail Call* (Armed Forces Radio Service): Made guest appearance as himself, with Dick Powell.

December 31, *"Amos 'n' Andy"* (NBC): "Mister."

1944

April 3, *Lux Radio Theatre* (CBS): "Destroyer," with Marguerite Chapman, Dennis O'Keefe.

June 5, *Lady Esther's Screen Guild Theater* (NBC): "The Amazing Dr. Clitterhouse," with Claire Trevor, Lloyd Nolan.

October 2, *DuPont Calvalcade of America* (NBC): "Voice on the Stairs."

1945

March 1, *Suspense* (CBS): "My Wife Geraldine."

April 8, *P. Lorillard Comedy Theater* (NBC): "A Slight Case of Murder."

April 16, *Lux Radio Theatre* (CBS): "Only Yesterday," guest producer.

April 19, *Command Performance* (Armed Forces Radio Service): Appeared with Kay Kyser.

April 30, *Dupont Calvalcade of America* (NBC): "The Philippines Never Surrender."

June 25, *Lux Radio Theatre* (CBS): "The Woman in the Window," with Joan Bennett, Dan Duryea.

October 13, *Lady Esther's Screen Guild Players* (CBS): "Flesh and Fantasy," with Dame May Whitty, Vincent Price.

1946

March 11, *DuPont Calvalcade of America* (NBC): "The Man with Hope in His Hands."

March 26, *Colgate Theatre of Romance* (CBS): "The Woman in the Window."

October 17, *Suspense* (CBS): "The Man Who Thought He Was Edward G. Robinson."

November 18, *Lady Esther's Screen Guild Players* (CBS): "Blind Alley," with Broderick Crawford, Isabel Jewell, Frank Albertson.

November 24, *The Jack Benny Program* (NBC). Appeared as himself.

December 7, Procter and Gamble's *This Is Hollywood* (CBS): "The Stranger," with Ruth Hussey.

1947

March 18, *The Family Theatre* (Mutual): "Work of a Lifetime."

November 25, *Gulf's We the People* (CBS).

1948

March 14, *The Eternal Light* (NBC): "The Island in the Wilderness," narrator.

March 18, *The Kraft Music Hall* (NBC): Appeared as himself.

April 12, *Camel's Screen Guild Players* (CBS): "The Great Man Votes," with Edmund Gwenn, Frank McHugh.

November 4, *Sealtest Variety Show,* (aka *The Dorothy Lamour Show,* NBC): Appeared as himself.
November 11, *Camel's Screen Guild Players* (NBC): "All My Sons," with Burt Lancaster.

1949

January 28, *Ford Theater* (CBS): "The Woman in the Window," with Linda Darnell, Stephen McNally.
February 27, *NBC Theater* (NBC): "Night Has a Thousand Eyes," with William Demarest.
March 31, *Suspense* (CBS): "You Can't Die Twice."
November 28, *Lux Radio Theatre* (CBS): "Key Largo," with Claire Trevor, Edmond O'Brien.
December 2, *Screen Director's Playhouse* (NBC): "All My Sons," with Jeff Chandler.

1950

June 1, *Suspense* (CBS): "A Case of Nerves."
February 3, *Screen Director's Playhouse* (NBC): "The Sea Wolf," with Paul Frees, Lurene Tuttle.

1951

January 25, *Screen Director's Playhouse* (ABC): "House of Strangers," with Victor Mature, June Havoc.

1952

December 7, *Eternal Light* (NBC): "Trial and Error," appeared as Chaim Weizman.

1953

September 17, *Lux Radio Theatre* (CBS): "Witness for the Prosecution" (simulcast from television broadcast).
October 21, *State of Israel Bond Program* (NBC): "Jerusalem Is Her Name," with Paul Muni (taped broadcast of special Madison Square Garden show).
December 7, *Lux Radio Theatre* (CBS): "Man on a Tightrope," with Terry Moore.
December 20, *The Eternal Light* (NBC): "Face to Face with Gabriel."

1954

January 24, *NBC Star Playhouse* (NBC): "A Slight Case of Murder," with Elspeth Eric, Pat Hosley, William Redfield, Wendell Holmes, Larry Haines.

TELEVISION APPEARANCES

1953

September 17, *Lux Video Theatre* (CBS): "Witness for the Prosecution," appeared as Wilfrid Robarts.
October 11, *What's My Line* (CBS): Goodson-Todman Productions quiz show, appeared as the Mystery Guest.

1954

For the Defense: "The Case of Kenny Jason" (pilot for proposed weekly series). Producer, Samuel Bischoff; director, James Neilson; teleplay, Donn Mullally. Cast: Edward G. Robinson, Glenn Vernon, Ann Doran, John Hoyt.

September 20, *Operation Entertainment* (NBC): A star-studded tribute to the armed forces.

December 9, *Climax* (CBS): "Epitaph for a Spy." Producer, Bretaigne Windust; director, Alan Reisner; teleplay, Donald S. Sanford. Cast: Edward G. Robinson, Melville Cooper, Robert F. Simon, Ivan Tressault, Nicholas Joy.

1955

January 13, *Ford Theater* (NBC): "And Son." Story, I. A. R. Wylie; adapted for television, Peter Packer, Robert Bassing. Cast: Edward G. Robinson, John Baer, Erin O'Brien-Moore.

December 29, *Ford Theater* (NBC): "A Set of Values." Cast: Edward G. Robinson, Ann Doran, Tommy Cook, Paul Fix.

1956

September 30, *The $64,000 Challenge* (CBS).

October 28, *The $64,000 Challenge:* Edward G. Robinson and Vincent Price vie in the category of art.

The Ed Sullivan Show (CBS): Guest appearance as himself.

1957

The Steve Allen Show (NBC): Guest appearance as himself.

1958

October 23, *Playhouse 90* (CBS): "Shadows Tremble." Producer, Fred Coe; director, Herbert Hirshman; teleplay, Ernest Kinoy. Cast: Edward G. Robinson, Ray Walston, Beatrice Straight, Frank Conroy, Parker Fennelly, Robert Webber.

1959

February 3, *Goodyear Theater* (NBC): "A Good Name." Producer, Winston O'Keefe; director, Eliot Silverstein; teleplay, Richard Alan Simmons. Cast: Edward G. Robinson, Lee Philips, Parley Baer, Jacqueline Scott.

This Is Your Life (NBC): "Salute to Frank Capra." Appeared as himself.

This Is Your Life (NBC): "Salute to Mervyn LeRoy." Appeared as himself.

April 2, *Zane Grey Theater* (CBS): "Loyalty." Cast: Edward G. Robinson, Edward G. Robinson Jr., John Hackett, Robert Blake.

May 5, *Reflets de Cannes (Int'l):* Appeared as himself.

1960

October 24, *The Right Man* (CBS special): Historical revue of U.S. presidential campaigns; producer, Fred Freed; director, Burt Shevelove; narrator, Garry Moore. Edward G. Robinson played Theodore Roosevelt.

February 17, *The Devil and Daniel Webster* (NBC special, repeated CBS-TV April 30, 1962): Director, Tom Donovan; teleplay, Phil Reisman Jr.; story, Stephen Vincent Benet. Cast: Edward G. Robinson, David Wayne, Tim O'Connor, Betty Lou Holland.

October 24, *The Right Man* (CBS). A spry review of presidential campaigns. Producer-writer, Fred Freed; director, Burt Shevelove. Edward G. Robinson played President Theodore Roosevelt.

1961

January 9, *General Electric Theater* (CBS): "The Drop-Out." Producer, Stanley Rubin; director, Richard Irving; teleplay, Roger O. Hirson. Cast: Edward G. Robinson, Billy Gray.

October 6, *The Detectives* (NBC): "The Legend of Jim Riva." Producer, Arthur Nadel; director, Richard Carlson; teleplay, John K. Butler, Boyd Correll; story, Arthur Browne Jr. Cast: Edward G. Robinson, Rudy Solari, Butch Patrick, Robert Taylor, Tige Andrews, Adam West.

December 9, *Twelve Star Salute* (ABC): Benefit for Jewish Philanthropies seen on several ABC-TV stations.

Here's Hollywood (NBC): Daytime interview show hosted by Dean Miller and Jo-ann Jordan. Appeared as himself.

1962

March 18, *The Dupont Show* (NBC special): "Cops and Robbers." Producer, Don Hyatt; director, Don Hyatt; written by Phil Reisman Jr. Edward G. Robinson as the narrator.

April 1, *At This Very Moment* (ABC): Televised benefit for the American Cancer Society/Eleanor Roosevelt Fund.

1963

December 1, *The World's Greatest Showman* (NBC special): Tribute to Cecil B. DeMille. Hosted by Edward G. Robinson, Betty Hutton, Cornel Wilde, Barbara Stanwyck.

1965

January 9, *Hollywood Palace* (ABC): Dramatic reading of patriotic essay "This Is It."

February 19, *Xerox Special* (ABC-TV movie): "Who Has Seen the Wind." Producer, George Sidney; director, George Sidney; teleplay, Don Mankiewicz; story, Tad Mosel. Cast: Edward G. Robinson, Stanley Baker, Maria Schell, Veronica Cartwright, Gypsy Rose Lee, Lilia Skala, Simon Oakland, Paul Richards, Victor Jory.

December 5, *What's My Line?*. Appeared as the Mystery Guest.

1966

February 7, *Here's Lucy* (CBS): "Lucy Goes to a Hollywood Premiere." Cameo appearance as himself.

1967

March 2, *Batman* (ABC): "Batman's Satisfaction." Uncredited cameo appearance as himself.

June 17, 24, *Eye on Art* (CBS series): Edward G. Robinson as narrator of the first two of six parts of this series, a tour of the museums of Chicago and Los Angeles.

1969

April 17, *CBS Movie World Premiere: UMC* (movie-pilot): Producer, A. C. Ward; director, Boris Sagal; teleplay, A. C. Ward. Cast: Richard Bradford, Edward G. Robinson, James Daley, Kim Stanley, Maurice Evans, Kevin McCarthy, J. D. Cannon, William Windom, Shelley Fabares, James Shigeta, Robert Emhardt.

December 19, *The Name of the Game* (NBC): "Laurie Marie." Executive producer, Richard Irving; writers, Henry Slesar, David P. Harmon; director, Harry Hart. Cast: Peter Mark Richman, Carla Borelli, Edward G. Robinson.

1970

October 13, *The ABC Movie of the Week: "The Old Man Who Cried Wolf"*: Executive producer, Aaron Spelling; producer, Walter Grauman; assistant to the executive producer, Edward G. Robinson Jr.; director, Walter Grauman; teleplay, Luther Davis; story, Arnold Horwitt. Cast: Edward G. Robinson, Martin Balsam, Diane Baker, Percy Rodrigues, Ruth Roman, Edward Asner, Sam Jaffe, Naomi Stevens, Virginia Christine, J. C. Flippen.

October 23, *Bracken's World* (NBC): "The Mary Tree." Producer, Stanley Rubin; director, Paul Henreid; teleplay, Jerry Ziegman. Cast: Edward G. Robinson, Diana Hyland, Leslie Nielsen, Peter Haskell, Elizabeth Allen, Edward G. Robinson, Jr.

October 23, *This Is Tom Jones* (ABC): Dramatic reading of "I Will Not Go Back" and Kipling's poem "The Betrothed."

1971

April 5, *Hollywood Television Theatre* (PBS): John Dos Passos's "USA." Director, George Schaefer. Edward G. Robinson delivered the prologue and epilogue.

October 11, *Rowan & Martin's Laugh-In* (NBC): Cameo appearance as himself.

November 8, *Rowan & Martin's Laugh-In* (NBC): Cameo appearance as himself.

December 15, *Rod Serling's Night Gallery* (NBC): "The Messiah on Mott Street." Producer, Jack Laird; director, Don Taylor; teleplay, Rod Serling. Cast: Edward G. Robinson.

1973

America's Romance with the Land (ABC): Appeared as himself.

APPEARANCES IN ARCHIVAL FOOTAGE

1993

Rowan & Martin's Laugh-In: 25th Anniversary Reunion (NBC).

1998

Behind the Planet of the Apes (American Movie Classics): Produced by Foxstar Productions and Van Ness Films. Seen in makeup tests for Dr. Zaius in archival footage.

BIBLIOGRAPHY

BOOKS

Astor, Mary. *A Life on Film*. New York: Delacorte, 1971.

Bessie, Alva. *Inquisition in Eden*. New York: Macmillan, 1965.

Boyarsky, Bill. *The Rise of Ronald Reagan*. New York: Random House, 1968.

Capra, Frank. *Name above the Title*. New York: Macmillan, 1971.

Carey, Gary. *All Stars in Heaven: Louis B. Mayer's MGM*. New York: Putnam, 1981.

Caute, David. *The Great Fear: The Anti-Communist Purge under Truman and Eisenhower*. New York: Simon and Schuster, 1978.

Ceplair, Larry, and Steven Englund. *The Inquisition in Hollywood*. Garden City, N.Y.: Anchor Press, 1980.

Chayefsky, Paddy. *Middle of the Night: A Comedy in Three Acts*. New York: Samuel French, 1957.

Cogley, John. *Report on Blacklisting*. New York: The Fund for the Republic, 1956.

Cole, Lester. *Hollywood Red*. Palo Alto, Calif.: Ramparts Press, 1981.

Dies, Martin. *Martin Dies' Story*. New York: Bookmailer, 1963.

Douglas, Helen Gahagan. *A Full Life*. Garden City, N.Y.: Doubleday Press, 1982.

Eells, George. *Hedda and Louella*. New York: Putnam, 1972.

Finch, Christopher, and Linda Rosenkrantz. *Gone Hollywood: The Movie Colony in the Golden Age*. Garden City, N.Y.: Doubleday, 1979.

Gabree, John. *Gangsters from Little Caesar to The Godfather*. New York: Pyramid, 1973.

Higham, Charles. *Cecil B. DeMille*. New York: Scribner, 1973.

Hirsch, Foster. *Edward G. Robinson*. New York: Pyramid, 1976.

Hirschhorn, Clive. *The Warner Bros. Story*. New York: Crown, 1979.

Kaminsky, Stuart. *John Huston: Master of Magic*. Boston: Houghton Mifflin, 1978.

Johnson, Nunnally, and Tom Stemple. *Screenwriter*. San Diego: A. S. Barnes, 1980.

Lawrence, Jerome. *Actor: The Life and Times of Paul Muni*. London: W. H. Allen, 1975.

LeRoy, Mervyn, with Dick Kleiner. *Take One*. New York: Hawthorn Books, 1974.

Logan, Josh. *Movie Stars, Real People, and Me*. New York: Delacorte, 1978.

Madsen, Axel. *John Huston*. Garden City, N.Y.: Doubleday, 1978.

Navasky, Victor. *Naming Names*. New York: Viking Press, 1980.

Parish, James Robert. *The Tough Guys*. Carlstadt, N.J.: Rainbow Books, 1976.

Parish, James Robert, and Alvin H. Marill. *The Cinema of Edward G. Robinson*. New York: A. S. Barnes, 1972.

Parish, James Robert, and Steven Whiting. *The George Raft File*. New York: Drake, 1980.

Raft, George, with Lewis Yablonsky. *George Raft*. New York: McGraw-Hill, 1974.

Reagan, Ronald, and Richard G. Hubler. *Where's the Rest of Me?* New York: Dell Publishing, 1965.

Robinson, Edward G., with Leonard Spigelgass. *All My Yesterdays: An Autobiography*. New York: Hawthorn, 1973.

Robinson, Edward G., Jr., with William Duffy. *My Father, My Son*. New York: Frederick Fell, 1958.

Ross, Murray. *Stars and Strikes: The Unionization of Hollywood*. New York: Oxford University Press, 1941.

Schwartz, Nancy Lynn, completed by Sheila Schwartz. *The Hollywood Writers' Wars*. New York: Knopf, 1982.

Sennett, Ted. *Warner Brothers Presents*. New Rochelle, N.Y.: Arlington House, 1971.

Steffgen, Kent H. *Here's the Rest of Him*. Reno, Nev.: Foresight Books, 1968.

Swindell, Larry. *Body and Soul: The Story of John Garfield*. New York: William Morrow, 1975.

Trumbo, Dalton. *The Time of the Toad*. New York: Perennial Library, 1971.

Vaughn, Robert. *Only Victims: A Study of Show Business Blacklisting*. New York: Putnam, 1972.

Wallis, Hal, with Charles Higham. *Starmaker: The Autobiography of Hal Wallis*. New York: Macmillan, 1980.

Warner, Jack. *My First Hundred Years in Hollywood*. New York: Random House, 1964.

Wikerson, Tichi, and Marcia Borie. *The Hollywood Reporter: The Golden Years*. New York: Coward-McCann, 1984.

Zolotow, Maurice. *Billy Wilder in Hollywood*. New York: Putnam, 1977.

GOVERNMENT DOCUMENTS

United States Congress, *Congressional Record*: Remarks by Hon. Samuel W. Yorty of California, April 9, 1952, pp. A2713-14. Washington D.C.: Government Printing Office.

United States Congress, published record of Testimony to the House Committee on UnAmerican Activities. Pertaining to EGR: October 27, 1950; December 22, 1950; April 30, 1952; and executive session, January 25, 1954. Washington, D.C.: Government Printing Office.

Federal Bureau of Investigation files obtained under the Freedom of Information Act: Ronald Reagan, Edward G. Robinson.

ARCHIVES

Margaret Herrick Library of the Academy of Motion Picture Arts and Sciences, Beverly Hills, Calif.

University of Southern California, Los Angeles: Warner Bros. files pertaining to Edward G. Robinson and his films; Warner Bros. general files; Edward G. Robinson's papers.

William Morris Agency, Beverly Hills, Calif.: Files pertaining to Edward G. Robinson.

NEWSPAPERS AND MAGAZINES

American Legion, "How the Reds Made a Sucker Out of Me," Edward G. Robinson, October, 1952, p. 11, 6268, 70.

Baltimore News, October 22, 1930 interview notes EGR once wanted "to be a minister."

Boston Globe, review of *Under Fire* on January 9, 1916 only.

The Commonweal, article praising EGR, R. Dana Skinner, May 11, 1927, only.

Daily Variety.

Daily Worker.

Hollywood Citizen.

Hollywood Now.

The Hollywood Reporter.

In Touch, June 1974, EGR's final interview, published posthumously.

Jewish Daily Forward.

Life.

Los Angeles Examiner.

Los Angeles Herald-Examiner.

Los Angeles Reader, "Ronald Reagan's Forty Years of Friendship and Favor-Trading with the Moguls of Hollywood," Dan E. Moldea and Jeff Goldberg, November 2, 1984.

The Los Angeles Times.

Milwaukee Sentinel.

The Nation, "Hollywood Meets Frankenstein," "X," June 28, 1952; "Blacklist = Black Market," Dalton Trumbo, May 4, 1957; "The FBI's Forty-Year Plot," Robert Justin Goldstein, July 1, 1978.

New York Daily News.

New York Journal-American, page 1 banner headline "Edw. G. Robinson Stricken," June 18, 1962.

New York Mirror.

The New York Post, five-part series, "The Edward G. Robinson Story," David Gelman and Marci Elias, May 1957.

The New York Sun.

The New York Times.

New York Tribune.

New York World.

New York World-Telegram.

Screen Guild Magazine.

The Screenwriter.

The Theatre Magazine.

Variety.

The Word, Alexander Woollcott's praise of EGR, December 4, 1927.

PAMPHLETS

Alert, no. 157, January 25, 1951, pp. 625–26.

"Nazi Instructions for Our Friends Overseas," distributed by the German-American Bund.

"Handbook for Foreign Germans," distributed by the German-American Bund.

Red Channels: The Report of Communist Influence in Radio and Television. New York: Counterattack, 1950.

INDEX

ABOUT THE AUTHOR

Alan L. Gansberg is an award-winning writer-producer-director working in television, film, and documentary filmmaking. He is also a professor of film and Hollywood history and business practices studies at Columbia College Hollywood, Tarzana, California. He is the president of the faculty association of Columbia College Hollywood and dean of the faculty. In addition, he teaches acting workshops and privately coaches actors.

15378072R00201

Made in the USA
Middletown, DE
21 November 2018